BEN STOKES
FIRESTARTER

Me, Cricket and the
Heat of the Moment

with Richard Gibson

HEADLINE

First published in Great Britain in 2016
by HEADLINE PUBLISHING GROUP

First published in paperback in 2017 by
HEADLINE PUBLISHING GROUP

Cataloguing in Publication Data is available from the British Library

Paperback ISBN 978 1 4722 3672 2

Offset in 10.1/16.68 pt Bliss by Jouve (UK)

Printed and bound in Great Britain by Clays Ltd, St Ives plc

FSC
www.fsc.org

MIX
Paper from
responsible sources
FSC® C018179

Headline's policy is to use papers that are natural, renewable and recyclable
products and made from wood grown in well-managed forests and other
controlled sources. The logging and manufacturing processes are expected
to conform to the environmental regulations of the country of origin.

HEADLINE PUBLISHING GROUP
An Hachette UK Company
Carmelite House
50 Victoria Embankment
London EC4Y 0DZ

www.headline.co.uk
www.hachette.co.uk

To Clare, Layton, Libby,
Mam and Dad,
who mean so much to me

ACKNOWLEDGEMENTS

I cannot believe that at the age of 25 a book about my cricket career is going to hit the shelves – who would have thought it?! This would have been impossible without the support and guidance of so many people who I need to thank.

As a cricketer, sacrifices have to be made by your family, and no one has sacrificed more than my fiancée Clare, who has not only supported me through good times and bad, but also puts up with my mood swings – especially through the summer. Most importantly, she has given me two beautiful children – Layton and Libby – who are my whole world!

To Mam and Dad, who drove endless miles across the country when I was younger for me to take part in training and matches and provided me with kit until I was lucky enough to receive a sponsorship. They also gave me the kick up the arse when I needed it.

To Clare's parents, Jane and Arthur, for accepting me into their family, and for making it slightly easier for me when my parents moved back to New Zealand, knowing I had a back-up family here.

Neil Fairbrother has been my mentor, advisor and friend, and the whole team at ISM have been a fantastic support system. Without Harv at the end of the phone I might have lost my way.

Thanks must go to all my coaches at every level, especially Jon Gibson at Cockermouth where it all began.

To all the medical staff at the ECB and Durham, thank you for getting me through each injury, being patient when I'm not, and putting up with all my complaining. You guys are the best at what you do and I appreciate you every day.

Thank you to my fans – your loyalty and support has been amazing, you have no idea what a difference it makes. Cheers!

Thanks must go to my publisher Jonathan Taylor and everyone at Headline Publishing Group for allowing me to tell my story and making this book a reality.

And finally to Richard Gibson, who was so easy and amazing to work with, which surprised me as he's a Yorkie! All your effort (and trips across the Pennines) have not gone unnoticed. Cheers Gibbo!

Bor~ ~ C~ ~hurch, New Zealand, in 1991, Ben Stokes moved to
C~ ~~ ~~~ ~~'y at the age of 11. He made his d~'~ ~ ~
Du~ ~~ CCC in 2~~~ ~~ ~~~ ~~~ ~~~ ~~~ ~~~ ~ ~~~ d
shirt for the first time.

The highlights of his explosive England career to date have included
scoring the fastest ever Test century at Lord's and England's fastest
ever Test double-century. His bowling spell of 6-36 at Trent Bridge in
August 2015 helped England to regain the Ashes.

He has also played for the Melbourne Renegades in Australia's Big Bash
League and for Rising Pune Supergiants in the Indian Premier League.

He has a partner and two young children.

1

'I've just f**ked this up, completely. I've lost us the World Cup.'

I couldn't believe what had just happened to me. What should I do now? How should I react? It wasn't as if I had any experience to fall back on. Lots of guys get asked to bowl the final over in limited-overs matches. But how many have bowled the 40th of a World Twenty20 final?

Not knowing how to respond, I didn't. I effectively did nothing. I remained still in the middle of the pitch. When the battle is on, my reaction is spontaneous – I fight. But here the battle was over. I had lost. The fight had left me. I was empty.

Head bowed towards the Kolkata turf, hands over my eyes, elbows on my haunches, I stayed down. I did not want to get back up. Something held me there. In that snapshot of time, it felt like the entire weight of the world rested on my shoulders. Whatever entered my head was negative. How could anything be good? I had let everyone down.

When you are in a Twenty20 match, you are buzzing. As soon as it's over, all your energy is gone. It's literally sapped. You tend to feel a little light-headed after every single match. But for this particular one, that feeling was ten times worse.

People will talk about Carlos Brathwaite hitting me for four consecutive sixes for the rest of my life. I can deal with that. What I couldn't handle was losing the game. Yes, there were 50,000 people inside Eden Gardens on the evening of 3 April 2016, and millions across the globe watching on television, but I thought not of them but the England team I had failed.

It was a kind of numb feeling. I felt hollow. My England team-mates were the ones I had affected most with those four deliveries. We had all worked so well as a group. So hard. We had become tight. A genuine team, with genuine talent, genuine aspirations. We had gone all the way in the competition. All the way to the tournament's final over. But in a flash, all that hard graft had come to nothing.

Of course, the other lads were there for me. I felt their hands on my back; on my shoulders. I was aware of their kind and supportive words. Yet, at the same time, I was barely listening. And I couldn't say 'Thanks'. Actually, I couldn't talk at all.

All sorts of things were going through my mind. For the next three quarters of an hour, I had to deal with being the guy everyone was looking at. I had to come back out on the field, collect my medal and listen to all the speeches. I knew the cameras would be all over me, to see how I was holding up. I may have looked okay. That was an act. I was not. I was gutted. *Do not show it. Keep your head up.* Joe Root had said exactly that to me more than once as I crouched motionless on the square.

Later, as we sat in the dressing room reflecting on our defeat, I told Eoin Morgan that I had been more nervous bowling the last over of the semi-final than I was the final. That much was true. My confidence was high after doing the death job successfully a couple of times previously at this World Twenty20 tournament. Preparing to bowl against Sri Lanka and New Zealand had been infinitely more stressful. In the semi-final, I conceded only one run off the bat and took two wickets. I was more than happy to be in the firing line at Eden Gardens. I felt well drilled to construct the same kind of over as I had against the New Zealanders.

Nothing can help you get over the disappointment of losing in those circumstances. It was almost contempt that controlled me at the presentation. As the medal was placed around my neck, all I could think was that it was the wrong one. This one was for runners-up. Second place. I didn't want it.

Some time later, once I had retrieved it from under my seat in the dressing room, my view began to change. With me, some habits – such as throwing things in anger – die hard. Of course it was the gold one that we all craved, but during two hours together in the changing room, everyone sat with the medals around our necks, we agreed on one thing.

No one can take this moment away from us.

We had played for our country in a World Cup final. Let's be proud of that. I certainly was. What happened will be in my mind for quite a long time and with me forever. But in future, when I reflect upon the 40th and final over of that thrilling match, it will be a motivation, not a regret. I will use it to try to make sure it never happens again. I cannot say categorically that it won't. But I'm prepared to place myself in the same kind of scenario, again and again. Setbacks only increase my desire to get better, to train harder, to be a winner.

In the aftermath, people kept asking: 'Will you bowl the death over again?' It didn't need much thought. One hundred per cent I will. If the captain gives me the chance, that is. It's what I train to do. It's a skill I've practised a lot. I enjoy the one-on-one contest. Some days you win, other days it goes to the other guy. That was a bad day for me, but I will not shy away from the responsibility. In a funny way, I actually want to be put back in that kind of situation. It will mean this England team has been as successful as I believe it can be. And if I nail it next time, everyone will forget the past. Or at least it will give them something else to talk about.

Truth is, we had done unbelievably well to get to the stage where Eoin threw me the ball. The pitch was flat, the boundaries were not the biggest and the ball wasn't turning. And we knew we were light on runs. Not just a few, either. About 30-40 light. So to stay in the contest defending 155 meant we had to take early wickets. We did that and more, with three inside the powerplay, forcing West Indies on to the back foot at the start of their chase. As a bowling unit, we worked in unison. Until that last over – and the worst passage of cricket I turned in throughout the entire World Twenty20 competition.

My preparation for those final six balls – well, four – had been fine. Eoin didn't need to tell me I would be bowling it. I knew. I could tell that looking at other bowlers' overs on the electronic scoreboard. He brought Chris Jordan back with four overs to go. *It will be me if it gets there,* I thought.

For some time, the match was looking like it was going all the way to the death. I was totally in the zone – running from long-on to cow corner for 14 overs had kept me 100 per cent focused on every single ball. When the opposition is batting, a Twenty20 innings is intense, and concentrating on being in the right fielding position meant I did not start thinking about my fourth and final over until it was upon me.

But when it came to it, I felt ready. I knew exactly what I had to do. And no, there was no complacency from me. None whatsoever. Plenty of people have been hit for 19-20 runs in an over before. So not for one second was I walking to my run-up thinking, *Nineteen? This is all over.* What I was thinking about was my plan. The confidence of carrying out the job a few times before made me relax. All the nerves I had experienced bowling to Sri Lanka in the must-win group game just weren't there. I felt really good at the end of my mark.

Not for one second did I consider that we had already won. There was certainly no underestimation of my opponents on my part, as I knew a couple of heavy blows would make it game on again. So I just focused on my preparation for each ball, and what I wanted to do with it once I hit my delivery stride. I knew that if I got all six in the block hole, they were only going to score eight or nine runs maximum and we would win.

All I had to do was deliver. There was no real need to discuss things with Eoin in terms of setting the field. All our talking had been done in preparation. We set it for what I wanted to bowl – the yorker. Yorkers are what I back myself to get right in that situation. I over-perform those drills in practice, doing double workload to get them right, so my training feels transferable when it comes to a game. I had been doing it daily throughout the previous four weeks. It wasn't a case of holding anything back at this point. I felt ready to go. It wasn't a case of aiming and hoping. My radar had been good.

A field set for balls pitching on the batting crease is also ideal for slower balls bowled into the deck. So, third man and point were up on the single – the batsmen were very unlikely to be able to hit me through that region with any power and, because there is no pace from the bowler, it's hard to get the ball behind square on the off-side at all. All the deep fielders were set straight down the ground and in the leg-side hitting arc.

Yet, as soon as I let the first one go, I knew I had missed my spot. *Oh God*, I thought, as Brathwaite flicked it off his pads and over the rope at deep square-leg.

But I was still backing myself. I had confidence that I could hit the crease with accuracy. That I could deliver the ball exactly where I wanted.

For each of those next two balls, when I let them go, I thought they were in the hole – that Brathwaite could not get his ferocious swing of the bat under it. But they both soared over my head, and 90 metres into the crowd. I didn't feel as though I missed my target by much. But I had been punished, big time. As a bowler you have a feeling when you release the ball whether or not you have got a yorker right, and it felt like I had.

Between each of them, I had tried to slow myself down. I didn't want to rush back into things. As a bowler I am guilty of doing that at times: getting the ball back into my hand, turning around and running in, rather than trying to maintain a clear head by pausing. I knew Brathwaite's adrenalin would be going too, so I was just trying to play the game at my own pace.

Eoin had a chat with me after ball two. It was just his way of trying to alter the tempo a bit. Everything slowed further after the third ball, because it took that long to get it back from the crowd. Throughout I tried to stay as composed as I possibly could.

I kept glancing at the scoreboard: 13 needed off five balls, seven off four. At that point, I still fancied my chances of seeing it through. All I focused on was getting two balls away, for a couple of singles. Five off two and it would still be game on.

It was not until they needed one off three that I conceded it had gone. It was truly amazing hitting.

In the aftermath, it was natural to question my methods. I wondered whether things might have been different had I plumped for four slower balls into the pitch. But if they had sat up in the deck and been clunked, then what? I would have regretted not trying to execute on the field what I had practised so often in the nets. I know I can run up and hit those yorkers the majority of times I try. My recent performances boded well. Against Sri Lanka, I nailed six out of six. And with the dew I worried that the slower balls would skid on to the bat. By my reckoning, they would have been easier balls to hit. My regret was execution not selection.

Once back in the changing room at the Wankhede Stadium, I slumped back in my chair for several minutes with a towel over my head. All the thoughts I'd had on the field minutes earlier, in the immediate after-math, had gone. This room of silence was still an uncomfortable place to be, though, despite the constant taps on the back from team-mates to let me know – despite their own feelings of dejection – they were with me.

You come to expect that kind of thing from this England set-up. There is a lot of loyalty, and a sense of togetherness. But I knew I still had to get through the public spectacle of it all. The television cameras and photographers would be on me, commentators would be analyzing my body language. With that in mind, I didn't want to be walking out there with my shoulders down.

So when the time came, I made a point of lifting them high, and sticking my chest out at the same time. Inside that chest was a horrible feeling, but I wanted to at least make it look as though things were alright. Pictures that appeared afterwards made it look like Joe Root and I were boyfriend and boyfriend, with arms on each other. I was just trying to give off the right vibes. To show that I was not shying away, or sulking. I wanted to be seen as a character that fronted up. Even in defeat. Even though it was my fault.

Scrutiny was inevitable. But whatever people said about me, there was no way I wanted anyone thinking I was bitter. Respect for the opposition is important, whatever goes on during a match. When you leave the pitch, you have to let everything else go. Although I'm not sure everyone shares this opinion. I will come to Marlon Samuels later.

One of the things I was determined to do was to say well done to Carlos. I didn't know him but Chris Jordan did and said he was an absolute champion. If someone achieves something on the pitch in direct competition with me, I want to be the first to congratulate them. Given our contrasting emotions, and the magnitude of the occasion, this wasn't possible. I would have been steamrollered by a whole West Indies team had I tried.

But, as I was walking off the pitch, I noticed him celebrating on the boundary edge to the left-hand side of me. I simply wanted to go and tell him 'well done'.

He clocked me as I approached and made the effort to walk my way.

'Awesome,' I told him. 'Class.'

'Respect, man.'

He then asked me for my shirt, which I agreed to, although it was a strange situation to be in after he had just pulverized my bowling. I was never going to ask him for his in exchange. For a start, we don't need another duvet in our house.

True to his word, he came to our dressing room later to claim that shirt. Perhaps he wanted to write something funny on it? Nah, he's too good a lad for that.

When he spoke publicly about me after winning the match for West Indies, it showed him in an even better light. 'Ben Stokes is an absolute legend in his own right. You shouldn't forget what he has done for England in the past couple of months,' he said.

Neither should we forget how incredible his feat was. Naturally, we dwell on our disappointment when we lose. But to come in and strike 34 off 10 balls, hitting four sixes as cleanly as he did, was phenomenal. Anyone who plays the game, no matter the level, knows how hard it is to do that when you first go in to bat.

Yes, they might have been balls to hit for six for him because of his ability, but he still had to hit them for six. And hit them for six under pressure. There would have been plenty of times I would have bowled those same balls and got wickets. Nobody would have thought anything of it.

This was a guy making his debut in the tournament, but he kept his composure and cleared the ropes with ease. That shouldn't surprise you if you have seen the size of the man. He's an absolute monster. I literally couldn't believe how big he was. WWE wrestlers would fear him.

The third of the sixes emphasized Brathwaite's amazing power. It flew over J-Roy's head at long-off – but it was a mishit. You could see the bat turn in his hands, and it didn't make the perfect noise it does when you middle one. Yet it still went 15 rows back.

I would like to think I could replicate that kind of big hitting, but I tend to get into that sort of zone when I have faced 100-120 balls. He had faced six. That is what we were up against – incredible hitting from a standing start.

Cricket fans appeared to appreciate Brathwaite's extraordinary acts as well. Certainly judging by the reaction to me on social media afterwards. I expected a panning. So it was a pleasant surprise when, after plucking up some Dutch courage, I switched on my mobile phone as I got on the team bus back to the hotel. I refreshed Twitter every few seconds as we wound our way through the streets of Kolkata.

There was nothing like the anger directed towards me I had anticipated. You always get one or two who feel pretty tough sat in their bedrooms hundreds of miles away – but the keyboard warriors were in a real minority on this occasion. Nearly all the messages from England supporters were positive. They focused on their pride at watching us throughout the tournament, not the disappointment they felt at the very end.

I expected flak. I anticipated that I would soon be deleting the app from my phone. But I should have known that the England fans would stick with us. They always do. Their warmth made me want to interact. So I did so.

'Overwhelmed by all the support of everyone after a disappointing last over . . . So proud to have represented my country in a World Cup final . . .,' I tweeted.

Throughout those first few hours — firstly, as we sat drinking a few reflective beers at the stadium, later with our families at the Taj Kolkata hotel — the messages simply flooded in. There have been times when I have been pleased with a particular England performance and received more abuse. It had taken a defeat to really emphasize how much pleasure we have given to people in recent times. It was certainly appreciated.

It was not only support from English fans. There were kind words from Indian fans; cricket fans in general were taking time to say 'well played'. It almost took us to lose a major final to fully realize how much it meant to English cricket followers that their team was one to be proud of. It sounds an odd thing to say but if we had won, I'm not sure we would have appreciated that level of support as much. Of course, you are proud to play for your country. But you are also proud to have fans like that. They are certainly not just in it for the glory.

There were ones from fellow cricketers too, team-mates at Durham, lads I'd played with for England, and also some ex-players. To get one from Shane Warne, one of the greats of our game, meant a lot. 'It is hurting at the moment. Head high. Use tonight's match as motivation on every level, so you don't feel like this again,' he wrote.

Receiving reassurance that I should stick to the same path, from a player like Warne, was comforting. I had previously met him to say, 'Hi, how you doing?' but didn't know him any better than that. When someone who you've watched and admired as a kid offers you advice and support, it really means something. It gave me a real buzz to read it. For him to take the time out to contact me was pretty cool. By this time, I'd realized I could do nothing about what had gone before.

Other things had brightened my mood, like sharing a beer or two with the rest of the England lads – I was a bit of a late starter as I was cramping up in the hour after the game finished, meaning I had to drink a few Gatorades to rehydrate first – and chatting about the tournament as a whole.

It was not long after Trevor Bayliss, our laid-back coach, addressed us as a group that I was supping my first one of the night. Trevor was straight to the point, as is his style.

'We've played some unbelievable cricket in this tournament,' he told us.

'In parts, probably *the best* cricket of the tournament. Tonight did not go our way, but I hope when you look back you will think that we have achieved.'

He reminded us, as we sat with medals around necks, that the match we had just played in was a World Cup final.

'You haven't been together as a team for very long, so please think of it all in perspective.'

We had chased down 230 to beat South Africa, defended 142 against Afghanistan after being 57-6, then beat New Zealand and Sri Lanka convincingly, he reminded us. New Zealand had been the competition's form team.

'You should all be very proud of yourselves,' he finished.

Eoin Morgan took a similar theme, reminding us how far we had come in a year.

'It's scary to think where we can be another year from now,' he said.

Trevor is generally a man of few words. But I appreciated the ones he did say to me directly. After coming back from the post-match press conference, he revealed that he had been asked whether, if the game was to be replayed, he would have any qualms about me bowling that last over again.

'He'd do it tomorrow,' he told the reporters.

My mood was improving all the time.

Soon, once the beer was truly flowing, we all burst into song. Dressing-room karaoke versions of the personal ones sung by the crowd always give us a good chuckle. As a team we try not to take things too personally and tend to turn some of them into in-house jokes.

During downtime it's amazing what nonsense is hauled off the Internet. Some time earlier, one of the lads had found some YouTube footage of the Bhaji Army, a collection of passionate Indian fans, singing some of their ditties – the best from our perspective being about Stuart Broad's coating at the hands of Yuvraj Singh at the 2007 World Twenty20.

> It's the first ball of the over, Stuart Broad,
> And the mighty Yuvraj hits it out the park,

. . . and so on and so forth, all the way to six sixes. Funnily enough, as we sat there, this song was going through my head. It gave me the chance to get things back to normal in one fell swoop.

> *It's the first ball of the over Benny Stokes,*
> *And the mighty Carlos Brathwaite . . . la de da . . .*

Everybody around the room began creasing up with laughter. Then they joined in a new rendition.

It was an early event in a period of closure for me on a career-low moment. On the transfer to the team hotel, I got in touch with Clare, my girlfriend, for the first time. This was another step for me. Normally, when our phones come out of the ICC anti-corruption unit's locked box at the close of a day's play, she's the first person I look for in my messages. If I haven't got one, I tend to text her. But she knows me well enough. When things have gone wrong, she knows not to talk to me about cricket. At least until she thinks I might be alright. On this occasion, she left it until around the time we were leaving Eden Gardens.

She was with the other partners back at the Taj. 'On my way,' and 'You okay?' messages were exchanged before we met up. It was late and the hotel bar was shut when we got back. But this was a time for celebration not consolation. And we did so with our loved ones, who had been preparing for such circumstances by over-ordering vodkas, bottles of lemonade and requesting extra glasses.

It was nice that when we got to see the girls they were no longer upset – because as a team we were past that stage. We had come so close to achieving what we had set out to achieve when we left them back in the sub-zero UK just a few weeks earlier, and it was important to acknowledge the positive aspect of that.

We did so, in a private room laid on by the hotel management, until the early hours and beyond. The last drops were drunk at around nine o'clock the next morning.

Let's face it, if you'd told England fans at the start of a tournament that we would be playing in the final and taking the game right down to the wire, they would have been delighted. It was nice to be in celebratory mood about our achievements, rather than wallow in what might have been.

Everything that happened in those immediate hours after that final over helped me overcome the disappointments quicker than might have been expected. By the time we returned home, I had already come to terms with the fact that people would be talking about me. What others might say was out of my control. And that is the case when you do well too. Entering the dressing room to lavish praise can feel slightly embarrassing. You don't know quite what to say in response, so you either say nothing or give an awkward laugh. Just as, in that kind of scenario, I wanted to get back to being my old self again.

2

Marlon Samuels lacks respect. You get that if you have spent any time with him on a cricket field. It doesn't matter whether you are a team-mate or an opponent. You get it.

Compare his conduct after West Indies' victory over us in that World Twenty20 final to that of Carlos Brathwaite, his more inexperienced colleague. Where Carlos went with good grace, Marlon followed with a total disrespect for the game.

Without removing his batting pads, Marlon walked into a press conference, sat down and placed his feet on the desk. It was totally lacking manners. I don't think any other cricketer in the world would have done something like that.

There has been some bad blood between us over recent years, and it didn't require him to give me a character assassination – bizarrely claiming I am some sort of 'nervous laddie' – to help me form the opinion that I do not like him one bit. I believe in the saying 'Respect the game.' But I cannot remember him shaking hands with anyone on our team. I don't think he respects the game.

Yes, he played an unbelievable innings. The second time he had done that to us in international cricket. But because of our personal history, it stops me short of saying he's a good player. Yes, in white ball stuff Marlon has won a lot of games. But it's not my idea of a team player. Team players are the good players in my eyes.

With his feet still on the table rather than under it, he claimed, 'Stokes never learns', after our on-field exchanges during that final. Hang on. I was not the one fined 30 per cent of my match fee by the ICC for 'using language or a gesture that is obscene, offensive or insulting during an international match'.

This was all part of some very sad post-match behaviour all round in the aftermath of West Indies becoming world champions. I know their cricketers were discontented with their cricket board, and their participation was in doubt pre-tournament due to financial and contractual concerns, but to hear their chat, having just won the World Cup, was disappointing.

Instead of discussing what had been a glorious time, they were focusing on completely different things. In post-match press conferences, they should have been revelling in being the first international team to win two titles in the Twenty20 format. Instead, because of what had gone on before, they focused on other things – the wrong things. Marlon spent far too much time talking about myself and Shane Warne – whom he sarcastically dedicated his man-of-the-match award to three years after they had had a run-in at the Big Bash – while several other West Indies players aimed digs at those in charge of running their region's cricket.

Any verbals from me that evening had been in the heat of battle and were intended to gee up my team. Indeed, the first flashpoint came when we started brilliantly with the ball in defence of an under-par 155. In the past, sometimes this England team has had a tendency to ease off when we have got opponents three or four wickets down quickly, perhaps taking our foot off the gas in the mistaken belief we have already won. So there was me, Joe Root and Jason Roy – a three-pronged cheerleading squad – making sure that would not be the case this time.

I had drunk a couple of cans of Red Bull for an intake of caffeine during the interval, to try and get me up for the challenge. The adrenalin rush increases when you've taken a couple of them, and everyone else seemed to be on a high too. It was no wonder. We couldn't have wished for a better start than reducing West Indies to 14-3.

From my position back on the boundary, you could see the close fielders were bouncing. The ball was being pinged around the inner ring and at the wicketkeeper with real purpose. Some lads were wringing their hands, and when it's being thrown around with that much gusto, you know everyone is up for the fight. A team always looks good when individuals are feeding off others' energy. I had been as guilty as anyone in becoming submissive previously, but the pleasing thing here was that we maintained an aggressive collective approach and raised the intensity in the field a level or two.

When you have batsmen under the pump, it is important to maintain that position of dominance. Especially in Twenty20 when one big over can turn things round. I pride myself on trying to get the other lads going. I have certainly become more vocal since being recalled in the aftermath of last year's 50-over World Cup. Paul Farbrace, while he was interim coach, really drummed into me that I was a leader on the pitch.

'People will go with you,' he told me.

He gave me the confidence to speak more and encourage more while we were out there.

That is how I like to play – aggressive, on the edge. It is the nature of the game. Sometimes it goes over the line, but that can happen when playing for your country. In a World Cup final, the pulse is going and emotions can spill over.

It was when they were still 14-3 that I got involved with Marlon. Or rather his mannerisms got me involved. Although I'd started the tournament fielding in the covers, Eoin Morgan moved me to mid-off a couple of games in because he thought I might get a run out when batsmen hit the ball straight down the ground. It had worked against the Sri Lankans.

In my enthusiasm I found myself creeping in from my position and I noticed that Samuels, at the non-striker's end, was walking around like the big easy. I couldn't resist: 'You've got a bit of a swagger on here, Marlon, considering you're 14 for three.'

'Shut the f**k up, you little bitch,' came the reply.

I simply reminded him of the score, no more, and he came back with the same words again. At that point, Kumar Dharmasena stepped in. He told Marlon to chill out a bit. He didn't say anything to me but then again,

I had not really done anything to warrant being spoken to. As far as I was concerned, that was the end of it.

Not for Marlon, though, and when he was given out – caught behind, off the first ball outside the powerplay, sent down by Liam Plunkett – he decided to carry things on. I was fielding at long-off at the time, and admit to being tempted to have a word with him as I ran in to congratulate the other guys on what we thought was our fourth wicket. As I ran past him towards the huddle, I even considered giving him a farewell salute. Luckily, a voice in my head told me: *Don't do it, don't do it.*

It proved to be a good decision because, as we stood chatting, it became clear that Jos Buttler was not sure if the ball had carried all the way into his wicketkeeping gloves. Third umpire Marais Erasmus took an eternity over his decision; replays on the big screen showed it was a tight one. In our favour, we thought, was the fact that the decision on the field was out. In such an instance, there has to be comprehensive evidence for a decision to be over-ruled.

The more it was shown on the screen, though, the less out it looked, and, finally, after a lengthy stoppage, the decision was over-turned – Marlon had been reprieved with 20 to his name.

As I ran back to my position, he made a beeline towards me, staring me out. And this was without me doing anything untoward.

Of course, a lot is made of our history whenever we are pitched together. I tend not to waste too much time thinking about him, but I can see why the media have focused on the issue. Things had not been cordial since the very start of the 2015 Test series in the

Caribbean. Yes, even before he saluted me during the second match in Grenada – to send me off after I clobbered a long hop straight to the man in the deep.

I tried to see the funny side of that incident in the aftermath, truly I did, although it didn't stop me saluting back after we won the match in question. That was blatant points scoring. The Samuels salute even developed into a bit of a dressing-room mickey-take from that point on. Now, if one of us does something good we get the stiff-elbow military acknowledgement from our team-mates. Most famously, when Joe Root saluted me on the Lord's balcony after I got my hundred in the second innings against New Zealand in 2015.

● ● ●

Things did not go well for us at the start of the final, as we attempted to emulate the England side of 2010 in winning the World Twenty20. Eoin Morgan lost the toss and we were asked to bat by West Indies captain Darren Sammy. We too would have bowled first given the choice.

Cricketers can be superstitious. In the previous matches in Delhi, we had done well batting when I was positioned in the changing room, watching from the balcony. Naturally, I therefore wanted to do the same thing again. Only at Eden Gardens there is no balcony.

Without any viewing areas, it meant I had to watch on TV, and that made it a bizarre process. There is a five-second delay from the live action to the television broadcast, which means you hear big roars from the crowd uncertain what has occurred on the pitch. In India, the fans are so passionate and noisy that each 'yaaaaaaah' has the potential to be absolutely anything. It could be a single, it might even be a dot ball.

Unfortunately, there were a couple of uncertain moments during that opening spell that meant I soon had to change my position. Second ball: roar. Head up, I looked at the TV. Right, damn, J-Roy's out, bowled by a Samuel Badree slider. Not long after, more noise: Alex Hales nails a short ball from Andre Russell, straight to the man at short fine leg.

West Indies produce unconventional cricketers. Badree is one of them. He's so weird. As a bowler, he looks so innocuous, but he's dangerous as hell. I have never faced him. But he is very skilful in terms of pace variation and the different angles he uses to deliver the ball. He is not your classical leg-spinner, doesn't really give the ball much flight or a big rip, but his flat trajectory style is mightily effective. He regularly gets early wickets, and for him to bowl like he does in the powerplays is a massive bonus for West Indies. Even if he's not taking wickets, he can go for as little as four runs an over. We spoke about the danger he posed ahead of the game, and that if we did not lose wickets in that first six overs of powerplay we would be okay, because it would mean that we had seen Badree out.

Unfortunately, we lost three. From the moment Eoin Morgan lofted Sulieman Benn over extra cover for four I thought he was on, that he was going to bang a score, after struggling for one over the previous fortnight. He is that kind of player. But it wasn't to be – he was caught at slip soon afterwards.

I felt for Morgy during the tournament. It was so hard to listen to people criticize him for not getting any runs. Unfortunately, you can't see captaincy on a TV screen. Yes, some of his players performed well along the way. But it was Eoin Morgan who captained us to a World Cup final.

He made some really astute tactical decisions. The rotation of the bowlers, for instance, was something he judged brilliantly. David Willey would take the new ball to try to exploit any swing on offer, and would be kept on if either he was not going for runs, or looking likely to take wickets. But if there was not much doing, he would whip him off to bring him back in the middle overs and at the death.

He was flexible and seemed to have the knack of making the right calls at the right times. The one gamble against Sri Lanka – to keep the seamers on while they were dominating and hold the spinners back – would have been brilliant if it came off fully. It didn't. The Sri Lankans counter-attacked them, as the situation demanded they must. But we still won.

His best quality as captain, what has earned respect from the rest of us, is that he listens to the bowlers. So, if he wants a certain field but you don't, he won't force it upon you. He will ask if you are sure. If you are, all he will say is 'Good luck.' He also constantly reinforced the same message, saying before every game: it's all about us, we don't care what they do, let's be brilliant.

After our sticky start, Joe Root held the innings together superbly with Jos Buttler in support. It was just a shame that the rest of us could not capitalize on what was a really important stand. In fact, it took the depth of our batting order to get us up to something like a reasonable score. Even then, at the halfway stage, we all knew we were short with only 155 runs on the board.

During the break, I was having a slash out back when Morgy walked in. Our victory over South Africa was in my head. That day, we got hit for 229 but did not dwell on what had gone before in the match, only what was to come. Crucially, we managed to switch off from what happened in the first innings to concentrate on the second. I told him we needed to repeat that, to do exactly the same again. We needed to get out there committed to what was required for victory over the next 20 overs.

Yet when we walked out onto the field together, it was obvious that our team-mates were already fully focused on what was to come, not what had gone before. Every one of them was out there throwing, bowling or catching. There was a really positive vibe about them. You wouldn't have sensed from any of the body language that this was a team feeling behind in the game at that stage. There was a buzz around the field. Both Morgy and I were of the opinion words needed to be said when we discussed things in the toilets moments earlier. But on this evidence, any concerns that the team would get into our halfway huddle looking jaded or down from the first innings were dispelled.

Joe had been bowling a bit in practice that week and I knew he was going to bowl in the game itself because he only bowls in the warm-ups if he has been given the nod. His old man's back gets a rest otherwise. When it became obvious that we were going to bowl an off-spinner in the powerplays, I had thought, *Why not bowl Mo, then?* After all, Moeen Ali was in the team as our specialist offie.

But, when Johnson Charles skied the first ball of the second over, the first sent down by Rooty, straight to me at mid-on, those thoughts switched to *Morgy, you genius*. As I was shoved back to long-off for Chris

Gayle to take strike to the next ball, it crossed my mind that it was as likely that he would mishit a delivery from Joe down the ground as one from Moeen. Gayle has a reputation for getting out to part-time spinners and although the danger is he murders them with his power, it was obviously a gamble worth taking.

And one that paid off for us, handsomely. As soon as Gayle wound up his long levers for that fourth ball of the over, I looked straight down at the rope behind my feet. I knew I had to get my boots as close to it as was possible and not go any further back. Even Gayle's mishits tend to test the boundary edge and I wanted to make sure that I gave myself maximum room to work with as the ball went up into the night sky. Double-checking with a downwards glance one second and judging the flight of the ball the next, it then struck me that I need not be right back on the line at all. Its trajectory told me it wasn't going to reach me.

Christ, I need to run in for this.

Luckily, it went so high that I got there comfortably despite my panic, set myself and held on. It was a great feeling.

At that stage, it felt as though all my hunches were coming to fruition. From the moment I set foot on the plane out to India I believed we were going to be one of those top teams contesting the prize. Our first game against West Indies had been a bit of a reality check on how well we would need to play to live up to that, having been Chris Gayle-d in Mumbai.

Then, halfway through the South Africa game at the same venue, I was thinking, *Oh God, we're going home here.* But we made a habit of getting out of the crap. In previous tournaments I'd watched, often the teams that went on to be crowned champions were the ones that chased down ridiculous targets, defended unrealistic scores when they had no real right to, and kept finding ways of winning against the odds. It's amazing how often this kind of thing happens. Equally, while teams that scrape through and show character to win games that look lost prosper, ones that sail through groups winning every game never seem to do so.

Destiny was on our side when we got to the final, I believed. Australia were a whisker away from being eliminated by South Africa in England in 1999 and went on to lift the World Cup. They came back from the brink to take the glory. As a fan, you recognize from afar the patterns that develop in major tournaments, but I had gone from watching top-level sport to being one of the people involved in the drama as our own story unfolded. When it's happening to you – victories snatched from the jaws of defeat as they were against the South Africans and Afghanistan – it feels quite weird.

One of the lessons I learned on my first full England tour to Australia was that you've never won until you've won. Equally, you have never lost until your last chance has got up and walked right out of town. How many games have you seen that look dead and buried, that have resulted in teams, that should never have won, winning? Believe me, you don't want to be that team that it happens to – as we were in Brisbane in early 2014.

It was the second one-day international of a five-match series, and we had not won an international match on tour. Whitewashed in the Ashes, then defeated in the opening 50-over game in Melbourne. We put a much better performance together at the Gabba, and were on the verge of getting a first victory on the board. Australia were nine wickets down, required 57 more and there were only six overs left. Unfortunately, however, one of those last two men was James Faulkner, who earlier that winter had stolen a match off India with a display of extraordinary hitting. Now he showed us just why a game is never done. Clint McKay, his last-wicket partner, contributed just two, and faced only nine of the deliveries as Faulkner farmed the strike expertly. I was on the receiving end of his big hitting, which came between him nabbing singles to ensure he faced the majority of the bowling. By the end he was on such a roll that he took 25 off his final seven deliveries, and all 12 required off the final over from its opening three balls.

We had arrived in India on the back of a 2-0 Twenty20 series defeat to South Africa. Of course, there was the usual talk of 'England can't play spin, and they're heading to India next', after Imran Tahir bagged four wickets against us in the first game, a share of which slipped through our fingers literally when Reece Topley fumbled a throw from the deep off the last ball. Then, after making a mess of the death overs in Johannesburg, where we scored 14 from the final 22 balls for the loss of seven wickets, South Africa showed that good teams punish mistakes.

The annoying thing was that we knew we were better than that. In the privacy of the dressing room, Trevor Bayliss, our coach, was not throwing tea cups or anything like. Both he and Eoin, our captain, are men of few words, who keep calm, and in any case we didn't really need telling where we had gone wrong. As a team we trust ourselves to deliver at crucial times more often than not. We had come up short.

As a partnership Bayliss and Morgan are pretty cool. I mean cool in the sense of not panicking. There is no bullshit from them. And there is no bullshit back to them from us, either. I think that's why we had such a successful first year under Trevor, why we have had such a united changing room and why we are all really close.

They both kept telling us ahead of the World Twenty20 that the boldest team would be the one that won, urging us not to go into our shells after two defeats. Equally, they were realistic about the make-up of our squad. We were young – only old man Liam Plunkett was in his thirties – with nowhere near as many caps as some of our rivals. They know Twenty20 cricket in India. Many of the Indian players were together at the Kolkata Knight Riders and won the IPL.

'We've had some good performances, and there's a lot of potential there. But potential never won anything,' Bayliss said to the media when we left South Africa in late February.

Within 24 hours of being on Indian soil, all thoughts of South Africa were out of our heads, and we wanted to show that potential could win something. We were straight into training sessions the day after we arrived, and everyone was feeling really confident. These conditions were different from what we had been playing in recent times, and it felt like we had properly moved on. The conditions were also different from what you might expect to find in India.

Our first session at the Wankhede Stadium in Mumbai proved to be a real eye opener – the practice wickets were so flat. The ball was going through at a decent pace, and there wasn't much turn. It was nothing like what we were expecting. Not many of us had played in India before, myself included, and we were anticipating them to spin quite a bit more.

If the pitches were as immaculate as those given for us to net on, we said amongst ourselves, the batsmen would have a field day.

Of course, the ones at the Wankhede were as true – the one given to us for our first group game against West Indies absolutely identical to those we had been practising on. In a Twenty20 tournament like this, you would take a score of 182 for your first outing and there were no complaints from us in terms of runs on the board.

Unfortunately, though, West Indies possess Chris Gayle, one of those players who can make any total shrink. When someone like him is going full tilt, it is so hard to stop. Some people say he has an intimidating factor about him. I wouldn't necessarily agree with that. It's not like he psychs you out, as some might think. He is just highly talented, and it is a cold stone fact that if you don't get your bowling right when he is in touch, you're going to get punished.

Certain players around the world will completely take you apart if you don't get things right. Gayle is one of them. If you miss your yorker, and it's a half-volley, he gets that huge swing of the bat of his under the ball so easily you can bet it's going to be six. He's so powerful that even his mishits go the distance. Mind you, on this particular night, he didn't mishit many. Only once, when he lobbed one over Joe Root's head – if the boundary rope had been two yards further back it would have been a different game – did we have a sniff of getting him out.

Gayle's muscle actually obliterated our pre-tournament bowling plan. The bowling attack had bought into a slightly different way of doing things in this tournament. Dot-ball percentage is one of the chief statistics coaches look for from their bowling group, and of course you are trying to bowl as many of them as possible. Stringing them together puts opposition teams under pressure.

However, our ploy – chiefly for the opening six overs of powerplay when the fielding restrictions were on – was that if we bowled two dot balls, instead of running and hoping to bowl another, we would feed the on-strike batsman a single. We figured giving them one got the guy off strike, and was a much better option than conceding a boundary. It also gave us the chance to bowl at the other batsman. With only two guys outside the 30-yard circle, if a batsman gets two or three dots on them, you know they're going to be looking for a boundary as a way of relieving the pressure.

Our job was to try to think a step ahead of him: to commit to a certain delivery at the end of our mark, whether it be yorker, bouncer or slower ball, and try to get him to hit it straight to your fielder in the deep. If they hit it for four or six, well played. If on the delivery in question your opponent was better than you, so be it. But if, as the bowler, you nailed it, all the better – trying to keep them to a single is not negative, you can also pick up wickets. The yorker keeps bowled and lbw in play, a bouncer can result in a top edge straight up or a catch on the rope at deep square leg.

We tried this in the first game in Group 1; we just didn't execute it properly. I made this point in the post-match debrief. As far as I was concerned, there was no point analyzing what we could have done better, what we didn't do well, because we headed into the game with a plan. We weren't good enough on the day to execute it. It was important not to go against what we had agreed in the build-up. Sure, it hadn't worked, but I didn't see any value in dumping it after one match.

However, losing that first game opened our eyes to a very harsh reality. We couldn't keep getting things wrong. The way the tournament was scheduled – with only the top two countries progressing to the latter stages – now meant we had to win every single game to guarantee our hopes of being crowned world champions alive. One more slip-up would mean needing favours from others.

While there was a pledge to keep the bowling tactics the same, however, Jason Roy and Alex Hales committed to change at the top of our batting. If surfaces were going to be this good, they needed to trust them and hit through the ball from the start. In Twenty20 cricket, realizing you are playing on a belter four overs in can be too late. They accepted their jobs were to take advantage, not survive, and that self-assessment was crucial in the way we were to play from then on.

To be honest, there was no choice in our second match, against the South Africans. The size of South Africa's total forced our hand. They had 96 after seven overs, for goodness sake. It was complete madness. Every ball was pinging off the middle of the bats of Quinton de Kock and Hashim Amla, it seemed, and either threading through the infield or clearing it altogether. There were so many runs scored in the first third of the innings that the task became restricting them to something that was not completely ludicrous. At one stage it must have looked like they were going to surpass Sri Lanka's 260-6 against Kenya and bang a new world record T20 international total.

From the position we were in, we managed to drag things back but, let's face it, when you are talking about that volume of runs everything is relative. Being asked to score at 11-and-a-half an over was still pretty steep – not so long ago 230 was considered a good one-day score.

The best thing at the halfway stage was how we switched off from what had just happened. Hales and Roy ran off to get their pads on, as if they couldn't wait to get started, there was an energy about the team and there were lots of shouts of, 'Come on, boys, let's do this shit.' There was no moaning, no heads went down.

Before we left the pitch Morgy told me: 'Stokesy, you're batting three.' So I was focused from the first ball. Seeing it sail over mid-off's head for a one-bounce four, then the same treatment again second ball, set a crazy tone. Kagiso Rabada took some real punishment from J-Roy, then Hales collared Dale Steyn. We had 44 on the board after just two overs. No bowler was to be spared.

I was in during the third, and wasn't going to play any other way than foot to the floor. I knew what I had to do. There was no subtlety required, no time to play myself in. I had been promoted in the order to take advantage of the powerplay, to try to drag the run rate down as much as I could, and it was a nice challenge going in to bat against a hard ball with only two South African fielders out for protection.

Frustratingly, I managed to pick one of them out, hitting a full toss straight to the man at deep-square, when I had so wanted to play a bigger part in getting us to that target. When Rabada hit the pitch I managed to swing him into the stands at deep midwicket earlier in the over. This one, if anything, I hit too well. It was one of those flat hits; it spent about two seconds in the air. All the intense sessions of power hitting against length balls, slower balls and yorkers – and a full bunger had done for me. Shame we never have anyone throwing the ball at our hips during those drills.

To worsen my mood, the shot split my bat just under the splice. Safe to say the crack in it got considerably bigger back in the dressing room – to the extent that it ended up not so much a crack but two different bits.

Jase and I were dismissed in consecutive overs, but from a position of 87-3 in the sixth over, Joe Root was typical Joe Root. The start to the innings had got the lads on our bench buzzing – it had been absolutely class to watch the ball getting blazed around everywhere at the head of our reply. But by the 12th over there was a different noise level altogether. It was around that time that the realization kicked in – *We're making a good job of this*. Now there were a few nerves where previously there were none.

Root's innings was incredible. Not once did he slog, yet he was hitting boundaries every third ball. For a guy who is not a big power hitter, his strike rate of 188.63 was ridiculous. Whenever we needed it, he anticipated the delivery that was coming down and found the gap.

What sets him apart from others, and what has taken him to a level alongside the very best batsmen in the world, in whatever form you nominate, is that he is such a brilliant reader of the game. The reverse sweep off Chris Morris that flew for six over third man and into the crowd was probably the shot of the tournament. It was so inventive. The match situation meant he needed to exploit whatever open expanses of grass were open to him whenever he could, and he was able to manouevre the ball into them every single time.

That six not only brought up his 50, it also dipped the required run rate below 10 with five-and-a-half overs to go. He's freakish, really. Others get noticed for their range of power hitting, but he is so adaptable. On the occasions when he doesn't anticipate the delivery bowled, he is able to compromise and produce a shot to suit it and the field that's been set.

I grew up playing junior cricket with him and what has changed him into the amazing player we see today is his ability to score quickly whatever the colour of the ball, the length of the game or the match situation. He never used to be able to hit the ball with any great power, whereas now he can go aerial, in addition to his deft touches and vision. It has made him a really special player for this England team. He has the class of knowing where the gaps are, the ability to hit them, and a big enough strike in him to take those gaps out of the equation and clear the boundary.

Faced with a required run rate of 10, sloggers like me think only of sixes, but his take on the situation is different. While I will swing hard, sometimes too hard, at each ball, he will try to manipulate a couple of boundaries and make the over a profitable one that way. He's in a class of his own at the moment.

Everyone got a bit fidgety in the dug-out, and I found myself wandering up to our changing room at one point. But Paul Collingwood, on the coaching staff for the tournament, sent me back down to where I had been sitting.

'Go back and sit in your seat, man, because I've been stood in this f**king place the whole time we've been batting.'

Colly, my county captain at Durham, is one of the biggest enforcers of retaining your position in the ground while things are going well on the field. Mind you, we all do it. I was to remain in the dressing room at the start of the final. During the series-clinching win over New Zealand in the one-day international at Chester-le-Street the previous year, I didn't move a muscle while Jonny Bairstow steered us home.

Joe had reduced things to a run a ball when he followed my lead and hauled a full toss into the hands of a fielder in the deep, trying to finish the game with an over in hand, as the best players do.

Tension remained because, whatever had gone before in those three hours on the field, we still had to make sure we got over the line. Only a win would do, remember, so there were still a few nerves amongst those waiting to bat. I refused to believe we could do anything but win. *Game over*, I thought, even when we had the late drama of losing wickets.

It was an amazing feeling to win. As we sat there in the dressing room, someone said: 'Imagine how good tonight's going to be.'

There were to be a few more nights like that during our time in India. At Delhi's Feroz Shah Kotla, six wickets down against Afghanistan, we were effectively in the departure lounge again. But this England team is not only good, it has great depths of resolve, and we showed them to get out of a trough once more. Winning games of cricket like this, from seemingly hopeless positions, gives you immense belief, no matter the identity of the opposition.

And let's be honest, England always seem to have trouble against unfancied opposition in major tournaments. The Netherlands; Ireland; the Dutch again; Afghanistan. Heaven knows why.

What I must tell you is that there was no under-estimation of our opponents' talents. We knew Afghanistan possessed quality players, some of the most naturally gifted of limited-overs players doing the rounds. They bat all the way down to number nine; they all hit the ball so cleanly; a couple of their bowlers hit close to 90 mph and are seriously skilful with it; some of the best spinners in the tournament wore their blue shirts.

Even so, we knew should be beating them, and when you are up against a team like that, and don't start well, a fear of failure can creep into your mind and you become tentative. I cannot speak for others, but that wasn't the case for me. I just had a howler. My up and down time took in the run out of Joe Root, for which I was more than slightly culpable, by the bowler Mohammad Nabi at the second attempt, he was so far short of his ground. Then, just as I was trying to rebuild the innings alongside Moeen Ali, I received an absolute stinker of a ball that left me looking like a right idiot.

The World Cup was ever-present on television in India – games were shown live, highlights seemed to be on a reel 24-7 and everything that happened on and off the field was debated. There were montages of the best of this and that – sixes, catches, wickets. Somehow, and I could laugh about it later, the grubber that the leg-spinner Rashid Khan snuck through me managed to make it into one of the best deliveries of the tournament! You what?

The ball simply didn't bounce and I dragged it via an under-edge into my stumps. Stuff like that tends to happen for teams when fortune is favouring them. Afghanistan were on a roll and that effectively gave them a bonus wicket. Not that they needed any bonuses. We were six wickets down, there were only 57 runs on the board and more than half the overs remained. Sprawled on all fours, I was annoyed with myself for trying to hit the ball far too hard.

What we did learn as a team from that incident, though, was that shorter-pitched spin deliveries sat in the Feroz Shah Kotla wicket for longer than other surfaces we were used to. As a batsman, you therefore had to be more clinical when facing up to it. I'd received another drag down the previous ball and pulled it for four. Now I had been done by a repeat dose. You can imagine how I felt – no matter what the game situation, if you get one of those off a spinner you need to punish it. Unfortunately, I didn't, and in the process of adjusting to the comical bounce had fallen flat on my face.

I was furious I'd managed to get out to a ball like that. 'Why is it always me?' as Mario Balotelli would say. A full toss, now this; I was finding ridiculous ways to get out.

It left a lot of work for the tail to do but Mo, Chris Jordan and David Willey kept their composure to give us something to bowl at. Once we got to 107-7 with a couple of overs remaining, we knew we could get 125-130. Whereas a score below a run a ball would have resulted in almost certain defeat, that would be enough. Put it this way – it *had* to be enough.

We were well and truly back in the game. Outsiders, yes, but we had a chance, and that chance improved when Amir Hamza, Afghanistan's left-arm spinner, came on to bowl the 19th over.

He was bowling to two left-handers. On the bench there was a collective 'Wow'. We knew it was good for us. We had two very good ball strikers at the crease in Mo and Dave and they would both be hitting with the spin. That one over went for 25. There is no doubt that it won us the game.

There had been media talk of our need to improve our net run rate during this match, how boosting it would improve our chances should teams like us, West Indies, South Africa and Sri Lanka finish level on points.

To be frank, that never came into our heads. A lot of things can happen over the course of cricket matches, and it's important not to get too far ahead of yourselves. We just knew where we had to be at the end of our next match, the final one of the group against Sri Lanka – on the winner's podium again. South Africa's defeat to West Indies the previous day, in Nagpur, simplified the equation further. If we secured victory, everything else would take care of itself. It was high stakes, I guess. But at the same time, the demands on us had not changed. Win and we were in the knock-out phase. Losing meant a plane ticket home.

From the brilliant start we had, we should never have lost that game. Yet in the end it got quite tight. People are a lot better at hitting the cricket ball nowadays, plus there is a lot more diversity in terms of shots, and where a batsman can hit it. So there tends to be less panic if wickets are falling early on and the required run rate sky-rockets. You can't change what has already happened, so players have become a lot more accepting of the circumstances they get thrown into. So even though Sri Lanka were plunged into a position of 15-4 after only three overs, chasing 172, they knew they were not out of it.

From our perspective, the energy in the field early on was really positive. That tendency to slacken off after a couple of early wickets was not there to restrict us, and we seized on Sri Lankan mistakes. To play my part was pleasing. Hours of practice goes in to executing run outs from drop and runs, and to be able to exploit Angelo Mathews' indecision to leave Lahiru Thirimanne short at the non-striker's end with a diving underarm throw, felt absolutely class. Only two things had been asked of me at that stage, the end of the 23rd over of the match, and I had done both of them. Having slammed the final ball of the innings from Thisara Perera for a leg-side six, I had now bought us a wicket.

Even then we knew what a dangerous side Sri Lanka could be. They were reigning champions, and although they no longer had the class of player of four years previously, in Mathews and Perera they possessed two massive ball strikers. Mathews did not get off to any kind of start at all. He didn't even try to keep up with the rate – partly due to the fact we didn't let him, partly because he knew he had to take the chase as deep as possible for his team to retain their own chances of a victory.

He faced 24 balls to get into the 20s yet ended up getting 73 not out off 54. In Twenty20, all it takes is one big over for teams to get right back in the game. Sri Lanka got a couple of them, and with Mathews still there we were under pressure to perform with the ball.

At that stage, my death bowling was really pleasing me. Twenty20 is a game that is frustrating but one that actually requires a sense of humour. You can bowl four overs one day and get hit for 20. Next day you can bowl the same four overs and go for over 40. There are very fine margins that exist.

But I practise my slower balls, yorkers, bouncers, everything, heavily – probably more than I do length. You bowl so much in first-class cricket that your normal length looks after itself. It's the specific change-up skills that you need to work on, and I had been concentrating on this every training session for quite some time.

In the first game against West Indies I didn't really need to bowl any death stuff. I was just trying to bash a length and change up my pace. It didn't work. The dew made it difficult to bowl anything with real confidence. I had never bowled with a ball that wet before. I asked Mo what it was like for him as an off-spinner. He told me he couldn't bowl anything on the seam. He had to grip everything cross-seam. It was no use making excuses, that's the way things go in a tournament – you lose some tosses and suffer, you win others and gain an advantage – it just didn't help our cause that we couldn't hold the ball comfortably.

Thankfully, for the next game they sprayed the outfield to stop the dew settling. It is not something we are used to in England. I moved on knowing that on another day things could have been completely different. Here, with a drier ball, I knew I needed to bowl my yorkers and slower balls more. The situation called for that. Reece Topley began the tournament as one of our death bowlers but was no longer in the side, and that meant David Willey, Chris Jordan and I were vying for the job.

I love the responsibility. Eoin Morgan knows I practise it heavily. I had done it a couple of times for him and delivered before, most notably against Australia the previous year, and he always seems pretty confident in my ability to deliver. Equally, I think he knows that some days it won't come out as right as others. From my side, I had made it a goal at that tournament to show him as captain that I was capable of bowling at the end. It was the same for all the seam bowlers in our team. They all wanted to show their versatility.

Sri Lanka entered the final two overs needing 22. It was game on. If ever there was a time to deliver those skills, this was it, and fair play to CJ because he did. His accuracy in hitting the block hole improved the rate in our favour. When I was thrown the ball for that final over, it was 15 needed from six balls. Mathews was on strike. I knew that I had to prevent him getting under the ball. Everything had to be full. I delivered. First up, a dot; a couple of twos; another yorker found its mark; another and victory was ours.

I was relishing the chance to influence games. I'm the guy who wants to make a difference at every opportunity. So to be asked to be one of our go-to men at the end of innings was exciting. Sure, the heat is on and you can get burnt – that's the nature of the job – yet it also comes with the massive appeal of being a hero.

Against New Zealand, Morgy left me and CJ for the final assault once again. Only this time, I got two overs rather than one. My first couple had been wicketless and cost 20, although they might have been quite different but for a couple of inside edges from Colin Munro's bat that missed the stumps and flew for four.

When I got the ball for my second spell, none of that was in my mind. I felt ready to deliver what I had done in practice over the past fortnight – what I had been able to produce against the Sri Lankans just three nights earlier on the same ground. On that pitch, I knew that a combination of full balls and off-pace deliveries would be the best option – and I was not wrong. With confidence high that I was a successful end-of-innings bowler, I either targetted the base of the stumps or a shorter length when I was bowling slower balls.

You have to have a ticket to win the raffle, they say. Three times the ball was mishit into the Delhi night sky. Three times it landed in hands of my team-mates. To finish with figures of 4-0-26-3 was awesome. If you are going at a run a ball from the 16th over onwards, you are well ahead of the game. I had only gone at three an over. But like I said, that's the nature of the beast. Had I deserved figures of 2-0-20-0 earlier in the innings? No, that was harsh. But the beauty of Twenty20 is that every-thing can change in a flash.

Restricting New Zealand to 153-8 was a massive bonus. They had been scoring in excess of nine runs an over for the first 10, so it was a great team effort in the second half of the innings. Once again, Jason grabbed the initiative at the start of our reply. The way he bats against the new ball is a pleasure to watch from the dug-out. I think players like him rub off on others. Taking 16 off Corey Anderson's first over set the tone, and meant we were always ahead of the rate. I like guys that go through red lights, if you know what I mean, and Jason is one of them when he bats.

If it feels like you are meant to be scoring at eights, he will go at nines or 10s just because he can. When he bats he just sees ball, hits ball, and his method was worth 78 off 44, plus the man-of-the-match award. Within a flash, it seemed, Jos Buttler was booking our place in the final – and a shot at a second World Twenty20 title – in typical fashion. A late flurry of sixes meant we were through to meet West Indies with 17 deliveries to spare.

Ultimately, we fell short but there is so much hope for the future. We don't play Twenty20 internationals that often, but there is no reason why this England team shouldn't win every single game over the next couple of years. What we have shown is that we are one of the best teams in the world. The challenge now is to take that up a notch. Opponents fear us. We don't worry about anyone else. And we are so young that we have a lot of growth in us as a team. In terms of global names, we don't have a lot of those, but there is definitely something about us, and the way we play.

We have the ability to be challenging for trophies again, and I want to be in that situation trying to win the World Twenty20 again, and to experience the feelings West Indies players felt. They received some criticism for the way they bounced around the field in the aftermath, but you have to let the winning team have their five to 10 minutes together in that situation. They wanted to celebrate as a group because they had just won a World Cup and we had to respect that. Let's face it, we would have been overcome by emotion in the moment too. Unfortunately, the emotion that engulfed me was quite a contrast.

On the night I was not good enough, and it hurt like hell. But, immediately after I had gathered myself, I knew it was the right thing – the sporting thing to do – to shake everyone's hand. It is what I will always try to do.

After I got stuck into Temba Bavuma with a few choice words during the Test series in South Africa in early 2016, I made sure I was straight up to congratulate him when he reached his maiden hundred. His performance deserved that. As far as I am concerned, what is said on the pitch stays on the pitch. It's a shame not everyone shares the same view and carries on the same way.

3

It took a while for me to accept the kind of cricketer I am. There was quite a lot of frustration along the way. Over the years there was a lot of head scratching, and some head banging too, before I was persuaded that with the way I play comes a tendency for my form to veer from one extreme to the other. Where I am concerned, there will be moments of heartache but also moments of great triumph. There will be highs and lows, and in the case of early 2016, an ability to fluctuate from one end of the spectrum to the other.

Of course, I would rather not go from the level of performance I managed in England's first Test of 2016, to that which left me disconsolate in Kolkata four months later. Naturally, the challenge is to improve my consistency, so that the talk in future tends to be like it was after my Test-best score of 258 at Newlands rather than my Brathwaite mauling. It's not that I'm after appreciation from others — although that's nice — it's just that I want to be the best I can be. And pushing your personal threshold of achievement higher is one of the beauties of playing professional sport.

If that process was easy I would be there already, of course. Lots of us would, wouldn't we? It's far from easy, though, and who knows how far any individual can go. I am committed to having fun finding out, and what I can promise is that while I am out there on a cricket field I will always give my all. That pretty much sums me up – it might be penthouse one day, shithouse the next, but it will never be for the want of trying.

Thankfully, the England coaching duo of Trevor Bayliss and Paul Farbrace fully accept the characteristics I bring. They back me to be me. One of the things that picked me up in those first few days of April was when Trevor said in the World Twenty20 final post-match press conference that I was 'the heart and soul of this team'.

'If everyone put in half as much as Stokesy does, we'd go a long way. You can't fault Ben's leadership in the team or the effort he puts in. It doesn't matter whether he is batting, bowling or fielding, he gives you 100 per cent until there's nothing in the tank. The more of those type of cricketers we can produce, the better for England cricket,' he said.

It's an unbelievable boost to your confidence to hear your coach speak about you like that. And Trevor has played a huge part in understanding what it is that I deliver as an all-rounder. Now I am able to sum myself up as a cricketer. Yes, I'm going to go through a period of low scores and not go too well. But all of a sudden I know something can just happen for me. I'm not necessarily a form player, more of an in-the-moment player.

In the past, I perhaps fell into the trap of expecting something to happen for me every single match. But I no longer expect to score runs, make hundreds, bowl well, take wickets, every time. Obviously I want to, and I try to, but even the best players have been unable to do it on a daily basis. People like Brian Lara, Jacques Kallis have been through bad times, and I am finally understanding that now.

Cricket is such a hard game and mistakes are magnified because of it, particularly when you're batting. One mistake, your pads are off and you are sat watching the rest of the innings. I'm probably going to make more mistakes than others because of the way I want to play, but the management team know that if I under-perform skill-wise, it's not because I am under-performing effort-wise.

Just occasionally, skill and effort combine to create something special. In those moments, it feels like you can cope with anything thrown at you by your opponents. On days like 3 January 2016, you feel almost invincible.

I had no idea about the number of records that had just fallen as I went to meet the assembled media that evening.

It was only on the walk to the press conference that I got a grasp of it all. That was when Rhian Evans, the England team's media manager, told me all the things that I would be asked, and reeled off the statistics that had been surpassed both individually and as a partnership by Jonny Bairstow and me during our 399-run stand in Cape Town.

My innings of 258 against South Africa in the second match of the series was the fastest score of 250 in Test history; I had registered the fastest double-hundred by an England player; the highest score ever by a number six; the 130 runs I contributed before lunch on day two was the most by a single player in a morning session; the combined tally between us was a new high for the sixth-wicket across all Test nations; and no England player had previously struck as many as 11 sixes in one visit to the crease.

Not that any of this stuck in my head, particularly. I have never been good at revising. Swotting up on numbers? Nah, not for me. A couple of the facts may have sunk in but, to be honest, I found it all a bit of a blur. And what are you supposed to say in that situation? I don't find it easy to speak in public about personal achievements. Saying things about myself does not come easy, and can make you sound a bit goofy. It's the doing part I like best. Others can talk about it.

Whenever I walk out to bat with those three lions on my chest, I want to do the best I possibly can, to put England into a dominant position, to entertain the fans that give such unbelievable support. I didn't do anything differently at Newlands. It was just that things fell into place for me on this occasion.

It's pretty transparent from seeing me play that I thrive on opportunities to attack, and if I think it will enhance the team position I tend to go for it. On this occasion, the cards fell perfectly for me.

I was far from gung-ho at the start. My immediate concern when I went out to bat was to survive the hat-trick ball Kagiso Rabada was about to send down. Then it was time to rebuild with Joe Root. I feel comfortable batting with him. We know each other so well and when we're together in the middle we have a laugh – trying to relax by taking the mickey out of each other. We shared a 50-stand playing normally, refusing to take risks. South Africa were bowling well and it wasn't particularly easy during that period. Early on I survived a review for lbw by Morne Morkel that was missing leg-stump.

But I did feel good at the crease. I feel I am playing well when I am hitting the ball straight down the ground, between mid-on and the umpire. It's my signature shot for being in nick. I played one off Chris Morris, on 24, and knew immediately I was on my way to a big one. Not 258 big but a big one.

Tactically, I was very focused on not letting Dane Piedt, South Africa's off-spinner, settle into a rhythm, wanting Hashim Amla, his captain, to feel under pressure to bring back his seamers more often than he might otherwise have done. It wasn't that I took a policy of all-out assault to start off with, far from it; I just wanted to be busy against him, always looking to score, to rotate the strike. If you take four runs across an over from an off-spinner, then follow up with boundaries whenever he over-compensates, you can find that the scoreboard flies along.

Because it was such a flat wicket, it was hard work for the seamers and I wanted them to bowl as much as possible. I wanted to make them work for everything they got. The only time I considered upping the tempo on that first day was, after Joe got out, when they took the new ball.

'I'm in, let's be positive, don't go into your shell, let's try to put them under pressure by attacking it,' I told myself.

Opening bowlers can occasionally run in with that second new ball expecting things to happen, confident that the batsmen are going to be watchful. They almost expect to get a few wickets. But, as I know from experience, it doesn't just happen, you still have to work for your rewards. And I wanted to take advantage of any complacency as well as fatigue.

If they bowled well at me with the new rock then fair enough, but in my mind I suspected they'd be tired. There might be a few scoring opportunities offered up to me as a result, and if I got them I was determined to cash in. It was that moment that triggered things for me.

We were 271-5 when Chris Morris took it. First ball, he put it right in the slot for a perfect cover drive; next up I went hard again and the ball flashed over the slips; the fourth one was a gift half-tracker outside off; and from the fifth ball I got my fourth boundary of a 17-run over as an edge went into the gap where third slip had been moments earlier.

My decision to be positive had resulted in the fielders being spread out over the field within a couple of minutes, and from then on, as the harder ball flew off the bat, there were men out everywhere. The catchers were gone, the danger had therefore been reduced and there was a deep point, a deep square leg.

From the second ball of that 81st over, I had reached my 50 off 70 deliveries. By the end of the day, I had 74 off 93. My mentality to make them suffer as they tired paid dividends. During that half-hour period, there were regular boundaries and our scoring went up and up, as it tends to do against a harder ball.

In one aspect, I did get carried away. I had been so focused on taking on the South African attack, looking to score as heavily as I could from each ball, that the time aspect of batting towards the end of a day's Test cricket had temporarily left my mind. In a brief moment of composure, I told myself to keep playing the same way until we got to within three overs of the close. That would be time to dial it in.

I was still unfurling pull shots right up until that point. Some I was nailing and others were flying off top-edges but they all seemed to be locating the gaps between fine leg and deep square or falling into no man's land. Yes, there were two guys back and if they were going to bowl short I would not try to control it, I would hit it hard. I was confident playing the shot. When I am 'in' my technique is different from when I first get to the crease, and I backed myself to middle it more often than not. If I hit it straight to one of them, so be it.

In terms of technique, when I face up to my initial deliveries of an innings, my back foot tends to slip towards the leg-side, as it always tended to when I was a kid. But it is a flaw I am constantly aware of, and one I can iron out fairly quickly. I am very conscious of old habits, and this one tends to be worse when I have just come off a lot of one-day batting – clearing my front leg to go aerial.

If everything is in good order, I am motionless. Whenever I feel as though I am shuffling a bit, I load up footage of my performance against New Zealand at Lord's in 2015. I find watching myself in those innings gives me confidence if I am in a bit of a rut with my batting. Standing still is important to getting my technique where I want it to be.

If I am hitting the ball well from the start like that, even from defensive shots, or leaving the ball as decisively as I was, it fills me with confidence, and I knew I was in decent nick when, in trying to make a nice contact with the bat on the ball, I was connecting with the middle and picking up fours. It felt pretty effortless.

Although I had given myself a cut-off of three overs remaining before pulling up the drawbridge, I was wrongly looking at the overs left on the scoreboard rather than the clock. Yep, I still believed we had six overs left when we had three. It was only when Jonny said, 'Right, two overs left lad,' that I realized. 'Shit, it's a good job you told me, I was going to keep playing like this,' I said to him. South Africa had been slow through their overs, and could not complete the stipulated 90 in six-and-a-half hours.

I was in shot-playing mode. Now suddenly, I had to keep telling myself 'No' to avoid temptation. Obviously, had I got a full toss I wouldn't have blocked it – I would have been going for it 100 per cent – but at that stage of the day it is about striking the balance. You don't want to go chasing a wide one or heaving one straight into deep square-leg's hands to gift them a wicket. That simply gives the momentum to your opponents and offers them a fresh batsman to bowl at the following morning.

Stepping off the gas at that point ensured the next morning would be fun. I got a handful of early drives away; a pull shot for a couple, an upper-cut to the third man boundary. I was motoring without trying. After just 12 balls of that second morning, I found myself on 97. In a flash, I was one shot away from a third Test hundred.

I got there at the first attempt, after watching Jonny take a couple of fours off Morkel. Morris offered me a length ball around off-stump and I managed to thread it into the gap. I knew it was worth at least three from the moment it left the bat, and even though Temba Bavuma stopped it hitting the rope at deep extra, I knew that we would make that third run easily – Jonny is one of the fastest men between the wickets on the world scene.

Every time you score a hundred for England, it's class. The feeling is mint. You've dreamed of it as a kid growing up, of course, but actually being out there experiencing it, throwing your arms aloft, is amazing. This time the sense of achievement was mixed with one of relief, as I had gone several months without one. I'd got to 60 in a Test in Dubai, but there were no further runs in that series against Pakistan. Then, there had been disappointment for me in the first Test of the South Africa series in Durban, because I had not been able to make good form count – after getting a start, I got out to a poor shot.

Not that I had been dwelling on any of this while I was out there. I had managed to get up to 100 without too much aggression. In my head, after celebrating the moment, I told myself, 'Right, time to pick it up.' That is something I have always done. If I get to three figures, unless the team definitely does not require it, I will go on a major offensive.

We were so far ahead of the game, already 1–0 up in the series, and that kind of thing tends to increase a team's confidence. We had a strong batting line-up too, so it wasn't the end of the world if they dismissed me. On the other hand, I could see the potential to add a further quickfire 40 before getting out. That would demoralize the South Africans, I thought.

My hundred had taken us to 350, and I knew 500 was comfortable from there on in given the strength of our batting line-up, even if I got out straightaway. Equally, I knew if I got us up to 400 quickly, we would get 550. I was already in three figures, seeing the ball beautifully, so I thought, 'To hell with it.'

I was intent on pushing everything on. It was like batting in fast forward. I had tried this kind of thing before – where I try to be ultra-aggressive – not in a Test match but against top-class opposition. While South Africa might have been missing Dale Steyn, they were still

Test cricket's world number one team at the time. But I was an opponent with nothing to lose and lots to gain.

When Piedt came back on, I decided to have a look at a couple first. Only a couple, mind. From then on, there were only two things in my mind: should I run at him or slog-sweep in my bid to clear the men in the deep? When I ran down I was swinging like mad, trying to get good elevation on my shots, no matter where the ball was pitched; and when I wasn't charging I was looking to get him over midwicket. In my head it was *boundaries, boundaries, boundaries*.

'Be decisive against the quicker bowlers,' I told myself. 'If they bowl short, do not back out, hit it. And when I mean hit it, I mean hit it for six,' I said. A top edge might not carry the distance, it might go to hand, but equally it could get me four. I wasn't worrying about the consequences. Everything was stacked in my favour. I just wanted to play.

There was a certain amount of pot luck to my career-best score. I could have missed one, poles everywhere, or hit one straight up. But it happened for me. And I just kept going with the flow.

The atmosphere was incredible too. Between deliveries the crowd would be split between chants of *Hashim, Hashim, Hashim, Hashim, Hashim, Hashim, Hashim Amla* to *Moeen, Moeen, Moeen, Moeen, Moeen, Moeen, Moeen Ali* depending on which set of supporters got in first. The battle of the beards was a constant hum for the whole morning session.

Otherwise it was pretty quiet in the middle. We might have shared a 399-run stand, but there was not much chat between Jonny and me. There was no need for it, really. We were enjoying ourselves, batting in our own rhythms and so, aside from regular chirps of 'Shot, lad', there wasn't a lot to say. When you are both in and your opponents are on the ropes, what is there to discuss?

Jonny stayed in his own zone so well, never once stepping out of his own mode of playing. His level of discipline was exemplary. For a batsman as aggressive as he is, the trap would have been to get drawn into a hitting contest. If I had been him, there is no doubt I would have been trying to hit every other ball for four or six like the bloke at the other end. Jonny didn't. He cruised his way to that maiden hundred without risks, playing textbook strokes and only freed up his arms in a search for those big boundaries towards the back end of the innings.

When he got to his own hundred there was a lot of emotion there, in terms of both his personal success but also his family history. It had been something of a wait for him to get to three figures in an England shirt. His dad David played and coached in Cape Town, and it was the anniversary of his death later that week. He had been shaken by the loss of his grandfather the previous summer. All this came together in his head, no doubt. The jump, the roar, a release of relief; the look skywards and the raising of his arms to the heavens, his dedication to his father figures; the pointing of his bat to one corner of Newlands, an acknowledgement of two of the 20,000 spectators – his mum Janet and sister Becky sat in one of the boxes, amongst the rest of our families.

I don't always get things right. Far from it. But on this occasion, my judgement was bang on. I know from experience what an unbelievable feeling it is to score your first England hundred, there is nothing quite like it. That special time doesn't come around again, so I held back until his personal celebration was over before I went up and gave him a hug. I felt it was right for him to have that time for personal reflection. After scoring a couple of 50s, including getting into the 90s against the South Africans a few years earlier at Lord's, you could see how he cherished his moment.

By this stage I was going hell for leather. Who wouldn't enjoy feeling so in nick, so well set, that they could disregard their captain's advice that morning? Before the start, Alastair Cook had told me, 'Play yourself in again.'

That was a distant memory by lunch, which was taken shortly after my reaching my double-hundred. Again, that was mint to get to 200, but at no stage was I actually thinking about landmarks. This innings was all about having fun. I managed to put Piedt into the brewery with one of my sixes – it was a monstrous blow, but the smile that followed was because I had finally managed it, having been trying for a while. There was a game going on within a game.

Towards the end, Jos Buttler came out with a message from Cooky saying, 'We are thinking of declaring at 630, do you want time to get 300?' To me, the question was irrelevant. If I got there, I got there. I was going as hard as I could, as long as I could.

'I'm trying to hit every ball for six now,' I shrugged. 'So it doesn't matter.'

True to my word, I just kept swinging. Rabada bowled a short ball and I swivelled to pull it high over square-leg. It took me beyond 250. The next ball was fuller and I got an even better connection over long-on. But then came the inevitable mishit from the third delivery of the over. Another attempt to hit the ball out of the ground got the height but not the distance. It was carrying no further than mid-on.

Now if I had played that shot when I was on a normal score rather than 258 I would have run, just on the slight chance that AB de Villiers was going to drop it. But I had already told myself that wouldn't be happening – 'AB de Villiers doesn't drop catches.'

So I stood and awaited my fate a few yards outside my crease, accepting the adventure was at an end. You can imagine when he picked the ball off the turf, after making a mess of it, and hit the stumps with his throw, what a chump I felt. It had gone so high in the air and I was only halfway down the pitch, standing still while watching it descend to earth. 'Ben, what are you doing?' I asked myself. But it was too late.

What a way for what I expect will remain my career high to end. Of course, it would be lovely to replicate my performance with the bat across two days of 2016's New Year's Test, but if I'm brutally honest it was a once-in-a-lifetime innings. Trust me, I'll be doing everything in my power to repeat it: to be able to re-live that kind of innings in real time would be class. But it would be remarkable if I ever manage something like that again, and I'm not just saying it to be humble, or appear modest. I don't want to be Mr Nice Guy. I genuinely don't think it will be possible.

This is an acknowledgement that I was able to enjoy it so much, and give pleasure to England fans at the same time, because everything fell into place for me. Yes, in one sense I brought my own luck. Yes, in another, I made it count. And it came when I was only 24 years old, so time is on my side. But I cannot shake the feeling that whatever else I achieve – and I have huge ambitions to win Test series and world titles with England – that will almost certainly be the innings of mine that people talk about once I am done in this great sport.

Not that it will be the innings that gives me the most pleasure. It's true enough that it was the one that gave me most fun, but it's not one that I'm ever likely to coo over. I mean, in terms of entertaining the people watching, yeah I get it. The ball disappeared into the stands 11 times. I hit 30 fours. I only faced 198 balls in all. Most cricket fans love big hitting.

To be honest, though, I have no urge to watch it back. I have done so only once between then and now, six months later as I put the story of my career so far in print. Not because I don't watch re-run footage of myself. I do, as it happens. As England cricketers, we have all this computer-generated technology at our fingertips, so we can download games from two or three years ago at the push of a button.

But if ever I'm feeling like a pick-me-up when out of form, or even if I've made a few scores but not felt as fluent as I do at my very best, I will kick back in my TV room at home and watch some of my technically best knocks. There was nothing technical for me to take from this one. Sure, there were elements in that first 100 runs, but even then it doesn't compare to the level of performance in making scores of 92 and 101 against New Zealand at Lord's in May 2015.

If I need a boost in terms of confidence, I will always revert back to watching the video of those two innings to remind me of the standards I can achieve. It's useful whenever I have technical issues, to recall the uncomplicated, classical positions I can get into as a batsman, and how still I am at the crease, when I'm striking the ball well. It was the purest kind of batsmanship I've ever produced – 100 per cent – and came against high-quality swing bowling.

What I did take from the Cape Town match was a memento. I'm not particularly big on memorabilia for its own sake, but this was slightly different. As I say, I'm not sure whether I will get another Test double-hundred. So, after hands were shaken on a draw three days later, I made sure I grabbed one of the stumps and threw it into my kitbag. Later, I took out my Sharpie pen and wrote the details across the wood underneath Sunfoil, the sponsor's logo: South Africa v England, Second Test, Cape Town, 2-6 January 2016, 257.

Yep, that's right. 257. I had written the wrong score down – in permanent marker ink! That's me, I guess: brilliant one minute, useless the next. It took a fair old working over with an alcohol wipe to remove and correct it.

Of course, lots of people were saying lots of nice things about me after that. Michael Atherton, writing in *The Times*, seemed to have some sympathy for the South Africans, saying it was my 'brutal and brilliant batting that pounded them into submission'. His article suggested I had joined the all-time greats. Sir Ian Botham, one of those greats, said that I was a better player than him at the comparative age of 24. All I can say is, he must have been drunk.

Obviously it was a nice thing to hear, but as a commentator and a former all-rounder himself, I guess he had to say something. Others were comparing me to him, and I had just scored 258. He was just being generous with his praise, and to me it was no more than a sound bite. I believe you achieve things across a career, not over three sessions of a Test match, so I don't tend to take anything from that kind of thing.

It's not that I want to be disrespectful to someone of his standing, or dismiss his opinions, I just think he was being supportive towards an

England player who is trying to follow in his not-inconsiderable footsteps. There have been several outstanding all-rounders in the world of cricket, but Beefy has always been the benchmark in terms of volume of runs and wickets. His statistics were amazing.

In contrast, Andrew Flintoff's career numbers were inferior, but I have always viewed them with a similar level of respect. Flintoff to me was someone who won games for England with what he did in short, sharp bursts, and that is something I would like to emulate. He changed the course of contests with three quick wickets, a catch, a run out, a rapid 70 off 70 balls with the bat. People that focus on stats alone will never see that – because his career record is not as impressive as others.

All I know is he won games of cricket with eight-over spells. He didn't get five-fers but he got good players out. And he always seemed to raise his game against the best opponents. He had the knack of doing enough to help England win. Stats, who gives a monkey's? That's how I feel. When games needed breaking open, he was the man. To me, if you could get Flintoff and Botham and combine them half and half – Fred's dynamic impact plus Beefy's long-term class and ability to produce time and again – to make another person, that person would be some cricketer.

At any rate, I know how hard it is to perform consistently with both bat and ball, across different formats. Yes, there have been highs and the stump from Newlands reminds me of one of those. Equally, though, the World Twenty20 runners-up medal that hangs above my bed at home reminds me of the lows. The up from Cape Town was soon followed by the down of Kolkata. The trick is, I believe, to sweep all things under the carpet once they've gone, good or bad. You can't live off your last innings or your last spell, whatever its outcome.

And there were still the usual jitters just a week after that innings against South Africa when the Test series moved to Johannesburg. Even though I felt like I was in the best form of my career with the bat, I was really nervous when I walked out at the Wanderers.

Perhaps it was because it came so soon afterwards and the expectation was on me to reproduce. It's a stupid thing to allow into your head, but as I was going out to bat I was thinking, 'I probably won't do well this week.' As if my runs for the series had been used up already.

Perhaps it was because of my tendency to experience the troughs immediately after peaks. I just kept thinking, 'Surely, it can't happen again. I can't get another good score.' Let's face it, if ever I have a run of something, it's usually ducks. I'm the guy that wants to string 50s and 100s together, of course, but to this point in my career I haven't managed it. I'm moving towards that, yes, but you always want to stay in top form when you hit it, and three or four games has been the longest stretch I've managed.

Don't get me wrong, I want to be the best I can be. I want to be the very best. But self-doubt has always been there in the background holding me back. It has always been the same for me. For example, every time I have gone up a level, there has always been a little devil on the shoulder telling me, 'You're not good enough.' In my first game for Cumbria, I puked. On debut for Durham, I was scared stiff.

You would have thought an innings like that in Cape Town would have been the turning point, yet when I got to the crease in Johannesburg it was almost like the double-hundred belonged to someone else. I wasn't walking with the swagger of a man who had just played his best-ever innings against the bowling attack I was just about to face. It was as if I was starting from scratch. It might as well have been my debut.

But it didn't take me long to get into that attacking mindset. Sometimes I play shots, then think, 'How did that happen?' I don't necessarily think about taking them on. It's just instinct. In this innings, I just seemed to be throwing my hands at everything. Morne Morkel put one up my nostrils that I managed to flap down to fine leg, and it clearly stirred me up.

If it was there, I was taking it on. We were 91-4 at that point, but I attacked. Down at the other end, Kagiso Rabada bounced me and I pulled him over the rope at mid-wicket. Later on, just before I got out, Morkel returned to the attack and I lofted him over extra-cover for four. I even questioned myself as to how that had happened.

Once in the heat of the battle, I don't think. I just do. I try to bat and bowl the same way in every game – that means if someone bowls short I will look to whack it. From my perspective, I play so much better when I'm looking to hit the ball. In Cape Town, it just lasted a lot longer than it ever had done before, and perhaps longer than it ever will again.

Throughout my childhood, I thought my dad had lost a finger to a hungry crocodile.

As kids, my cousins and I were always spellbound listening to the tale of how Dad had been out in a boat when the croc attacked. His sacrifice for trying to push it away, by bopping it on the nose, had been the loss of his middle finger of his left hand from the knuckle up.

It was certainly a story that was in keeping with his tough-guy image, and of course we believed him. We were kids. And kids love that kind of story. Tell us again, we'd say. We would lap it up and were always asking to have a look at his half-finger. Only later did I discover this particular story was a tall one. There had been no boat trip, no snapping monster, no heroic fight. He had lost it following an accident at work.

My father Ged was a full-time rugby league player during the 1980s, an era when a career in the sport was comfortable but far from a get-rich-quick profession. Sure, he'd given his bravery a bit of tap with that fight in the water, against the monstrous beast and its snapping jaws, and the escape to shore. But the reality was just as fantastical.

Rugby league had a bit of a weird set-up back then. As an overseas recruit, you couldn't sign for a full 12-month spell with clubs like Workington Town. There were not opportunities to agree deals that would take you across a couple of seasons – from one September to the May, 18 months later, say – which meant players from New Zealand had to return home, then go back the following year afresh. Obviously that denied blokes the security of having a guaranteed return to an English club season after season, year after year. Later, the rules were relaxed a bit, but even then they only applied when you had a dozen Test appearances to your name. Only established internationals could sign a full-time contract of, say, three to four years in length. Otherwise it was season-long agreements.

One year, within the first five minutes of his final game in New Zealand before leaving for Workington – a representative Wellington versus Christchurch match – he badly dislocated his finger. Badly enough for it to be sticking out sideways from the joint, just like mine would do several years later following a fielding accident in a County Championship match, with me on the verge of my first England call-up.

He went off the field for treatment, but the medical people told him they weren't allowed to put it back in. As far as they were concerned, it would have to be done in hospital in order for it to be done properly. Of course, typically of a rugby league player – and even more typically of my dad, I guess – he didn't want to go off. So he popped it back in himself.

Unfortunately, he didn't do it properly. Not the first time; or the second; or the third for that matter. He reckoned it dislocated four or five times in all, with his unsuccessful attempts to put it back each time doing irreparable damage – he basically broke the joint. Not that it mattered too much to him. He'd just wanted to get back onto that field. So he simply taped the finger up and dealt with the pain.

Next day, he boarded a plane for the 26-hour journey to England, arriving on the Monday, in time to play his first game for Workington on the Wednesday night. Wary of losing his contract on fitness grounds if he made a fuss, he simply strapped that finger up for that evening debut and continued to do so on a weekly basis. All season he played that way, with the aid of painkilling injections. Without them, each bang on it hurt like hell.

Not once did that injury stop him running onto the field with his team-mates. In fact, his string of appearances only came to a close four games from the end of the season when he dislocated his knee, damaging the cartilage at the same time.

It was then, and only then, after returning home to see a specialist about his knee, that the subject of his finger came up. The surgeon who was to perform his knee surgery saw the state it was in and advised having an operation on it at the same time. He was told that they could break it again, and re-set it, but it would always be bent.

Now a bent finger isn't much use to a rugby player. It only serves to get in the way, and he couldn't do much with it in that condition. And there was another downside of following the surgery option for the finger – it would keep him out for several weeks. In those days, when it came to rugby league contracts, you got an appearance fee on top of your basic money, plus win money as a bonus. So, getting on the field each week and winning was a real incentive. Appearance money made up quite a big proportion of the contracts. He couldn't afford to miss a handful of games. So Dad came up with another option.

'Can you chop it off?'

In its present condition, it would be no use at all. It was more a hindrance than help. If it was bent, it would be of no use in the future. An amputation? Now that seemed a lot easier. So, as well as getting his cartilage trimmed, the finger was removed. It was a case of needs must. Not playing meant no pay and he couldn't afford that. It was a practical decision. He thought he didn't need a middle finger. After all, he had another one if he needed to give someone a proper telling off. He was playing again in next to no time.

Dad was capped once by New Zealand and had a decent playing career. Unfortunately, it came to a slightly premature end when I was just 11 days old. A knee to the head in a tackle left him with a broken neck. It meant he moved into coaching in his mid-30s, probably a couple of years before he would have planned to. By the time I was five, he was an established coach on the domestic scene and developing a new reputation.

People have often commented on my combative spirit. How aggression is an essential ingredient of my style. There is no doubt I inherited that from Dad – that desire to defeat the opposition no matter what, striving never to let others get one over on you. He epitomized this. Literally nothing could keep him from the field of play. No one could intimidate him.

One story that emphasized what a hard nut he was – perhaps he told me to impress me, to make him look cool, I'm not sure – related to him on a tour to Australia. Whenever new guys came into the team, established players would prank the newbies. One of the pranks involved being stripped naked, tied up and left in public somewhere. On an away trip this would usually involve being dispatched down to the lobby in the hotel lift. It was a well-known prank and everyone took their medicine. Except Dad, that is. He warned them, 'If you ever try this with me, I will rip your f**king face off.' They never did.

Not that he avoided punishment altogether. He went to private school but had a very similar attitude to me towards learning, by the sounds of it. He got the cane a fair few times. For either not going at all, or sneaking out to go and play rugby for Canterbury on a Saturday morning. He knew what was going to happen to him every single weekend but couldn't help himself. He simply loved the game, and nothing was going to stop his enjoyment of it.

Rugby is a way of life in New Zealand. You start playing not long out of the womb. At four years old, kids are involved in full-contact games of rugby league, and with my family background I was destined for it as soon as the quartet of candles were blown out. The first grade you can play in is Under-7s, but four is classed as old enough.

According to Dad, I loved it from the start, although as you can imagine at that age I didn't do too much other than run around the pitch. For two seasons, my try tally remained at zero. Not once did I cross the white-wash. But I loved tackling. I'd tackle all day long. Mam, Dad and Granddad would watch me every week. But for the very last game of that second season for Marist, my local club in Christchurch, Nana also braved the cold to take her place on the sidelines. Everyone laughed about it afterwards. Suddenly, I couldn't stop scoring. Six times I crossed the line in that one match. A double hat-trick!

In subsequent years, Dad's best mate John Sheehan would watch too. He used to say to me, 'Every try you score, I'll give you a dollar.' This appealed to me, like it would to any kid, I guess, and sure, I got a bit greedy. Scoring tries became money for sweets. He was true to his word, and I did get a dollar for each one. In hindsight, though, this bonus scheme meant I didn't always make the best decisions from my position at stand-off.

Obviously Dad was keen for me to do well at rugby. It was his passion. Listen to him now and he will tell you that I was a very clever league player. To tell the truth, I loved it too. Like most lads, I wanted to do what my father did. And I spent a lot of time with him during our spell in Christchurch. The company Mam worked for had sites throughout Australasia, and every single site had a different computer system. They wanted to incorporate one universal system across the lot, and as Mam headed up the team that facilitated the change, she was constantly on the road. It meant Dad was pretty much a single parent in the week, while Mam came back at weekends.

Dad worked as a plasterer during the day and coached Canterbury Cardinals – a team in New Zealand's national competition – at night. All I ever wanted to do as a young lad was help him, be around what he was doing. So when he decided to completely renovate our bungalow in Bourne Crescent one year, I was his go-fer. At eight years old, I was a good size to get under the floorboards, to run cables and pipes. So I'd dress up all in black, pull on a black beanie hat, and be dispatched under the house. Dad would knock and I'd make my way towards where the noise was coming from, find the hole and feed the wire through it.

If I wasn't working with him on the house, I would be on the sidelines as he took his team for rugby training. Generally, while he was coaching, I would kick goals. Left foot, right foot, from straight in front, out wide, longer distances. I would break off to talk to any of the players who were milling around. Then, I would be back kicking more goals. It was a relentless process. It was my daily routine.

Rugby league remains a winter sport in New Zealand. It was always cold, wet, and blowing. I would be covered in mud and shivering, but that didn't matter. I was out with Dad. It was sport. It was what I did. Dad was prepared too, shoving a spare pair of clothes into his kitbag for me every single night. There was no way I was allowed into our house in the state I got into.

He was strict about stuff like that. I wasn't allowed much time in the back garden either, as it was his pride and joy. So it meant grabbing my rugby ball and kicking tee and heading to the front whenever we were at home. We had a wooden fence out front, held up by two concrete posts. It also had a concrete join across the middle – making it a perfect replica for rugby posts. I would move the cone around the garden, trying to kick the ball through the gap from all different angles and distances.

I reckon that fence had to be replaced at least ten times by the time we left Christchurch. I peppered the damn thing, smashing little pieces off those planks. The Chinese family next door went ballistic every single time.

Every day I worked to a tight schedule. It would be home from school, grab some tea, and then head off to training. As I got older, I used to have a quick look at my homework, but it used to suffer quite a bit because of my commitments to other things. Not that it bothered me. I was doing stuff I loved all the time. Most nights we wouldn't get home until nine o'clock, so it was straight to bed. There weren't enough hours in the day for it. As a sportsman you have to time-manage, Dad says, and during that time he reckoned I got used to working to a schedule. Once you play sport professionally, you do it all the time.

● ● ●

Then there was cricket. In New Zealand most kids get plastic bats for Christmas and I had mine at the age of one, not long after I started walking. Dad says I picked it up really naturally, and swung it really well from my very first go. I couldn't talk, other than a bit of jibber-jabber, but I could hit a perfect straight drive. Dad would get me playing in the hallway, rolling the ball to me so that I could hit it back past him, and according to his story I rarely – if ever – hit the walls, more often than not striking it as straight as a die. Whenever anyone came round to the house, such as my older brother James – both my parents had children in previous relationships before I came along – they would be tormented with demands of 'play cricket' until I got my way.

At other times, Dad would instigate a knockabout, telling visitors to come and watch, before lining me up at the bottom of the hall to show off my party piece. He actually tells me one of his regrets was not recording me batting in nappies, in the same way Tiger Woods was filmed by his dad, hitting a golf ball. He just wasn't savvy enough.

Dad's sport was rugby league. It was Mam who played cricket. In fact, she still played while she was pregnant with me. I was obsessed with it, too. I was also obsessed with disappearing. If there had been a junior hide-and-seek championships, I would have been a contender. There one minute, I would be gone the next. That was me. Mam and Dad would regale friends with stories of my temporary absences. I rarely stayed still, and so they got used to me being out of sight.

Only one day it got out of hand. I was about two-and-a-half years old. It was pretty normal for me to be somewhere else, not too far away, but on this occasion Mam and Dad completely lost track of me. Nothing untoward, they thought, at first. Bourne Crescent, as the name suggests, was a cul-de-sac. All the neighbours knew me and were used to me appearing in their gardens. So they did their usual traipse from house to house, popping their heads over fences, asking the other families if they'd seen me. After half an hour, when no one had, panic began to set in.

Soon, there was a search and rescue mission in operation, people out in their cars, patrolling the neighbourhood, looking everywhere. All to no avail. The police had just been informed I was missing, and it was only on Mam's last trek over to the local park that I was spotted. There I was, sitting in my stroller, dressed in a nappy and T-shirt, with a Tommee Tippee cup by my side and a biscuit in hand.

Mam had been frantic. As a parent, I totally get that. I might not have before my own children Layton and Libby came into my life. But once you have kids, they become everything to you. She yelled at me in relief more than anger.

'WHAT are you doing?'

'Me watch cricket.'

It all seemed pretty normal to the 30-month old me. But although Edgar Macintosh Park was a relatively short distance away, I had to cross a really busy thoroughfare, Condell Avenue, to get there. How I had managed that with no one stopping me on my journey totally baffled Mam and Dad; a toddler being allowed to push their own pram like that unchallenged was frankly ridiculous.

I was always an adventurer. When I was in a cot, I spent most of my time trying to get out of it. On one occasion, I was found outside, stood on the carport roof. To get there had involved climbing up a trellis. Once again, Mam demanded what the hell I was doing.

'Me fly like duck.'

Sure, that Perspex roof was strong enough to hold ducks. They sat on it regularly. And it was just about strong enough to hold me. But Mam wasn't taking any chances, so she clambered up very gingerly and shuffled across it to get to me, concerned that either it would give way or I *would* make good my promise and try to fly like a duck.

Another time, when I was four, I had been sent to my bedroom for a time-out. Even at that age I could never bear to be penned in, so I made a dart for the window, only for Mam to grab my ankles and yank me back in. Backpack on, teddy sticking out the top, I was off.

'Going to Nana's,' I told her, defiantly.

If Mam wasn't going to be nice to me, I would go elsewhere. If she hadn't entered the room at that exact moment, I would have too. Yes, it was miles away, but I knew how to get there, and as I had shown with my first cricket expedition, I didn't mind a trek. I was totally independent. A free spirit, you might say.

At five, I got my first bike. Mam and Dad both worked, so that meant I would get dropped off at some family friends five minutes down the road prior to going to school. Cheryl, Mam's friend, would drop me off each morning and I would often go back there after school until my parents got home from work.

One day I was given permission to make my own way to Cheryl's on my bike. Only I didn't follow the instructions. Much cooler, I thought, to cycle all the way to school. Later that morning, Mam phoned Cheryl to let her know she would be back later than normal that evening.

'Oh, I thought you must have taken Ben today,' came the reply.

I was banned from that bike for quite some time.

Breaking the rules, or at least testing the boundaries, was a little bit of a recurring theme for me. I was always a bit of a free thinker. I knew pretty much what was right or wrong, which my parents had instilled in me, but if I had an idea pop into my head I tended to follow it through.

For example, when I was six, I took a fancy to the new girl in school. So had one of my classmates, and it was me versus him for Chloe's affections. The competitive nature of the contest forced me into action. I needed something to close the deal in my favour.

Mam became aware of what that 'something' was one afternoon when she got a call from the teacher asking her to come down after school. The teacher in question had been walking behind me in the playground when she noticed a couple of items drop out of my pocket. They were shiny and glistened in the sun. Turns out, they were Mam's wedding and engagement rings.

I noticed them on the side one day when she was doing the dishes, and they were to be part of my perfect plan. Women were won over by men bearing jewellery, clearly. So I borrowed some of Mam's to win Chloe's heart. I would give her the rings, and that would be that. A few diamonds and then she'd be mine forever. Or so I thought. Of course I was brassed off when my plan was foiled, and Mam laughs whenever we talk about that story – I'm not sure she would have reacted the same if those rings hadn't come back in one piece.

Later, the worth of things became a lot more obvious to me. When Dad became one of the national coaches, the New Zealand rugby league team's changing room turned into something of a second home to me. I was totally comfortable in that environment, never star struck. Of course, I idolized the players but retained a self-confidence in their presence, to the extent that after one game, when I was one of the ball boys, Ruben Wiki, the captain, offered me his socks as a keepsake.

'Nah, I'm not bothered about the socks,' I told him. 'I want your boots.'

This was during our time in Wellington. We moved from Christchurch when I was 10, after Dad became coach of New Zealand A, in addition to his positions as assistant coach of the New Zealand side and co-selector. Having led Canterbury Bulls to grand final success in the inaugural Barter-card Cup competition, he was asked to move to Wellington Orcas and that meant a complete change of scene.

Dad reckons the way things turned out led to a really good couple of years for me – because I met a whole new raft of friends, standing me in good stead for what was to come later in life. I was constantly in or around sports teams, whether playing or tagging along with him. I lived in dressing rooms, and that, he reckons, has shaped how I behave in them now. I still went to virtually every training session, every match when Dad was coaching, picking up how a team dynamic worked almost subconsciously.

I would sit quietly at the back, listening as he gave his team talks. Then, I would slope off back outside, to kick the ball around and have a good time. From 30 metres out, I'd be putting them over the bar, left or right-footed. All that practice at Bourne Crescent was paying off.

It wasn't just the Stokes family that relocated when we switched cities, from New Zealand's South Island to the capital. Dad recruited a group of his Christchurch backroom team to go with him too, which meant there was a really tight group of friends to hang around with outside of work. They would invite me out to play in their games of basketball, or touch rugby – I was included in lots of adult stuff from a young age. It filled up to the brim a life that was wall-to-wall sport.

We lived in Porirua, a beautiful place, a couple of hundred metres from the beach; from the hill you could see the harbour full of boats, and it was 10 minutes from where I played cricket and rugby. Everything was pretty cool. I was already playing age-group cricket and rugby league for Canterbury's representative teams when we moved north, so I was picked up by Wellington immediately. I was also selected in the rugby union squads. In Christchurch I had mainly concentrated on rugby league, but here I began to take the other code more seriously with my local club Plimmerton.

I was giving everything a go, and enjoying success at most of it. One of my best mate's dad was well into his rugby league but also heavily involved with Australian Rules Football. He worked, and still does, identifying talent and coaching in the Wellington region. So I used to go off and play without Mam and Dad knowing too much about it. Until that is, I was nominated for the national trials for New Zealand's Under-16 team. I was never going to be an academic. As far as I was concerned, I went to school to play sport. That was something my senior school would come to recognize when I got older.

For the full 40 minutes of every lunchtime, we played rugby – in our socks, so we didn't ruin our shoes. Well, that was what we told the teachers if ever they questioned us. Secretly, we believed that running barefoot somehow made you faster. That's kid-logic, I guess.

These impromptu games were full contact, with no supervision, and kids of all ages would get involved, which often meant heading back into lessons stained by smatterings of blood from nose or mouth after being cleaned up by the bigger guys. They didn't take any prisoners and occasionally there would be red eyes too, from the crying.

Rugby was tough and rough. It was in my blood, though, and that love of the physical side of the game has been with me ever since those early games in Christchurch. In every match, I made a point of trying to tackle the biggest unit on the opposition. I was never big myself until I was 15 or 16, but I maintained a no-fear attitude whenever I walked onto the field of play.

And I took regular punishment. Wellington is quite a cultural centre, so there were a lot of islanders who lived there, as well as a big Maori community. Let's just say I stood out as being different, possibly the only *different* kid in the entire Wellington grade competition – with my pale skin and ginger hair. I couldn't believe it when I first turned up. These Maori lads were huge; absolute monsters. The guys at Porirua Vikings were all really cool and accepted me straightaway. The problems I had were never with them. The problems were with the players on other teams, who made it their number one priority to take me out. Every opposition wanted to play the same game, and it appeared to be called 'Kill the white guy'. From my position at stand-off, I was an easy target for these hulking forwards. So much smaller than everyone else, I would get properly beat up, going home bruised and unable to move properly for a couple of days.

Perhaps subconsciously, it was this that spurred me into playing more rugby union in Wellington. Plimmerton, the club I joined, had two teams in each age group and I played for what was effectively the B team. All the best players played in the other one, including my best mate Freddie Robinson. Both teams were in the same competition and Freddie always got the better of me in our direct battles. When I left New Zealand a couple of years later, I truly believed he was destined to play for the All Blacks, he was that good. But although he went to trials for the New Zealand Under-17 team, and he's still playing rugby, he's now switched to semi-professional rugby league and I paid him a surprise visit during the 2010 Under-19 World Cup.

Freddie was a real rugby union kid; a typical New Zealand kid. Everyone in New Zealand likes rugby union, even a dyed-in-the-wool league enthusiast like Dad. He just never coached it. Too slow compared to league, he said, and I have to agree with him on that. He's always liked the speed and the skills that rugby league has to offer, not that it stopped him enjoying watching me play whenever he could. I was a fly-half, the equivalent of stand-off in league, and getting to control the game suited me down to the ground. When it comes to sport I like to be in the midst of the action, not on the periphery.

● ● ●

From the moment I picked out my first bat from the kitbag at the local club, my attitude towards cricket did not really alter. That first bat in question was a Kookaburra Sword. I made a few runs with it; enough to make sure I used it every game for the rest of the season. With it in my hands, I was invincible. I wasn't, of course, but just like now I didn't die wondering when I got to the crease.

I loved swinging a bat just as much as I loved kicking goals. The first bat I owned, a Slazenger V500, with its blue stickers, was ruined by my addiction to hitting stones. I would throw them up and ping them as far as I could. Ping, ping, ping. Dent, dent, dent.

It was always my style to try to hit as hard as I could, every single time the ball came down at me. Again, not much has changed, really. I always wanted to see how far I could hit the ball, how powerfully I could strike it. Things have become a lot more serious, opponents have become considerably higher skilled, but the method and technique I used as an 11-year-old in the Milo Cup, a Wellington schools competition, hardly changed at all until 2015, when I tinkered with it after my England recall. My back leg used to splay out to the leg-side, I would free my arms and try to launch the ball over the top.

The Milo Cup proved to be a successful venture for Plimmerton High School. Matches were played with a four-piece cricket ball. And the same one was used to bowl with throughout the entire tournament. We got to finals day but weren't quite good enough to win it. On a personal level, I was beginning to make my mark in a relatively new environment. Along with recognition in rugby union, I had been picked out for extra training with Wellington's cricket academy.

Then, just as I was making progress on two fronts, came the news that I would be jacking it all in. I was enjoying playing sport in Wellington, just getting used to the new city, when I was told we would be moving to England. It was something I just didn't want to do. I'd already moved from Christchurch where I had loads of mates. I was just beginning to feel settled. I didn't want to move again. Moving somewhere in the same country wouldn't have been too bad, I guess. But moving halfway around the world did not appeal to a 12-year-old.

Dad was already over in the UK, on a New Zealand A tour, when Mam broke the news to me that he would not be coming back. During that trip, he had been offered the job of coach at his old club, Workington Town.

He'd rang Mam to chat it over, and the decision had been made that we were going overseas before they told me. He was staying over there to sort out his visa and begin a new job.

I was just like, 'Nah, no way.' There were plenty of tears. At that age, you are starting to get a little streetwise. Beginning to know what you want to do in life. I had developed ideas about playing sport as a career. It was something I was going to stick to. I was doing well at both cricket and rugby. Moving country was non-negotiable.

For the next couple of months, Mam and I were on our own, as she had wanted me to finish the school year in New Zealand. After the initial bombshell, when she sat me down to tell me the news, I was pretty ho-hum about it. As a kid you tend to deal with what is immediately in front of you, and as we were not due to leave immediately, I put it aside and got on with things.

It was on 21 December 2003, the day before we were to depart for England, that I had a complete meltdown and Mam was left in no doubt about my feelings.

'I don't want to leave Nana,' I insisted.

I hadn't seen Dad for about three months, but the thought of flying halfway around the world — leaving behind everything I had known — distressed me. It was a hammer blow to my emotions. Until then, I remained immersed in sport. But once school stopped for Christmas, everything hit home. Mam finished up her job to coincide with the end of term, and spent her last few weeks packing up our house in Wellington. Even while that had been going on, things felt pretty normal.

Now, I realized that although our immediate family would be reunited, I was leaving everyone else behind, most importantly my maternal grandparents Stewart and Pauline in Christchurch, but all my cousins too.

Mam was obviously concerned about my reaction. To the extent that she did me a deal: 'We'll go — because we need to see Dad. But if you don't want to stay after Christmas and New Year is over, then you and I will come home. Please understand, though, that if you choose that option Dad will be staying. He has a work contract that he cannot break.'

Mam wanted me to feel like I had a choice, so I began that plane journey believing there were two options open to me. I was either heading for a new life in England or beginning a fortnight's holiday.

5

I have had to get used to the circumstances in my life. We moved about a lot during those formative years of mine. Mam was away a lot. Then Dad was away a lot. We moved. Then we moved again. Only this time it was bigger. This was much bigger. The UK? No way. There was nothing great about Britain in my eyes. But for the first time in recent memory, all three of us were going to be together.

The annual school holidays were about to start in New Zealand and that meant seven or eight weeks of fun. Unfortunately, we were going somewhere where it wasn't school holidays. Within a fortnight I would be continuing my education in Cockermouth, Cumbria. All I knew about the place was that it was somewhere in the north of England.

Kids tend to be resilient and adaptable, I guess, and pretty forgetful too, so Mam's promise of a return home was never pushed for on my part. I never once asked to take her up on that promise. Moving 11,500 miles across the planet wasn't such a bad thing at all, and all the tears were left back on New Zealand soil.

During that Christmas period, Dave Smith, the football director at Workington Town, arranged for us to go to Cockermouth School, meet the teachers and be registered for the next term. Within a fortnight my education was continuing in England. Mam came to collect me that first afternoon feeling apprehensive. As it turns out, she needn't have been. She pulled up in the car, wound the window down and simply looked at me.

'I'm alright,' I said, trying to convey an image of cool as I walked home with my new mates.

Despite all the fears of the unknown, it didn't prove hard to settle into this new environment at all. On that first day, I was put with a group of lads who all played cricket. I don't know whether this was tactical on the school's part, but I suspect so, because they knew I was really sporty, and sitting me with those lads undoubtedly helped me settle. I would hang around a lot with Hugh Gimber, Matty Jones, Greg Barnes and Humayan Zaheen in the coming months. Playing sport always helps you to get to know people and build bridges. It was not long before Cockermouth felt where I belonged. Despite only living there for around five years, it's the place I now think of as home.

In Cockermouth, everybody knows everybody. You can't walk down the street without bumping into someone. It's your typical small market town: main street, a few pubs, a church, a sports centre, and, most importantly for me, a cricket ground. One of those towns with a single nightclub that shuts down for refurbishments every year, then reopens just a few months later under a new name.

All my best mates are Cockermouth lads, and I go back there as much as I can. I love it. Where you grow up, where you make your memories, no matter what type of place it is, is always special. The lads are sick of it, because it's the same old stuff every day for them. But for me it's something different. If a shop front changes, I notice. To them, it's like 'whatever'.

Mam and Dad are now back in New Zealand, but there are people close to me in Cockermouth. If ever I needed somewhere to go just to get away from things, or organize a spur-of-the-moment night out with my marras – that's Cumbrian slang for mates, by the way – I could turn up at the Smiths' house, tell them, 'I'm staying' and that would be that. There'd be no need to ring in advance. It'd be like, 'Okay, no worries.'

Dave Smith was one of Dad's former team-mates, and the man who persuaded him to relocate to Cumbria and take the Workington coaching position in the first place, back in the autumn of 2003. Years later, when Dad went to Perth, Australia, in the search for work after leaving his second coaching job at Whitehaven, Mam moved in with the Smiths. We've known them for years. They're like family.

I was in a new gang from the start. Only a few days had passed following our arrival in the north-west when those lads I was pitched with at school invited me down to Cockermouth Cricket Club's winter nets. Cool, I thought. Life here was going to be pretty sweet. Not so different from what I was used to back in Wellington after all. The session took place at Keswick School's indoor centre, and it was at that first practice that I met Jon Gibson, a coach who was to become influential in my development.

I'm not sure how I shaped up in that net practice, really. At 12 years old,

I was not into analyzing my game in any way whatsoever. I just did what I'd always done. I ran in and bowled as fast as I could and tried to give the ball the most almighty crack when I got a chance to bat. Some of my bowling was wayward, some was on the mark and quick. There would have been no deft touches to my batting, but I crashed it around enough for Jon to take note immediately.

The spring that followed would see me play my first games in Cockermouth's Under-13 team. It was not long before I was playing in the club's third XI on a weekend too. Had traditionalists seen me bat, they would have told you there was no method to my game. To me, there definitely was a method, however. My method was to try to whack it. It was about hitting boundaries. It's always been that way for me.

Junior cricket rules in Cumbria encouraged that too. Once you reached a certain point you were forced to retire, and that certain point was 29 runs plus your next scoring shot. It meant if you were in, and getting close to the mark, you kept an eye on the scoreboard. Only when in the 20s did I think about anything other than the big shots – the skill, you see, was being able to get to 28 and then nudge a one. That way, you could hit a six and finish up on 35. To be fair, manipulating this situation was what most people tried to do, and it made for both inventive shots and interesting decisions. For example, if ever you hit an obvious two that would take you to 30, you just wouldn't run. Certainly, personally speaking, I would wait for the ball that I could hit out of the ground. At worst, I would want to hit a four, and walk off in glory.

● ● ●

In one sense, age-group cricket encouraged freedom of expression, and that was in keeping with how I had always approached the game. However, Jon Gibson recognized during those early sessions that to get the most out of my talent, I could benefit from specialist one-on-one coaching. He was intent on addressing my technique – I was very raw but he could see there was plenty to work with. The only problem was that specialist coaching did not come for free, nor would you expect it to, and Mam and Dad could not afford to pay for those extra sessions – a rugby league coach's wage was hardly comparable to one of a football manager.

We didn't have the money, and that should have been that. But then something out of the blue happened. A person, to whom I will always remain grateful, came forward, and thanks to his generosity those sessions took place. Now, I cannot tell you his name as he has insisted on retaining anonymity. I also know, from conversations with my parents since, that he would never want me to approach him and offer my thanks. I will always respect that, even though I would love to be able to do so. I am not even supposed to know what he did.

You might call him an observer of cricket. One of those guys that you see at various club matches around the country, one of the older generation who stand in the same spot at their local ground every single week. If you went down to Cockermouth Cricket Club you would probably see his footprints on the grass on the boundary edge. He places them in the same position every single game, and has done so for years and years.

I knew him before he pledged the money. He's a permanent presence at Cockermouth matches, whether juniors, third XI, second XI, first XI. Whenever we were practising, he always seemed to be there, stood at the back of the nets, watching. Clearly, it was what he liked doing, and him being around was pretty normal. But at the time I did not realize he had a vested interest in me.

The national press got wind of my mystery benefactor in December 2013 when the *Daily Mail* ran a piece about my childhood, following my maiden Test hundred, in Australia. Later, after I scored my double-hundred against South Africa in January 2016, some newspapers revisited the story by sending their reporters to Cockermouth to unmask him. But his determination not to be revealed was highlighted by the fact that even though several people in the town know of his identity, those reporters left none the wiser.

He simply doesn't want any credit for the contribution he made to my career. He has also donated money to other young sports people, musicians and young entrepreneurs — but clearly not for a pat on the back.

I'm not sure why he chose me. I can only guess that he watched me and saw some potential. I can only imagine that he believed I was worth backing. It's certainly flattering. From my side, I just hope I have been able to give him some pleasure and a sense of fulfilment that what he did was such a massive help in transforming me into the cricketer I am today — that he helped that ginger-haired kid, freshly arrived from New Zealand, achieve his dreams. It takes a certain type of person to be so selfless, And not to seek an ounce of gratitude for truly amazing support.

Although technically I do not think she was supposed to, Mam felt I needed telling about the funding as I got older. Not only did his cash pay for private coaching, it also contributed towards me getting to places like Loughborough whenever it was necessary to report for representative training. She thought, despite the request for the information to be withheld, it was only fair that I, as the beneficiary, should know.

'It's not just us who have helped you over the years, not just your family – there has been someone else,' she informed me one day.

As I say, our family was not awash with cash. We lived up in Cumbria. In my world everything was happening up there. But everything in the English cricket world was happening miles away, sometimes hundreds of miles south, and he was a massive help towards being able to attend everything I was invited to. It was quite a financial commitment to cover all the petrol and hotel costs involved, and Mam and Dad began embarking on four-hour round trips from Cockermouth to Chester-le-Street once a week for nets with Durham once I was 14. Then, there was North of England stuff, not to mention England training from the age of 15, following a successful Bunbury Cricket Festival. His money got me where I needed to be, and provided me with every possible chance to climb each rung on the ladder towards professional cricket.

I cannot exaggerate what a massive role those one-on-one sessions played in my development. Jon Gibson initially worked on my front-foot batting and also addressed a mixed bowling action. He would go on to do all sorts of things in those personal sessions, including fielding drills. They went on for two years or so.

Meantime, my progression up the ranks continued at speed. From the third XI I got promoted to the seconds, but didn't stay long as I was fast-tracked to the first XI – albeit initially as a specialist fielder.

That really happened by chance. I was sat watching a match one Saturday afternoon when calamity struck. Our opening bowler was getting

Above: It was Mam who was the first cricketer in the family.

Left: Two-and-a-half years old and raring to go.

Below: The Stokes Building and Renovation Crew – me, Dad and my brother James.

Above: Home in Christchurch. From an early age I loved swinging a bat – as hard as possible.

Right: Aged about four and in my Uncle Chris' police car. He showed me around the cells to scare me into behaving myself.

Below: Rugby league was my first sport as a youngster.

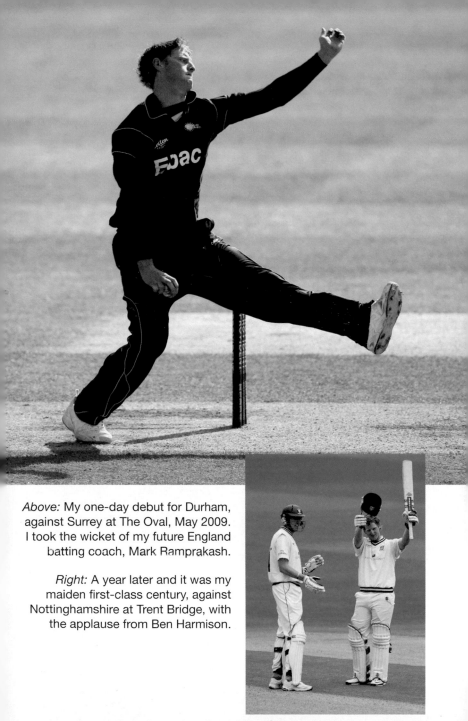

Above: My one-day debut for Durham, against Surrey at The Oval, May 2009. I took the wicket of my future England batting coach, Mark Ramprakash.

Right: A year later and it was my maiden first-class century, against Nottinghamshire at Trent Bridge, with the applause from Ben Harmison.

The fifth ODI v Australia at the Rose Bowl, 2013, where I took 5 for 61.

Above: One of my proudest moments was Durham's County Championship win in 2013, which included this spellbinding tussle against Yorkshire at Scarborough.

Below: Handbags with Haddin. So what if it was my England Test debut at the Adelaide Oval? I wasn't backing down.

Below: In Perth for the third Test, December 2013, I celebrated my maiden Test century. A false dawn? Probably.

Who needs anger management? A reminder of my altercation with a locker door on the 2014 West Indies tour. Thanks, Ian Bell.

Above: Royal London One-Day Cup, Lord's 2014. To help Durham beat Warwickshire in the final was huge.

Left: 'Where do you wanna bat, mate?' Number 3 will do nicely. That knock of 77 for the Renegades against the Hurricanes in the Big Bash was a turning point for my batting.

Above: 'Does this hurt?' Craig de Weymarn and Rob Young help me off after my shoulder popped in the UAE on the Pakistan tour of 2015.

Left: Dodging a chin tickler on my way to scoring the fastest-ever Test century at Lord's, 101 off 85 balls, against New Zealand in the summer of 2015.

Below: It's a shame you can dish it out but can't take it in return, Marlon.

Right: To be a true all-rounder, apart from batting and bowling you need to throw yourself around the place, like I did here against the Black Caps.

Below: Maybe I get a little bit pumped up at times. Still, winner takes all isn't a bad way to live your life.

loose at the end of his mark, bowling the ball to mid-off, who failed to take one cleanly and broke his finger. Being as keen as mustard, I told everyone: 'I'll go back and get my whites.' We only lived three minutes' walk away from the cricket club. Such was my enthusiasm, I was back within five, kit in hand and out of breath. I don't think I've ever sprinted so fast.

I fielded well that day and although I had only got into the team on a temporary basis, I didn't fall out of it following selection the next week. That was my first season in the first XI but the following year, the one in which I turned 15, I was clearly being picked on merit, chiefly for my ability with the bat. It was a good feeling, despite my relatively tender years, to be chosen on merit.

It didn't take long until my ability was being recognized slightly further afield. Jordan Clark, who would go on to play for Lancashire, was the real star of our area, regularly smashing hundreds in representative cricket and playing first XI men's stuff well ahead of lads like me. He played for Cleator, a club universally recognized for having the best junior set-up around. Everyone knew who Jordan was.

Cockermouth weren't supposed to do well against a team like Cleator. All the talk in our dressing room before my first meeting with him was, 'That Jordan Clark's awesome, He's so good, Did you hear about when he did this? Did you hear about when he did that?' It was like he was some kind of junior superstar. Unbeatable. Some kind of God.

His reputation certainly psyched out a lot of kids. And yes, of course, he was a bloody good player. So good, in fact, that he would open the bowling, sending four overs down at what seemed to all the other

13-year-old kids in the competition to be the speed of light, then take the wicketkeeping gloves for the rest of the innings. He was a ridiculously good wicketkeeper back then, standing up to every single one of his team-mates, even the ones with a bit of pace about their bowling, trying to take stumpings. He was a real freak.

My first combat with him was memorable. He grabbed the new ball and charged in as usual, but when it came to my turn to face him I gave as good as I got. First ball, I cut him hard for four. Then, when he followed up with a fuller one, I smashed a drive through the covers for another four. Nobody was meant to do that to him, of course – I had been left in no doubt about that from the pre-match talk in the changing room. So, with a little bit of encouragement from his dad on the sidelines, he hurled down a bouncer next ball. Luckily, I was on to it quickly, connecting with my hook well enough to send it over the boundary at square leg for six.

It led to Ian Clark, coach of Cleator in addition to being dad to their star player, hurtling around the boundary edge to speak to Jon Gibson.

'Who is this guy? Where did you get him from?'

The answer was something understated, like: 'His name's Ben, and he's from New Zealand.'

It was the kind of performance to get people talking, although not quite to the level they were already talking about Jordan. He scored runs at every level at which he was selected, and was playing first XI cricket, opening the batting at age 14. Whereas I was in the Cockermouth team as a super fielder, he was a super batsman. Watching him smack our opening bowlers through the covers left me in awe.

A lad of my age batting so well was simply outstanding. To put it into context, I only ever got one 50 for the Cockermouth first XI and to this day everyone laughs about the circumstances. It was the summer of 2006, I was 15, and we were challenging for the North Lancashire & Cumbria Premier League title. It was a match against another of the top teams, Workington, there were only a few weeks of the season left and we were so close to the line. Defeat to a rival and we could wave goodbye to the silverware.

Workington dominated the match, which meant we were batting to salvage some draw points. I was left with the tail for company and took the innings as deep as possible. It went down to the wire – we were nine wickets down, I had moved into the 40s. Soon, I was within just one scoring shot of my first half-century. A 50? Wow. I knew I was just one blow away from it. Trouble was, if I got out, it would mean defeat to one of our title rivals. Our season would be cooked.

As you can imagine, the situation was tense during those final few overs. Workington's off-spinner was bowling, and they were trying to give me a single to get our number 11 on strike. I wasn't interested in singles, though. I was waiting for something bigger and despite both mid-on and mid-off being posted back on the boundary at long-on and long-off, I couldn't resist going for it. Here it was. A ball was offered up into my slot – I swung through it and connected half-decently to send it towards the straight boundary. I can see the ball sailing narrowly over the fielder's head to this day.

If I had been caught, that would have been that. The team was desperate for a draw to keep the challenge for the league going. I was desperate for that first 50 in men's cricket. In the end we both got what we wanted. Cockermouth were crowned champions that September and I had played my part.

The club had really strong links to Cockermouth School. And I was happy at both. Not long after we arrived in the UK, I got offered a sporting scholarship from Sedbergh. Jordan got one too, and took his up, yet I was never going to go. Let's be honest, me and public school was never going to be a tidy fit. I wore black pants, a polo shirt and trainers. That was my kind of uniform. To go from that to wearing a blazer, shirt and tie would have been a culture shock, not my cup of tea, and the only reason I went to speak to Sedbergh at all was because it meant two days out of lessons.

The first was spent playing cricket, so they could check out whether I was any good, and the second was for the entry exam. Excuse me, a couple of days off? You bet I was up for that, even though I had no intention whatsoever of switching. I wasn't focused on school or scholarships. I was just focused on cricket. I played for a really good cricket club and went to a really good school when it came to sport.

Everyone did their best to help me fit in from day one at Cockermouth, although initially my Kiwi accent was a bit of an issue. It was as broad as you could possibly get, and as word got round about my background, it followed that more and more people were asking the new kid to read out signs. It gave a bunch of Cumbrian lads a good laugh. But it didn't amuse one of the teachers. Geography lessons used to be taken by Mrs Tickner. It's fair to say I wasn't one of her better students.

During my first lesson she asked for my name.

'*Bin* Stokes,' I said, in my New Zealand drawl.

Mrs Tickner was rather posh. 'You spell your name B-I-N?'

I don't think we ever got onto better terms.

With each passing week, school became more of a means to an end. I ended up in the head of year's office quite a lot. It wasn't that I was disruptive. I was not the class clown, or anything like that. I just tended to sit there and not do my work. I certainly wouldn't go out of my way to distract anyone else. But given a choice I would much rather be talking to the person next to me, who generally tended to be a good mate. Until I ran out of mates that is, and ended up sat at the back by myself.

It's not that I didn't see the point of school, either. I just knew I wanted to be a professional sportsman very soon into my life in England. From my first full school year of 2004–05, whatever I did in lessons at school was nothing to do with the career I really wanted to pursue.

You hear sports people asked what they would have done had they not become Tiger Woods, Sachin Tendulkar or Dan Carter. Now I'm not pretending to be in their ballparks in terms of ability, but I guess their answers would be similar: I never gave another career a second thought.

I came alive in the sports hall and playing fields during PE, and out of hours when we played against other schools at rugby and cricket. When it came to cricket, we played in a polo shirt and black pants. That was all the gear we had. In terms of equipment, we had one kitbag and an Astro-Turf pitch with cigarette burns in it. But we were good, and certainly not to be underestimated.

Those that did underestimate us got their comeuppance. We beat private schools, several of them. A good number of our team were also playing for Cockermouth Cricket Club, and we had team spirit as well as talent. When we drew Royal Grammar School Newcastle in a cup semi-final, they acted as if it was the equivalent of a bye, and began making travel arrangements for the final. They learned their lesson when we humped them.

If anything my upbringing taught me that owning all the gear was not necessarily the be all and end all. Each year the Cumberland age-group teams would play against a collection of the next best players from the region in a kind of trial match. In my first match of this type, as a 13-year-old playing for the best of the rest, I hit 40-odd. Dinger Bell, Cumbria's Under-13 coach and one of the bluntest men you could ever meet, told me afterwards, 'I want you back here next week.'

So there I was a few days later, back at Sedbergh School, playing for Cumbria against Yorkshire. Joe Root, with his little blond hair and permanent grin, was in the opposition. I turned up, not knowing anyone from either team, excited about the chance to step up a level. How big a step that was became evident when I warmed up with my new team-mates.

While we were decked out in whites at one end of the ground, our opponents were at the other, in full training gear. All we had was our playing kit and a jacket that had integrated red and yellow triangles as its motif and Cumbria written across them. The Yorkshire lads had badges on their helmets. We had a couple of helmets between us. The regulars in that Cumbrian team were mumbling, 'Look at us, man,' with embarrassment as we sat in the dressing room.

It looked like we were from completely different set-ups. And we were, of course. That didn't bother me. I had other things to concern me. I really wanted to make an impression with runs and wickets. I spewed up, I was so nervous. As it was, rain wrecked my chance to impress. The weather had stopped me where my new team-mates could not.

At the same time, I was playing representative rugby league for Allerdale, the local borough council, as well as for my club Broughton Red Rose. I was selected for trials in several big regional games, and even got picked in England squads for my age group. But the truth was, I was never really that bothered – never as serious about that pathway, especially when it was compared to the one that was opening up in cricket.

Evidence of that came in matches. Towards the end of my schoolboy rugby league days, I was playing at full-back, and whereas I had tackled everything that moved when I was a Kiwi kid, now I was literally letting people run past me. It might be an exaggeration to say that I was letting other players in to score tries – but I certainly wasn't doing all I could, making that extra lung-busting effort, to stop them. I just couldn't be bothered. Cricket was what I loved. I enjoyed it so much that everything else was going by the wayside.

I braced myself for what I anticipated being a difficult conversation with Dad. I had to tell him I no longer enjoyed playing rugby league and, given it was his sport and had been more than just a game to him – it had been his life, his lifestyle and his livelihood – I wasn't sure how he would react.

Actually, he was pretty cool about things. 'Right,' he said, 'you need to ring up your coach and do things properly.' So I made that phone call, and that was that. Up until this point, I genuinely believed a career in rugby league remained open to me had I pursued it with enthusiasm. However, giving it up was to become a significant step on my journey to becoming a professional cricketer.

● ● ●

Around this time, I was impressing sufficiently in representative cricket to gain higher recognition, and I was picked for an England Under-15 winter programme. Perhaps my rise was on Dad's mind in accepting my premature retirement from rugby league so calmly.

While it was undeniable that cricket was becoming more and more serious, however, I was still involved playing rugby union at school. One day we were doing tackling practice with Matthew Woodcock, the head of PE, who just happened to be one of Dad's players at Workington Town. During the session, I dump-tackled someone straight onto my knee, knackering it up to a degree that I couldn't participate in the first few weeks of the England camp.

Dad was furious. He said I should have been more mindful of the fact that I had been picked for an England squad. There was no sympathy for me whatsoever. God knows what Mr Woodcock got for it at training. Dad could be pretty frightening when angry.

When he eventually calmed down, there was a serious message from him: 'Son, you cannot play rugby any more.' With his background in sport, he knew that it was a no-no from that point. If I was as serious about cricket as I made out, and he was witnessing my progress at first hand, I would have to sacrifice other sports. The problem was that even though I had racked off rugby league, I still played union at school, and there was plenty of potential to get hurt.

I had discovered this to my cost on several occasions during schoolboy sport in Cumbria. During the third year we went over to Maryport to play Netherhall School. No one ever wanted to go to Maryport. If you have seen the *Lion King*, you may recall the Circle of Life talk between Mufasa and Simba in which the father tells his son about the dark and menacing Shadowlands:

'That's beyond our borders. We must never go there, Simba.'

Well, there was a social media meme doing the rounds that substituted Maryport for the Shadowlands. It was a pretty gruesome place, and the lads that grew up there seemed to use rugby union as an excuse to fight. They would pull hair, gouge and punch in the rucks, pushing the boundaries whenever they could, and caring little if they crossed them.

In this game, they pushed the boundaries even further than usual – the match ended in an abandonment and yours truly a victim of an unprovoked assault.

We scored an early try, and as I was lining up the conversion, I was shoved from behind. I swung around, straight into a scrap. I tried to give as good as I got, but within seconds two more Neanderthal players were throwing punches at me too. I took a bit of a beating before the referee got between us and took the most drastic action possible.

While there were plenty of normal school matches, however, to tell the truth, I missed not playing for a club side at weekends. The only trouble was, carrying on meant defying Dad. So it took covert operations to prevent him discovering I was doing so.

On a Sunday, I used to say I was going out to watch Cockermouth Wasps Rugby Union club play, and at first I genuinely was. But the more I watched, the more I wanted to be involved, so after a few weeks, I asked the coach, 'Can I play?' Turned out there were no forms to sign, which made my secret matches easier to play in, and Mam cooperated. Dad was pretty busy with his own rugby stuff on Sundays, so I just slipped back into my old fly-half role like nothing had changed. Don't get me wrong. I had other commitments myself by now that meant I didn't play every week, but whenever I could I would be there, always making sure that I showered well afterwards and got back into the same clothes.

There was once a 'Why have you got a black eye, Ben?'

'Oh, the ball hit me in the face.'

But other than that, Dad didn't have a clue. I'm glad he didn't find out as he was always a fairly formidable presence. Nobody ever messed with him, me included. Cross him and you'd find trouble.

One bloke, who played cricket for Workington, found this to his cost. He did not say a great deal to the older guys in our team but picked on me, the young lad. It might surprise you that I did not say a bean back then. Not a word. I just got on and played the game. But my old man happened to be one of the spectators watching his attempts to intimidate me, and the next time that fixture was played the guy appeared to have undergone a vow of silence. Suffice to say, Dad had approached him for a word or two.

As I have got older, I have recognized how similar we are. Whenever we talk to each other, on the phone or Skype, it's quite short and sweet. It'll be like alright, yeah, sweet, cool, speak to you later. He's pretty chilled out away from a sporting environment. There'll be a text from him every other week.

In contrast, Mam texts me every other day, reminding me of my responsibilities: how to do this, how to do that. Yes, Mam, I will wash my hands after I've been to the loo. I guess that's pretty normal mother stuff. And don't get me wrong, she is as involved with my career as Dad. She watches every single televised game I play and probably swears more than I swear on the pitch, sat in her front room in New Zealand. When things don't go right, or I get a bad decision, she turns the air blue. When I was younger, she never used to watch me bat, but now that she's on the other side of the world she uses it as her way of seeing me.

She was the same when Dad was coaching Workington. Mam and I used to watch games from one of the boxes in the stands. She used to cop a bit for her accent and I have to admit she could be pretty loud when a match was in full swing. She played a lot of sport herself and has a similarly feisty nature. But it's not quite the competitive level of Dad and me.

Yeah, of the two of them, I'm definitely more like him. We are both pretty quiet in everyday life but introduce the adrenalin of sport, and particularly confrontation, and you see a completely different side flare up. I'm sure that's the person you recognize when you see me on the cricket field. It was the person Dad was during his rugby league career. Nothing tends to bother us in everyday life – but that all changes in a working environment.

I witnessed this at first hand from a young age on those freezing nights in Christchurch. There was a determination about Dad. He was totally focused on one thing: winning. Sometimes he would explode. The number of times he was sent from the touchline during matches, to watch the rest of the game from the stands, was unbelievable. His competitive spirit would just overflow. Call it white-line fever, a game face, whatever. In the moment, when the competitive nature hits you, it sparks a huge change. Like a fire has been lit inside you. Sat at home with the kids, nothing could really annoy me. I'm as calm as anything. Once that kit goes on, though, everything changes.

That inherited volatility has definitely helped my cricket. It has meant I have never gone into a game on the back foot. For the manner in which I want to play, it's important to be in the heat of the battle at all times, to never shy away from any challenge. I've attacked every single opportunity I've been given in playing cricket.

And when that passion, that desire to win, overtakes me, I don't care who I'm up against. It could be the best player in the world standing 22 yards away from me, but their identity is irrelevant. I couldn't care less what their name is. I will never let anyone defeat me – whether with bat or ball – on reputation.

I have never cared who people are. Yes, you might be pitched against players who have played 100 times more matches, or be ranked number one in the world. But I have always viewed it as being one of them against one of me. On that basis we are equal, and that attitude has been a massive help to my development at each level up through the English cricket system.

It was what I applied when I first went to the Durham academy, again when I was given an opportunity in the Durham first team and once more when I was first picked for England in the 2013-14 Ashes. I didn't care who those Australian guys were; didn't care I had never faced someone bowling 94 mph before, as Mitchell Johnson was; didn't care that these were guys who were at the head of the world game. In the heat of the battle, in direct competition against them, that is all irrelevant. It becomes me versus him.

6

One thing I should clear up in case you have any doubts is that I am 100 per cent English. Yes, I know I was born in Christchurch, thousands of miles away. No, I never wanted to leave New Zealand. My parents are both unbelievably proud to call themselves Kiwis. And I only arrived in England as a boy of 12. All I can say is that to me, nationality is about feel.

If I ever get into a conversation with people in everyday life and they ask me where I'm from, I tell them I am from Durham. After all, that's were Clare and I have set up our family life. Only when the chat develops further, and turns to subjects like 'Where did you go to school?', stuff like that, would I mention my past, and the fact I spent my first dozen years on the planet in New Zealand. I am happy with my life in England. Everything I do is very English. I call my mother Mam, for goodness sake.

Of course, all of this does not diminish my family history. I am so proud of my heritage, don't get me wrong. I know exactly where I came from and will never forget that. But since the age of 15, when my dream of becoming a professional sportsman took in my first involvement with England representative squads, the three lions have been all to me. As a young lad, earning the right to wear them at international level represented a long-term goal.

You can see who I am, my identity, from my tattoos. They say some people wear their hearts on their sleeves. My sleeves are my life story. Where I came from, where I have been, who's been with me, are all recorded in ink.

I had still not turned 18 when I asked Mam whether I could have a tattoo. She reckoned – wrongly, as it turns out – that I would have gone and had one done anyway whatever her answer. So I was sat down and told that even though they were not overly keen at my age, if I could come up with something that meant something – not a dragon breathing fire, an anchor or a bulldog – it was a goer. If it was a design that had relevance to me, and always would in the future, it was okay by her and Dad.

Those are words that I have kept with me ever since. From that day on, I have always contemplated long and hard about each piece of artwork I have had done. To get to work at the start, I thought about what made me 'me'.

Amongst my mates, I was known for being a Kiwi, and it was public knowledge that I wanted to play for England at cricket. So I wanted something that contained both those aspects of my life. The problem was, what? And how would I put them together? I was set on the three lions, because I have always associated them with English cricket, but told my parents that I would also like a New Zealand connection. Any ideas?

Between them, they found some Maori designs on the Internet that, if put together, made a rugby ball. So, for that first tattoo on my back, I have those three lions as the central focus with the two halves of the rugby ball incorporated, on the outside. It is English at heart with the Kiwi history surrounding it.

Mam actually got one done at the same place back in Cockermouth, immediately before I was worked upon. Typically of Mam, given her patriotic nature, it was the outline of New Zealand's north and south islands on her back. She went first, and grimaced all the way through.

'You big softie,' I told her, anticipating a world of pain.

Only I never encountered it. Now, I'm not saying this to sound macho whatsoever – but for a first tattoo I couldn't believe how little it hurt. It felt like a kid drawing a sketch with a pencil. It was nothing compared to the soreness I have experienced since on my subsequent inkings.

Getting tattoos with meaning has become a bit of a pastime for me, each and every piece of artwork possessing its own significance. The initial ones contain a lot of traditional Maori symbols within the overall pictures. As a sportsman, I also believe deeply in motivation, and as I progressed with Durham, I wanted an inspirational quote.

I found an obscure one I liked but had to re-word it to make it sound more like me: *Being the best that you can be, Is only possible, If you desire to be a champion, And your fear of failure is non-existent.*

Dad then did more research into the tribe our family evolved from. In Maori culture, each tribe has its own mountain called a maunga. You can see mine in the Kirihuti art on my left arm, wrapped around that quote. There is also New Zealand's silver fern at the top, and a cricket ball in there too, with Maori markings as its stitching.

This one has been a work in progress over the years, starting with the words, ahead of my first England Lions tour, to the Caribbean in 2011.

The tribal stuff is particularly relevant to Mam. In Maori culture, everyone knows their own place stretching back hundreds of years. Your extended family is called the Whanau, then there is the Iwi, literally translated as bone, which is the tribe to which you belong, then there is the Hapu, which is the community of tribes throughout the whole of New Zealand.

The part Maori blood that I have, from my Mam's side, is really quite strong – stretching back to the Treaty of Waitangi in 1840. My great, great, great, great grandfather is a signatory on that, the most important document in New Zealand's history, drawn up between Maori chiefs and the British Crown, resulting in the declaration of British sovereignty.

Mam and Dad emphasize that I have no family history unless I embrace the past. My future will be in the UK, that seems certain enough, but they insist I keep some focus on where I came from, and their backgrounds. In the years to come, my own children Layton and Libby will no doubt ask me about that and I don't want to lose touch with that. It would be a bit tragic not to have a grasp of it, and so I am forever being reminded not only of my time in New Zealand but my heritage – who my relations are, the history and geography of it all – so I can pass it on to generations to come wherever they may settle.

Trust me, my mother is the biggest Kiwi going. I've had a couple of tiffs with her over the years when, after my international matches, she has been interviewed back home. She will say things like, 'Yeah, Ben's playing for England, he's English but . . . he's not, really, he's a Kiwi.'

I have had to tell her: 'Mam, I am playing for England. I would appreciate it if you refrained from saying stuff like that.'

I am not sure, if I was an England fan, that I would be wanting to hear parents of a player to be saying stuff like that. She knows exactly how I feel in terms of my nationality, and the pride I have in playing for England. I cannot believe that anyone could be prouder. Problem is she is equally proud of her background and I respect that.

Dad is more relaxed about the whole scenario but whenever they watch me play, they kind of hope that England win, apart from against New Zealand when they also sort of want the Black Caps to win too. I guess draws, ties and washouts for them are the best results . . .

At home, we laugh every Christmas about what Maori artefacts we will be receiving as presents from Mam and Dad. It's a way of constantly reminding me of my roots. We have a picture on the wall signifying knowledge and wisdom. It's a reminder of how the Maori race has developed. We've had carvings out of greenstone – called Pounamu in Maori culture – as well as whale bone. People back in New Zealand wear Pounamu pendants round their necks. Every design has a different meaning, and everything means something – whether it is how each is shaped, its engravings, whatever.

When I was younger, Mark Grisedale, a close school mate from Cockermouth, died in a car accident. Years previously, when I left Wellington for England, I was given a greenstone necklace by my best friend Freddie

Robinson, which represented 'safe travels'. Its symbolism struck me when we lost Mark, so I went round to the family house and placed that necklace in the casket ahead of his cremation.

In the autumn of 2014, I decided to start tattoos on my right arm. I have always liked angels, so I wanted to combine that with my own family. The main feature is a huge angel with Layton's name above it and Libby's below. As my Mam got a star named after Layton when he was born, there are stars to represent him, and I have always liked roses, so they finish it off. For the words this time, I borrowed some lyrics I picked out listening to the rapper Drake. It's a line from 'Shot for Me': *May people respect you, Trouble neglect you, Angels protect you, And heaven accept you.*

I may have mentioned that I'm not a big statistics man. However, numbers that do mean something to me are 658, my Test number, and 221, where I stand on England's list of capped players in one-day internationals.

Most recently, I added a phoenix from the ashes on my right forearm. I have always liked big designs and Clare reckoned the phoenix symbolized me perfectly. Whenever I am down, I always try my best to get myself back up – to rise again. It's in my character to strive as hard as possible to come back from bad times. I wanted lots of fire, and the phoenix to look mean. The rest I left to Mel, my tattoo artist, and her imagination. The timing? That seemed appropriate too. It was immediately after the World Twenty20, and I intended to come back strongly.

When stuff happens like that, it's nice that I can seek solace in my family.

People can be quite shocked when they find out I have two toddlers at the age of 25. These days it's not the norm, and I guess some would argue it doesn't fit my image. Not that I have let having a family get in the way of enjoying myself, or committing myself 100 per cent to my career. But they are placed first, ahead of everything else, when cricket is not involved.

It's what I was accustomed to growing up. Rugby league dictated our destiny. We followed Dad's job opportunities and landed in Cumbria. As a family, we were happy there, but unfortunately things did not end so well.

Dad's job at Workington lasted four years, finishing acrimoniously when he was dismissed following an altercation with a Barrow fan during a Northern Rail cup tie in February 2007. Even though he was cleared by a Rugby Football League investigation, the club stood by their decision to fire him for disciplinary reasons.

This fan had got really stuck into him, really in his face, and later claimed, 'He punched me.' Dad would never do that. He is just too professional to get involved with that kind of thing. The whole episode involved several hearings and at the end of it, the net result was that Dad was sacked. In the circumstances, they would not have to pay him a penny.

It all seemed a little bit convenient. A contravention of a disciplinary code meant no obligation by the club to pay someone off, and Dad still had two years of his contract to run. To think it ended for him in that way made me so angry. He had done so much for the club. Obviously, it was a bad time for Dad, and for us as a family.

Even then, as much as they did him over, he didn't want to bring the club down. He played for Workington, coached them, had an affinity with the people who worked there, and had a decent relationship with the supporters. So even though the actions of the club bosses were potentially going to ruin him, he didn't want to take them to the cleaners.

He just wanted something to compensate for his loss of income, which is why he took legal action against them. Thankfully, it didn't get to the High Court, as Workington agreed a settlement less than 48 hours before the scheduled hearing in November that year.

Dad always believed he had been thrown under the bus because the club had seen an opportunity to get rid of a coach on a long-term contract without giving him a bean, and for some reason that appealed to them, even though he was doing wonders for them. When he'd arrived in 2003, there were only seven registered first-team players. Only 12 turned up for his first training session. Remember, it's a 13-a-side game. Over the next couple of seasons, he turned them into a proper rugby team.

He was a prop but he has a creative side to his coaching too, always wanting to play attractive rugby, to entertain. He coordinated all the moves, and got people in with decent track records. Jonny Limmer and Lusi Sione, both brought over from New Zealand, are still talked about fondly at the club a decade later. Over the years, several guys who played for him at Workington and Whitehaven told me, 'He's the best coach I've ever had.' He had a real rapport with them.

Dad was the guy that got everything done. He would be out scouting players, assessing how they would fit into his system, signing them up. There was no talent identification network, or other guys sealing the deals. He did it all from start to finish. In one of his four seasons at Workington, he even designed the kit.

As you can tell from that, there was not a lot of money to work with, and when they drew Leeds Rhinos at home in the fourth round of the 2004 Challenge Cup, it was a bit of a godsend. The match drew a bumper crowd of almost 5,000 to Derwent Park. Workington got humped but there was some pride retained in the fact they were mega-competitive in the second half – Leeds shading it 22-18. They had trailed 52-0 just after the break but hit back with a hat-trick of tries and lost 68-18. Workington were part-time; Leeds were crowned Super League champions that season.

There were positive vibes around a club that was barely a club at all when Dad took the job. He turned around their fortunes, signed players who had played higher level in Australia or in Super League, guys that wanted to play for him because he was Ged Stokes.

If nothing else, his out-of-court settlement set the record straight. It also served to clear his reputation. And that made him employable again. However, the destination of his next job was a real surprise.

● ● ●

When, in late March 2008, Dad told me he was going to be taking the coaching position at Whitehaven, it was the weirdest thing to digest. Paul Crarey, the coach at the Recreation Ground, had just quit for health reasons. It was like Dad was joining the enemy. You see, Mam and Dad were Workington through and through. There was no love lost between Cumbria's two biggest clubs, and they had bought into the culture of it all.

It was a historical rivalry stretching back to the first half of the twentieth century, a period in which the county's coal industry was thriving. Pit workers from Workington called their equivalents from Whitehaven 'jam eaters'. It was to signify that they were of a lower class. Those from Workington, it was said, could afford meat in their sandwiches at lunchtime. In contrast, people from Whitehaven could only afford jam. It was all a bit tit for tat, though, and over the years I learned that those from Whitehaven inverted the taunt. There were jam eaters on both sides of the divide.

From a work perspective, it seemed like a good break for him because although Dad was loyal to Workington, it was clear that Haven were the best team in Cumbria. Over the years I had become accustomed to the rivalry between the two. Although it was incomparable to the City and United rivalry in Manchester football, when the two of them were up against each other, it drew decent attendances, and ensured tensions ran high. Everyone in Cumbria, it seemed, wanted to watch those games. It was a good standard of rugby league, with the odd elbow thrown in, and skirmishes kicking off around the field – the people up in the north-west of England loved all that.

After Dad was removed from his position with Town, there were a few players and members of the management whose attitude was very much 'We're not having this'. So they followed him eight miles down the west coast. Gary Hewer, Les Ashe and Vic Semple were loyal backroom staff, and men who Dad rated as well as trusted. When he got there, there was also a guy called Karl Edmondson, a prop forward, who used to play under him for New Zealand A. He had joined the enemy but surrounded himself with allies.

Whitehaven were facing relegation when he took over, yet they made the Championship play-offs that season, getting to within 80 minutes of a Grand Final. They were the only team to beat Salford – who went on to claim a place in Super League – doing so live on Sky TV.

Dad's signings got Haven going again. They made the play-offs again the following year. But things were a mess off the field, and some of the decisions made by the club owner Dick Raaz, a cigar-chewing American, used to drive Dad mad. The pair of them did not work well together.

The third season saw the club plunge down the table, and as in any sport the coach takes the blame. Wins transformed into defeats, 13 matches were lost on the trot and Dad was sacked a fortnight before the club was placed in administration.

And that, aside from recreational stuff with Cockermouth some time later, was the end of his relationship with rugby league. It was sad because I could see how passionate he was about his career and how much he put into each of his jobs. He didn't deserve to be treated that way by either of those Cumbrian clubs after what he did for them. Twice he received approaches when he was at Workington – one of them from a Super League club – only for him to dismiss the advances on the grounds of loyalty.

It was pretty tough being an out-of-work coach in the north-west of England, and the economy was such that there weren't enough jobs for the locals, let alone foreigners, as Dad put it. So it wasn't as if he could put his plastering skills to any use. The only opportunity that came up was one with an old pal in Perth, Western Australia. It meant he upped sticks, and left me and Mam behind. Mam was still working for the Rising Sun Trust, a charity devoted to helping drug addicts and their families.

These days they are back in Christchurch, where my story began. Mam is a victim support worker, helping families who have suffered at the hands of crime, while Dad is a corrections officer and principal instructor of the Rebuild Project at a local prison. We might be on opposite sides of the globe these days but we're happy, and share one really significant thing in common: we are living where we feel we belong.

'For Christ's sake, Deborah.'

The air regularly turned blue during our family car journeys from Cockermouth to Chester-le-Street. How was a young lad curled up on the back seat meant to top up on his weekly sleep with that going on?

I had been playing a year out of age for Cumbria when, a few days after my 14th birthday, we were involved in a fixture against Durham Under-15s at Darlington. Scott Borthwick was the opposition captain. I bowled well, taking three for 28 from my 10 overs, we won the match by six wickets and some time afterwards John Windows, who has since become Durham's academy coach, approached me, offering me the chance to switch allegiances and start attending regular net sessions with them.

Naturally, that sounded pretty cool to me. But when it came to it, it meant a commitment by my parents to trek across the north of England, initially once and later twice a week during the winter of 2006-07. Now, navigating routes from the west coast to the east is a challenge if you don't know the roads, and two New Zealanders struggled to find a quick one.

They spent hours behind a wheel for the sake of those training sessions. A little too much time as it turned out: the journey became considerably shorter when Mam and Dad finally figured out the Hexham way.

On those initial Monday afternoon trips, I would be collected straight from school, and we would head off from Cockermouth to Penrith, then cross country, through the North Pennines, and on to Scotch Corner to join the A1 northbound. What we would have done for a Sat Nav. Instead, it was just an AA route planner, with directions jotted down on a piece of paper.

There are lots of little towns joined by narrow country roads in that part of the world, which meant there were lots of different ways to make it from A to B. Occasionally, Mam would try to snip five minutes off the travel time by telling Dad to head for such-and-such a place. It rarely went smoothly. The number of arguments that went on in the front of that car was phenomenal. I used to wake up with a jolt while trying to catch a nap.

'To this roundabout and turn left . . . Sorry . . . Double turn right.'

'For God's sake, Deborah!'

They used to go at each other something rotten in the front of that car – but the memories bring a smile to my face. I was grateful for their commitment. Even when I'd played for Cumbria, getting to training could prove a real drag. We would have practices scheduled in Millom, a 90-minute drive away. Then, there would be the odd session at

Whitehaven. Every now and again we would be at Sedbergh School. We certainly didn't lack training sessions. There were plenty of them. If anything, the thing that was missing was quality facilities. At the major counties, indoor cricket schools don't look like the ones we used. We trained in what was effectively a sports hall with basketball hoops at each end, on rolled-out mats. You had to go further afield for a better standard.

Growing up in Cumbria means a hike for any talented young cricketer. In fact, there are only two realistic choices as a schoolboy player. If you're good enough, you tend to get picked up by either Lancashire or Durham. Like me, Graham Clark headed to Durham; Graham's elder brother Jordan and Liam Livingstone went to Lancashire.

At the start of the 2007 summer, I was invited onto the club's week-long tour to Dubai. I was playing for Durham's academy team at the age of 15. Things were progressing pretty quickly, and school definitely didn't get the attention it should have. It wasn't that I was rebelling. Still, how can I put it? I didn't give it much attention when I was there. What good were Maths, History and English going to do me where I was heading? I was going to earn a living playing cricket.

Fortunately, Cockermouth School were brilliant about my situation. They understood that I was intent on a career in professional sport, and supported me by granting me time off when necessary to commit to that goal. I was putting everything into cricket; very little into other subjects. I left school with two GCSEs, in PE and Design & Technology. I didn't even turn up for one exam, just hung around on the streets instead.

● ● ●

By my fourth year of secondary school, I had become well established on the national radar. I was involved at the Bunbury Festival along with Jordan, Jos Buttler, Sam Billings and Joe Root. The majority of the lads on show went on to play first-class cricket. Some no longer play: Matthew Pardoe and Neil Pinner, who both played at Worcestershire, and Chris Jones, from Somerset. Others do: two more from Somerset, the left-arm spinner Jack Leach and all-rounder Calum Haggett, who has since moved to Kent; Zafar Ansari, who played despite being Under-14; and Matt Machan, of Sussex, who has since switched allegiance to Scotland. Jordan and I were the first cricketers from Cumbria to be selected for England Under-15 squad training in 20 years. It was from this pool of players by and large that an England Under-16 team was chosen to face the touring Australians in September 2007. We won 3-0.

During that Bunbury week, we made poor Sam Billings cry. David English, the competition's founder and financier, laid on a dinner for us, at Nando's, which obviously went down a bomb with a load of teenage lads. But being lads, we saw an opportunity for mischief, and when Sam went to the loo, some hot sauce found its way into his unattended Coke. Before you get worried about a potential bullying case, it was nothing of the sort. It was an ill-timed toilet break – he was just unlucky.

There has always been a camaraderie between the gang of us. The core of the Bunbury lads went on to play England Under-19 cricket together. And even though I only played against Sam a couple of times between those youth international days and the summer of 2015, when he walked into the England dressing room for the Royal London Series against New Zealand, it was as if we had never been apart, carrying on as we did when we were kids. Cricketers tend to be good at that. You walk out of one dressing room and meet up in another, years later, and it's like nothing has changed. It's as if you've chatted every week for the past four years.

County cricket is a good environment for developing relationships too – playing against some guys regularly means you get to know them, to an extent that it feels comfortable when you're selected for England together. Jason Roy is a good example. I'd never played any cricket with him by the time he came into the England fold, yet he was already someone I would call a mate.

Recognition didn't only come in the form of selection. By the time I was picked for seven two-day England coaching clinics at the national academy in Loughborough during the Ashes summer of 2005, I already possessed my first contract with a bat manufacturer – the reward for being named the player of the tournament, representing the North of England at the English Schools Cricket Association's Under-14 tournament. I didn't make massive scores or take bags of wickets, but I would do something every game: a 40 off 30 balls, a couple of wickets and a catch, stuff like that. It was not as if I was some sensational stand-out player, but those sessions with Jon Gibson were certainly paying off.

A deal with Gray-Nicolls provided me with full kit, and therefore as the start of each new season approached, I got excited. The catalogue would arrive and it would be like 'check this out'. It was a real thrill. A teenage kid getting to pick his own gear, free of charge – it was class. I got whatever I wanted up to a few hundred quid, and anything on top of that had 50 per cent discount on it. Once I broke into the Durham first XI it was all in; if I wanted it, it was mine, and I was like any other young cricketer, keen to have the newest bats and pads.

Only later, after a good debut County Championship season with Durham, did I leave Gray-Nicolls and sign with Puma. At the time, Ian Blackwell was in the first XI and both he and Phil Mustard used Puma equipment.

'This kit is mint,' I told them. 'What do you reckon? Can you set me up?'

When Blacky rang up the response had been fairly negative, apparently, with more than a few grumbles down the phone. Soon afterwards, though, I got 160 in a televised match against Kent. The following season I was using Puma.

For some reason, I had an ability to do well whenever I needed to. Twice I did it to seal kit deals. My first appearance for the second XI was in an annual friendly against Lancashire, a match which gave opportunities to a couple of academy lads. Just like that Cumbria trial match, I was nervous. Here I was, the new kid on the block, in my plain old whites, up against guys with names and numbers on the back of their shirts. They had professional contracts, some with experience of playing first-class cricket. In other words, everything I wanted.

Once again, I made a good first impression, scoring a hundred. I had been placed in a more challenging environment, but I was able to perform in the same way as I did for the academy team on a Saturday afternoon. I batted no differently from how I would in the North-East Premier League, but the feeling of achievement was completely different. I was so happy, absolutely chuffed. Not because I was getting carried away, thinking that a first-team debut would be just around the corner, or anything like that. No, I had scored a hundred for Durham's second XI. That was a big thing. It was almost with a sense of disbelief that I had done it.

• • •

A couple of weeks before my 16th birthday, immediately after school broke up for fifth form exams, I moved to Durham. Well okay, not permanently. I lived in a house during the summer months that followed, with two other lads from Cumbria, Paul Hindmarch and James Tincknell, who would go on to play rugby union for Leeds and London Welsh.

Being away from home gave me a sense of freedom. It's not for everyone, but I liked living away. The other lads were 18, and, naturally, I wanted to do all the stuff they were doing. So I would head out to pubs and bars with them, using someone else's passport for ID. Every now and again it would work. When it didn't, it was a taxi back home.

Whenever I did get in, I'd have the time of my life. Durham owned two houses on adjacent estates and used them for players from outside the area. The club arranged things so that at least one person from each house could drive, so at weekends there was transport to matches. Each weekday we would train. It was awesome. School was out and I was playing cricket every day. I was living the dream and loving it. I was learning to become an adult. It was class.

The club also did things to try to help our transition from home life to our new state of independence. We headed to the Lake District on an academy trip, designed to strengthen team bonding and also improve our domestic skills. We spent three days lodging in converted barns on a farmer's estate and were challenged to feed ourselves.

Split into two groups of seven, we were given just £25 to spend. The idea was to test our initiative. What should we buy? How could we make the money go round effectively? It caused a bit of a scene in the local supermarket when I got to the checkout with the rest of my group and the till reel read £47.50. Living to a budget was not something I or my new mates were used to, so, red-faced, we traipsed back down the aisles, choosing items to place back on the shelves.

I've always liked my food and Mam made sure I knew how to cook certain straightforward meals. That wasn't a problem to me. However, the cost of everything was. After a few weeks, Phil Dicks, one of the club analysts who worked with us on the academy programme, came to see me as it had come to his attention via my parents that I was going through my weekly £50 budget like water. Durham always kept an eye on things like that, because of concerns that young players might get involved with drugs, alcohol or gambling.

Phil came round to see me to make sure I was eating okay and was shocked to discover that I was eating more than okay. I was cooking myself steak nightly. He told me that whilst that was obviously good for a young cricketer to be eating, there were other ways to get a decent diet without spending so much. He gave me a lesson on alternative meals and invited himself round for dinner the next day, challenging me to cook something both affordable and edible.

A couple of years later, after I had signed my first professional contract, when players were split into pairings for accommodation purposes, it looked like I was going to be living with Phil but ended up in a flat with Chris Rushworth instead. Rushy had just got back onto the scene after being released in 2006 without playing a first XI game, and sharing a flat with him had both its positive and negative sides. During that year we enjoyed ourselves, no doubt about it. If there was time away from cricket, we made it our business to turn it into a good time. Whenever I got paid, I would take a couple of hundred quid out of the hole in the wall and go straight down the bookies, to see if I could double my money.

If it was a Friday or Saturday night, you would find us out on the town. It's fair to say we both relied on talent rather than fitness. Our lifestyles were pretty ropey. I can't say what changed things for him, but I'm guessing the first good season he had in 2010 coincided with him losing a few pounds through sheer workload, and altering his off-field habits in subsequent seasons. With the majority of cricketers, you have some success, and you want to maintain it or improve upon it, so that would have no doubt had a big role in it as well. When I was shacked up with him, you wouldn't have believed this was a man that could go teetotal through an entire county season, as he was to do in 2014. Nowadays, he's one of the best bowlers in the country. Being stronger and able to recover quicker after matches has undoubtedly made a difference.

Throughout that 2010 season, my debut one in first-class cricket, I was scoring fifties and hundreds, taking the odd wicket here and there, while living like any young single lad would. Beer was the most constant thing in my diet. It was my first England Lions trip the following winter that changed me. Getting to see how they operated one level higher up was an eye opener.

There were some guys who had already played international cricket on that trip to the Caribbean – we played in the first-class competition – as well as some established county performers. Guys like Ravi Bopara, Craig Kieswetter, Liam Plunkett, Adil Rashid, Andrew Gale and Jimmy Adams. Previously, I had been mixing with my team-mates at Durham, the England Under-19s. Now I was seeing a rise in standards across the board.

Suddenly, I was being told 'this is where you need to be at' in terms of fitness. Without telling me what my target was, the conditioning coach Mark Spivey made it clear that I needed to lose some weight.

'We know it'll take a while,' was one of the comments that came back to me.

The same people who had spotted my potential as a future England cricketer believed I was too podgy. So, what do you think I did? Argue back? No, I accepted what they were saying. It only strengthened my resolve to shed the pounds even quicker.

When I get handed a target, I set my mind to achieving it, and failing was not an option for me. Sure, I wanted to make an impression on Mick Newell, the England Lions coach, and David Parsons, the England and Wales Cricket Board's performance director, but I also wanted heads of department back at the National Cricket Performance Centre in Loughborough, such as the medical team and nutritionists, to know I was getting better at the extra-curricular stuff too. That I was taking everything related to cricket seriously.

Previously, I did the training asked of me, but fitness was not a priority.

I did it, because I knew I had to. You need to be fit to play cricket. I just didn't do things away from the club that would help me in terms of diet and lifestyle. To get better, I was being told that I had to put in the extra effort – and I wanted to get better.

To be fair, Dad had been on my case in previous winters before I signed professional forms with Durham in December 2009, making sure I was not turning up for pre-season training less fit than I had been the previous September, forcing me into the gym from nine o'clock every morning.

I might have wasted two or three years, and several opportunities, had he not done so, and it's true to say I might not be where I am but for his intervention. But it was the regime I began on the 2010–11 England Performance Programme in Australia and stepped up in the Caribbean, rather than my on-field performances there during the three first-class draws against Leeward Islands, Guyana and Jamaica, that helped me going forward. I dropped from 110 kg to 95 kg over the next 12 months.

● ● ●

By this time, Clare was in my life. We had met the previous August while I was at work.

Clare's family all love cricket and Arthur, her dad, always told her that she should marry a cricketer. He was born and raised in Manchester, a big Lancashire fan, but lived in Somerset. Each summer they went back to visit their northern relatives for a week, and looked to include a County Championship match in their trip. In the year of 2010, the fixture that happened to correspond was Lancashire v Durham at Old Trafford, and I was fielding on the boundary. I noticed her, she noticed the name on the back of my shirt, and before the end of the game she was submitting a friend request on Facebook.

Our relationship was a long-distance one to start with. In fact, geographically we could hardly have been much further apart. Durham at one end of the country; Somerset at the other. When a 640-mile round trip is involved, keeping things going might be a struggle. But we showed that need not be the case. We met up a couple of times over the next month and hit it off. Then, I asked Clare to be my plus-one at Durham's 2010 end of season dinner.

I was only 19 and I wasn't necessarily looking to settle down, but we enjoyed being around each other and we made it work. Clare, a couple of years older than me, was finishing her studies – a PGCE to become a teacher – at university in Taunton. I was living in a flat with Rushy, and couldn't drive. Other people would give me lifts everywhere, so I didn't see the point in learning. When Clare had a few days off between lectures, she would drive up to stay with me. During the first couple of months that winter, I regularly jumped on the train down to Bristol.

As Christmas approached, things were getting more serious between us, and Facebook would play its part again. I was going away with the England Lions in the new year and Clare wanted to know whether we were serious.

'Are we boyfriend and girlfriend?'

'Well, my status says "In a Relationship".'

That makes things official, doesn't it? Well it did, as far as we were concerned. I am an instinct kind of person. Being with Clare felt right.

It was a similar feeling in the spring of 2012 when she phoned to tell me she thought she was pregnant. Clare still lived in Weston-super-Mare, and was calling to let me know her suspicion. It was a bit of an odd conversation. It started with Rushy and another couple of the Durham lads in the same room, and ended without any certainty.

Whoah. Oh, shit.

That had been my initial reaction. I was still young, we lived hundreds of miles apart, and most of my time was spent living out of a suitcase. What the hell would my parents say? What would Clare's parents say?

But the negative images subsided as quickly as they'd arrived. I have always been someone that meets challenges when they present themselves, not someone who worries about what might be. I have always lived in the moment. So when Clare took her pregnancy test on Mothering Sunday and sent me a photo of the result, it was an amazing feeling – pure class. I was going to be a dad.

The scariest thing was telling Mam and Dad; or at least the thought of what they might say scared me. I told Mam and she burst into tears. She was obviously happy.

'Are you going to tell Dad, then?' she asked.

I was a bit nervous when she left the room to get him. Typically of him, though, he was pretty blunt. 'What you crying for, Deb?'

'They're happy tears. You're going to be a granddad.'

They both took it brilliantly. However, the reaction in the Durham dressing room was quite a contrast.

'Good one, mate,' was the kind of thing I got back. No one took it seriously at first. Some of the lads just burst out laughing.

'Stokoe, you are going to have to change, my boy,' old man Dale Ben-kenstein told me.

I didn't need Benky's words of wisdom to tell me that I would need to work on my maturity. That with parenthood comes responsibility. Before, everything I did was for me. But in October 2012 when Layton was born, I became a family man. I started to think differently about things. Events were making me grow up fast.

Layton was just five days old when I received a late-night phone call from Jane, Clare's mum.

'Clare needs to come home,' she explained. 'It's her dad.'

Arthur had been ill with various things over the previous couple of years. It had been one thing after another, and his health had clearly dete-riorated again. You can tell in someone's voice when something like that happens.

'Start packing some bags,' I told Clare.

It was just past 10 o'clock but we drove through the night. During the pregnancy, Clare had forced me to learn to drive.

'I am not driving myself to the bloody hospital.'

This was another reason I was glad that I had. Arthur got to see his grandson, and that was important to all of us. That week was happy for him, there was no pain, and he died when Layton was 12 days old.

People are genuinely surprised when they find out I have children. It's almost like they think I've been keeping it secret. Far from it – I am the proudest dad you can imagine, it's the best thing ever, and far from hold it back, I reckon my career has benefitted from being a family man.

Kids offer you a release for angst and frustration, and remind you of the important things in life. When you walk through the front door, they couldn't care less whether you've had a good day or a bad day. Whether you have been out first ball, or smashed a match-winning innings. They put a smile on my face no matter what's happened. And Clare is brilliant when she knows things haven't gone well. She will keep Layton up if I am due home and his excitement at seeing me completely changes my mood if I've had a crap day. It's amazing what a scream of 'Daddy' and a cuddle does for me. In an instant, everything that's happened that day is gone.

I found out Libby was on her way into the world in mid-season 2014. It was 18 June, and I was playing a County Championship match for Durham. Despite being defending champions, a combination of bad weather, some uncharacteristically poor displays from us and the upping of opposition games meant we were winless after seven matches. Talk was of us following the fate of Yorkshire, Nottinghamshire and Lancashire and getting relegated the year after winning the title. We knew that was nonsense. But we had to show it.

Our eighth match was against Lancashire at the Riverside, and it had been one of those matches with lots of momentum swings. We collapsed, and recovered through a 150-run stand for the ninth wicket on day one; Lancashire began well but collapsed from 206-2 to 266 all out on day two; we staved off another batting slump to set them a 340-run victory target; all results were possible when they began the fourth day on 41-2.

It was a tense finish. We took regular wickets but couldn't get Jos Buttler, and they needed 31, eight down, as he neared his hundred. Thankfully, we managed to wrap things up soon afterwards, and celebrate our first win of the season with a few beers.

Clare usually leaves me be after matches, but this time her messages were clear: have a couple but you need to come home. We were due to go out together that night, to a joint-benefit do for Gordon Muchall and Gareth Breese. But I had more than a hard-fought win to thank for the spring in my step as we headed back out. Getting the kids out the way early in life means we can all head to Ibiza in the future and hang out together.

Even at the age of three, everything is about cricket for Layton. I have tried to get him to play golf, but he taps the club on the floor before striking the ball, as if he's in his batting stance. He's been brought up watching sport. He's unbelievably aware of it. One day we were flicking through the Sky Sports channels. 'Oh, that's tennis,' he said. Goodness knows how he knew.

He's a real chip off the old block, a very active kid and we have thrown him into lots of activities. We need to tire him out somehow. It's like he's got long-life batteries in. And the power never drains from them. He charges around all day. He's all-action. If he runs into a wall, he just gets back up and carries on. And the Stokes genes are definitely strong in him. He's so impatient. If he doesn't get his own way, he carries on something rotten, just like I did when I was younger. He will discover, as I had to, that crying doesn't get you what you want.

But he's also quite smart. If he's naughty, and he's getting a telling off, he will react with a facial expression that he knows will have Clare and I unable to keep straight faces. It's hard to remain mad with him when you're laughing your head off.

Libby's expressions are quite a contrast. At 15 months old I still had no idea whether she liked me or not. She's that kind of kid. You know in those first few months, when you're talking baby to them – 'boo, boo, boo' – she literally looked daggers at me.

'What the hell are you doing? You weirdo,' her face says.

That's her default for me. On other days she can be a laugh a minute, running around, singing to herself. But once the switch flicks, there she is, stern-faced, bottom lip out, telling the world she doesn't want to be here.

I'm so happy that she is.

8

'You don't want to play for England. You just want to piss it up the wall with your mates, and have a good time.'

This was the summary of Andy Flower, a multiple Ashes-winning coach and one who had taken his team to the number one ranking in Test cricket, in delivering the news that I was to be sent home from the England Lions tour of Australia in February 2013.

It hit me like a sledgehammer. He was so clinical. So cold.

'NO. I want to play for England.'

'No, you don't.'

'Yeah, I do.'

I went back at him a couple of times. But he sounded adamant. He had come to his conclusion. The England coach was questioning whether I would ever play for his team again. The England coach was summing me up as a waste of space. The England coach was sanctioning my removal from a tour involving England's next-best players.

'I'll prove you wrong,' I said, finger-wagging, as I left the hotel room in Hobart, where Flower, David Parsons, the ECB's academy director, and Guy Jackson, the England Lions manager, had delivered the news.

There may even have been use of the F word too. I know it's not advisable to swear at your bosses, but I was so angry. Andy had really riled me, made me out to be some kind of little kid, messing about with his mates. Not a serious cricketer with an international future ahead of him.

I'll show you.

Of course, as I later realized, that was also exactly what Andy wanted, and I confess his words that day stuck with me, and always will. Over subsequent months, playing under him for England, I came to realize he didn't mean it. He said it to be provocative; to try to make sure I got my priorities right.

Being told I had ventured beyond my last chance proved a real shot across the bows for me. The message, as I was booked onto the next flight back to the UK was: 'Get your shit together.' The perception that I was just there for a piss-up with my mates really stung me. Funnily enough, the first thing Matt Coles and I did when we got to the airport for our flight home was to have a beer. But that was irrelevant in the scheme of things, really. The impression I needed to make was in the longer term. For now, it was too late.

'On a very challenging tour to Australia, both Matt and Ben have ignored the instructions given to them around their match preparation and recovery,' read a statement from David Parsons.

'Following previous warnings, it is regrettable that it has been necessary to terminate their involvement in the tour.

'Both are very talented individuals and it is hoped that, with the support of the ECB and their respective counties, they will take positive steps to give themselves the very best chance of fulfilling their potential. There will be no replacement players called up to the squad.'

Matt and I were roomies on the tour. We got on well. We were part of a sociable group. When I wasn't whipping his ass at *FIFA*, we enjoyed a night out. A feed; a few drinks; a laugh. Find me blokes in the first couple of years of their twenties that don't.

But the tour started badly – very badly from my point of view. We arrived in Melbourne and were due to have our first training session the following day. Naturally, there was the excitement of being on a tour, and in a pretty cool location, so we decided we would all go and have a few drinks. Naturally, a few drinks led to a few more, some of us stayed out late and myself and another lad – my usual partner-in-crime, not Matt – got back later than everyone else.

In fact, it was daylight when we arrived back at the apart-hotel. Who should be in the lobby but Kevin Shine, our bowling coach for the tour. My mate clocked him, ran back outside without being spotted and evaded detection by climbing up a drainpipe and into his room.

Unfortunately, after shambling in totally oblivious, I was in the thick of some trouble and had nowhere to go. Bear in my mind I had jeans and a shirt on. It was 5.30am. The panic set in. What should I do? Shiney – who has a reputation as an early bird, someone who likes to get up and hit the gym before breakfast – eyed me up and down and gave me a knowing look.

I excused myself, nipped upstairs to my room, dived under the shower, put my training kit on, and returned downstairs quick smart. *It won't look as bad if I appear ready for the morning. I'll tell them I couldn't sleep. Bloody jetlag.*

At any rate, I wouldn't be the only one looking ropey, and it was highly plausible that even those who had gone to bed at a reasonable hour had been awake all night.

Brilliant idea, I'll get away with it for sure.

So I sauntered down, trainers and headphones on. That way, it looked as though I was ready for a walk or a run. I had breakfast, making sure I was chatty with the other early risers, trying not to make it too obvious.

'Just off for some fresh air. I can't sleep,' I announced, making sure everyone heard.

I was so knackered, I ended up lying on a park bench for a bit. But the main thing was remaining undetected, and up until the point I arrived back at the hotel, everything had gone very smoothly.

Yes, got away with it.

We were on the way to training. Nothing further had been said. Once there, however, I pulled my calf. All the lads, myself included, were clanging catches left, right and centre.

Damn, not got away with it.

Perhaps they knew all along. Or maybe they put two and two together after witnessing our horrendous first practice session? It didn't really matter how they had got there. But they had. Confirmation came later that day when I received a text asking me to go to one of the rooms in the hotel. It's fair to say that those of us they suspected to have taken the piss with our timekeeping got a big telling off, and were reminded about the standards of behaviour we were expected to keep to. Others had got away with it but, naturally, we weren't going to dob them in.

That's the way it goes. Sometimes you get away with things, sometimes you don't. I wasn't going to cry about that. I had been caught red-handed. Crucially, though, for my part in the impromptu night out, I also received an official letter from the ECB setting out what I had done and warning me about my future conduct. That would come back to haunt me in Hobart.

It was a bit of shame for the tour in general, because the atmosphere deteriorated pretty quickly after the Melbourne incident, and everything we did felt like school. We were being treated like kids. The majority of us were 20 and 21. Some of the guys were 24 and 25. We weren't being allowed to do our own thing. Young blokes need some form of release every now and again. There were those in the squad fed up with it. Not me necessarily because, having been part of an England set-up previously, I knew that this wasn't what being around the full team was like.

The people we had on the trip were sociable. We enjoyed going out. I'm not talking about going out on the beer every other night until the early hours of the morning – just eating at a nice restaurant, having a few drinks, chatting and going back to our hotel. But we felt even doing that would result in a telling off. It meant we didn't really do anything at all. Our freedom had been taken away.

The tour was not a good one on the field. We played three warm-up matches against sides put out by Victoria. We lost all three. I managed to hit 41 off just 15 balls in one match, but I did no better than okay. Andy Flower joined up with us for the start of the five-match series against Australia A – he was on a stop-off on the way to the England tour of New Zealand. Andy is a big disciplinarian. So opting to head out immediately after the first match wasn't great timing on our part.

We lost that opening day-nighter at the Bellerive Oval by seven wickets. Afterwards we went out, had a few beers. It wasn't a ridiculous session. Because it was a late game, it meant a late start to our drinking. It was a Saturday night but we reached nowhere near the levels of that first night in Melbourne.

However, there were now rules in place about staying out later than midnight within 48 hours of a game. The second match, also in Hobart, was on the Monday. Rules are rules, I guess, and we'd broken them. We were already on a tight leash from the first night out, and we were told that if we wanted to go out we had to let our security personnel know – to report what times we were arriving in, especially on nights close to matches. There were half a dozen of us out on this particular night in question, and Colesy stuffed things up for us by ringing security.

The issue for us, and what was to make us suffer, was that we had already received warnings, and it was not a nice feeling reading a text the next morning that read: 'You guys are not needed at training today – so don't come.'

Instead, we headed to the driving range. Later, came another meeting. I knew my fate before I even headed into the room. Matt had gone in first, and came out pretty distraught.

'Shit, we're going home, here.'

That thought was already in my head when I began my hearing. I'd screwed up twice, and got the flick. If it had been anyone else transgressing, the same would have happened. I don't think Matt or I were treated unfairly, or made examples of. Neither do I suspect it was a very nice atmosphere after we went. The results didn't get any better, and whatever happens on the field influences the mood off it. But, of course, I, 100 per cent, would have preferred to have stayed, to try to help them be more positive.

For me, the whole embarrassment of being sent home made me think hard about where I was at. I knew I was not going to get where I wanted to be doing stuff like that. I knew I had a lot to do to get back: put in some performances that said 'Pick me', to win Andy's trust again, to get the real me across to him, and show him that, contrary to what he said, I did want to play for England. I wanted to play for England so much.

There were other people to deal with too. When stuff happens and it's going to be *news*, the hardest people to tell are your parents. It's almost like you have failed them. And this news certainly didn't sit well with Dad; providing one of those cartoon moments when you get the hairdryer treatment down the phone, and hold it away from your ear for a bit until there's a pause for breath.

'. . . Yeah, I know.'

Then, at arm's length again . . .

'. . . Yeah, you're right.'

The one positive from that Lions tour was that it provided my first proper meeting with my sister Linda. Her and Mam were separated when I was very young due to life circumstances. Therefore, in contrast to the relationship I had with my brother James – who lived up the road from us in Christchurch the first 10 years of my life – I didn't see or hear of her throughout my childhood.

Latterly, bridges were being built, however, and by the time I knew I was going to be in Australia, I was in contact with her through Mam. I had a vague image of her getting married, when I was young. Now, this was a time to get to know her.

Linda lives in Melbourne, and it was a nice surprise when I got a message from her to say that she was coming down to watch those warm-up matches. Later a catch-up over a coffee and a bite to eat was slightly surreal but pretty cool. Before I departed for the UK, I had also met my brother-in-law, and nephew and niece. I was 20 years old and it felt like my family was getting bigger and bigger.

Dad and James were scheduled to fly out to Sydney to see me too. The tickets were booked and everything. Unfortunately, it was now going to be Sydney minus me. Typically, they still went and watched at the SCG. Equally typically, of Dad, he wanted his say on the issue, and so he asked Scott Borthwick, who he knew from Durham, to ask David Parsons if he could have a word. Scott was worried it was going to kick off. God knows what DP was thinking when he got the message.

As it happened, the conversation was cordial. Dad told him, 'Even though he's my lad, I think you've done the right thing.' He knew what was required as a professional sports coach himself, and it was the course of action he would have taken. At that point, I imagine DP wiped some sweat off his brow.

The worst bollocking actually came from Clare, not Dad, after she unpacked my kitbag. To say she was cross with me was an understatement. Until the point of calling her to say I would be home ahead of schedule, I had not informed her of the precarious ground upon which I trod. She'd been sympathetic until she found that letter nestling amongst my gear.

This time, I had invited bother into my life. I could hardly argue to the contrary. Although circumstances had been quite different on the previous occasion, it had made me its companion 14 months earlier. And it ended with me spending a night in a police cell.

● ● ●

I had not been selected on an England tour that winter due to the fact I needed a third operation on my right index finger. I had time to fill, and people willing to fill it with me, and so I headed back to Cockermouth to catch up with a few pals ahead of Christmas.

It was the evening of 16 December, and I was left with my mate, just the two of us, after the pubs in town had shut. He was pissed, and carrying on like a bit of a knob quite frankly – shouting his mouth off, and attracting attention. I could see he was going to get himself in bother. Then, a couple of police officers appeared on the scene to tell him to be quiet.

Trouble was brewing, for sure, and he just wouldn't button his lip, so when one of the coppers approached him, I did what I thought best to stop the situation developing any further. I jumped from the wall I was sitting on and stepped in between them, facing my mate and urging him to shut his mouth.

I had never seen this particular police officer before, which was quite unusual for Cockermouth. Living in a town our size, you tend to know all the blokes on the beat. Next thing you know, it's me, not my pal, who's in the firing line. Not only have I failed to quieten him, I'm arrested for obstructing a police officer.

It was only a month after my third surgery and my hand was still tender, so I asked whether the handcuffs they had banged on me could be loosened.

'These are really digging in,' I argued, showing both my damaged hand, and the marks the cuffs were making on my wrists.

'No, sorry. If we do that, you might retaliate.'

Spending a night in the cell was the worst time of my life. No question. If you are going to get arrested, you might as well have done something to have warranted it. This was ludicrous. Before being driven away, there had been the bizarre spectacle of my friend, no doubt sobering up when he saw what was happening, pleading, 'Arrest me. It's me you want, not him.' Unfortunately, there was no decision review.

I arrived at the station in Workington in the belief I'd be interviewed, then sent home. Even when they put me in the cell, I kept thinking: 'When are they coming to get me? They'll be here in a minute.'

No such luck. I woke in the morning, and was given my breakfast through the meal flap in the door. There I was, with my plastic knife and fork, tucking into sausage and beans. It was like a scene from *The Shawshank Redemption*.

The guy who interviewed me next morning was a cricket fan.

'How's it going?'

'Well, I could be better, funnily enough.'

He asked me whether I wanted to make any complaints. Of course, I did. I showed him the cuts around my hands.

'There's not much we can do about that, really.'

The whole episode was a complete farce. I could not believe they would waste public money like this. I was trying to calm a mate down, and ended up being treated like I was a dangerous thug. Come on, what had I done to warrant it? Absolutely nothing. I had no problem with them putting the cuffs on whatsoever. All I had done was ask for them to be loosened.

Okay, so any idea of a complaint on my part was kicked into touch, and I was free to leave. But before one of my mates came to pick me up, I wanted to be certain none of this would be going any further. I didn't want Mam and Dad or Harv (my agent, Neil Fairbrother) to know. I was also concerned what others would think, if it went public.

'No, it's all in-house.'

Was it, hell. A couple of weeks later I received a phone call from Yvette Thompson, the press officer at Durham.

'You been arrested, Ben?'

Somehow, news had spread.

Concerned about my image being tarnished further, I rang Tony

Harrison, a Cumbrian sports reporter I'd got to know over the years. He managed to keep it out of the local paper. But there was little that could be done to stop it getting onto the Internet.

Later, when I told Harv, his main beef with me was not telling him immediately.

'If you had told me about the wrist situation, we could have looked into it.'

By this stage, I had played five one-day internationals and two Twenty20s for England. I had been involved at the end of the previous summer. It meant they were interested.

Andy Flower rang me in the new year.

'Howzit?'

'Hi, Andy. Good thanks.'

'How's that finger? You didn't punch anyone, eh?'

'No.'

'Okay. As long as your finger's alright, eh?'

Chinese whispers had reached the ECB that I'd chinned the police officer. It's amazing how these things develop.

By the end of the call, I appreciated the fact Andy made it himself. He reassured me that this incident would have no influence on my future. Although big on discipline, he is not a guy that dwells on your indiscretions, and that means that if you do get a bollocking, you can accept it and move on. I was so pleased, following that Lions trip down under, that he was able to select me in England squads in 2013.

I didn't spend much time with him when he was England coach, but I could see just how driven he was to make his teams better. In batting drills, you could feel his intensity. Every net session was turned into a competition. He would give you everything he had, in terms of knowledge and assessment, as long as you were giving everything you could. All he wanted was for England to do well.

At Alice Springs during the 2013-14 Ashes, he'd invented a four-over net scenario – if he got me out, then the forfeit was for me and Mushtaq Ahmed, the coach who I had been doing drill work with previously that day, to buy him dinner that evening. Avoid dismissal and we were getting the free feed. With four balls left, I shouted to Mushy at the back of the net, 'What do you reckon? Fancy the lobster?'

'You look like a lobster,' Andy joked.

He has an aura. It would be unfair to say that you feel awkward around him. But at the same time, there is something about him that means you cannot be entirely comfortable either. Or at least not be 100 per cent yourself.

I don't know whether I felt that because of his dominant personality, or the fact that he was England's head coach. But when I was around him, I would be slightly stiff, concerned I might say something stupid. During conversations, he would fix you with his stare, keeping you held in that way well after the talking was over.

We once had to do a Lion's Den exercise on an England Performance Programme – a bit of a twist on *Dragons' Den*, in which you were pitching your ideas on cricket, not products.

'What is mental toughness?' Andy asked me.

It was like being back at school. I wasn't sure what to say. But I found myself blabbing a load of nonsense for three minutes.

I've done all right, here.

Then, he fixed me with *that* look.

'Let me ask you that question again, Ben. What is mental toughness?'

I had not felt so intimidated since my first pre-season tour with Durham in 2010 when all my nerves centred around the pre-match speech, not the first-class debut that followed it. It is tradition on your first away trip for Durham to give a speech to the rest of the group. So there I was, a bag of nerves on this visit to the United Arab Emirates. Back then I wasn't very good at speaking in front of people, not at all, even if I knew them. This ceremony was due to take place over dinner at the team hotel and so I had as many drinks as possible beforehand. When it came to it, I delivered something in a style that wasn't mine at all. I was a bit too formal, thanking the club for my chance in the academy, and being a bit too nicey-nicey when I'd already given the group, the coaches, a glimpse of the type of person I was from the other nights we'd had together.

Thankfully, I was playing with no fear. I'd had a good winter with the England Under-19s, at the World Cup, scoring a hundred against India, and that form continued when we got to Abu Dhabi for the Emirates matches against local teams in the lead-up to the County Championship contest between us, the county champions, and the MCC. An unbeaten 81 with seven sixes and a strike rate in excess of 200 in a 40-over match made the coaching staff at Durham take note, I think, and that gave me the chance of making my debut in the pink-ball match under floodlights at the same Sheikh Zayed Stadium. It was unbelievable when I got told I would be batting at number six.

Ben Harmison had held a position in the Championship team at the end of the 2009 season but I had effectively taken it, and kept it with 51 in my maiden first-class innings. When we returned home, I scored 80 in a two-day game against Lancashire that was made the more memorable when I knocked Jimmy Anderson's off-stump out of the ground.

It was enough to keep my place for the first Division One contest of the season against Essex. That didn't go well, but I got 41 in the first innings against Hampshire the following week, and then hit an unbeaten 27 alongside Phil Mustard to win the game.

● ● ●

I was still only 18 years old but that made it easier in some ways. I was just a kid having fun. I loved playing cricket and just took every opportunity given to me. For example, I got thrown the ball in both innings against Hampshire and took three wickets. I only claimed five all season because it was hard to get a bowl in the line-up we had, and I became one of the guys who was used to allow a spell to be saved for one of the big lads. To be honest, I wasn't taking bowling seriously in that first season – partly because my batting was going so well; partly because we had such a strong attack.

I was certainly learning on the job during that 2010 season. My fourth match at Trent Bridge was memorable for two things: a maiden first-class hundred, and an absolute shellacking from a chap called Ali Brown. Well, that was his official name, although I called him every other one under the sun as he whacked me all over Nottingham. He kept looking at me, laughing and smiling, which only served to get me more angry. He was upper-cutting over the slips, pulling us all for fours and sixes. When I went fuller he pummelled me back over my head. It was a 'wow' innings. I didn't know much about county cricketers then, but I knew of Ali Brown's reputation as a dangerous player and remembered his one-day record score of 268 he set for Surrey against Glamorgan.

We had made 280 in our first innings but, thanks to Brown's hitting in the middle-order, Nottinghamshire piled up 559. We fought hard just to make Nottinghamshire bat again, and when Ben Harmison and I came together we decided to be positive, to look to score our runs quickly. Sure, the situation was a tough one, but only if we let it be, and so I ignored it and reverted to my usual game. I viewed Samit Patel as an option to whack, not because he's a bad bowler. He's not. But if a spinner is turning it into me as their stock ball, I have always felt better trying to hit boundaries.

It got me into aggressive mode. At one point, Paul Franks, who had a reputation for giving it out to the new guys on the block, gave me a bit.

'You still think it's 2002, pal,' I said.

'You're not playing for England now – f**k off.'

He got me out in the end, caught on the line. I think I was through the shot a bit too fast . . . But not before I'd experienced the ultimate high of getting that first professional hundred. When you make the step up, whatever the levels, it's always a big honour to make three figures. You want to impress as you go through the ranks, and it was the same feeling I had as I'd experienced making my first Premier League hundred for the Durham Academy.

I kept going with my same methods at Canterbury, where Durham had wrapped up the Division One title the previous season, and was rewarded with another hundred. The one thing I regretted about this one, though, despite it contributing to a win, was how I batted with the tail. I was far too placid. Had I been give the chance to play that innings again, I would have shown a lot more intent.

Kent put a good score of 424 on the board; Robert Key got a double-hundred. Our response suggested we thought the game was petering out towards a draw. Instead of moving the game forward, we were treading water, and instead of me taking up the mantle once I got to three figures, I became defensive, leaving anything I could, looking to take time out of the game. We lost a few wickets and, having taken just 119 balls for my hundred, went back into my shell. Taking time out of the game is not something I like to do. I should have been trying to take it on. I finished unbeaten on 161, we got within six runs on first innings, and Kent just fell apart second time around. This time, I didn't mess about. We needed 52 when I went in, I hit 42 of them and the match was over in half an hour.

Kent possessed a decent pace attack of Amjad Khan, Makhaya Ntini and Azhar Mahmood. They beat us by an innings, inside three days, the following week back at our place (yes, in a quirk of the ECB fixture list we played them in consecutive fixtures). I batted on one leg, after twisting my ankle badly in the field, although it didn't keep me on the sidelines. I just taped it and strapped it, and carried on with the season – the only difference being that I moved from gully and point to slip to reduce my running.

By this stage, I felt an established member of the Durham team. I had two hundreds within the first half a dozen County Championship matches, and there would have been a third at the start of August. I blame Gordon Muchall for denying me. We were playing Hampshire at Basingstoke, Danny Briggs was bowling, and they had a big gap at cover. I knocked the ball towards the off-side, it clunked off silly-point's pad, and we could have run the two I needed for my hundred easily. But Gordon, also in the 90s at the time, said no.

I was on 99, and considered it highly unlikely I would get out. Come on, the odds were in my favour. There was a short boundary on the leg side – the next ball was going for six – so I got the slog-sweep out, only for it to steeple off a top edge. I stood willing it to travel, 'Go, go, go', like a golfer on the tee. Only for Sean Ervine to steady himself and catch it on the line at cow corner.

Afterwards, I got a very simple message from our then bowling coach Alan Walker: 'Wanker.' He wasn't on the ground but he probably guessed what I had done. It was a joke; it wasn't serious. You can't take anything Whack says to heart. But it was a reminder of how important it was to never give things away.

One thing Durham are brilliant at is promoting young talent, sometimes when it's least expected. In my case, I was totally surprised to be called up for a couple of 50-over games at the start of the 2009 season.

I hadn't played much second XI cricket and when given chances I had done okay, no more. I was certainly doing nothing better than any of the other batters in the team but Geoff Cook, the director of cricket, called me up. Whether he saw something or the other coaches saw something, and reckoned I was ready, I have no idea. But it was a pretty random call-up. Scott Borthwick made the step up that year too. Mark Wood was an academy team-mate at this time, but although you could see he was destined for greater things – because he was one of the faster bowlers, could bat and field – it took him longer due to the strength of our bowling.

Look at the list of players to have come through the Durham Academy in recent years that have gone on to represent England at some level: Phil Mustard, Gordon Muchall, Graham Onions, myself, Scott Borthwick, Mark Wood, Mark Stoneman, Jack Burnham. Then there is Keaton Jennings, who came from overseas to join up. We must have one of the better conversion rates in turning academy players into established professionals. You get a lot of guys being produced at one county and representing another. We produce them and they stay. It's a turnover rate to be proud of.

● ● ●

My promotion to the England Performance Programme for the winter of 2010–11 – to shadow the Ashes in Australia and play in West Indies' first-class tournament – felt like a real case of fast-tracking. For example, if James Vince, someone of the same age and level as me, had scored 161 not out on television as I had against Kent in May, it would have been him instead. I am convinced of that.

Not that I wasn't grateful for the opportunity to step up the intensity of my cricket. There wasn't much to talk of in terms of performances, but the training regime was the biggest thing for me. Those of us who required it were put on extra fitness sessions, and I suddenly found the gym addictive. I spent two months with the England Lions in the Caribbean, and the reaction in the Durham dressing room when I returned was, 'Jesus, how much weight have you lost?' That's exactly the kind of reaction you want when you have worked your tits off – quite literally – all winter. I had dropped a load of flab and looked and felt fitter for the start of the 2011 season.

I had averaged 46.25 in first-class cricket the previous summer, and I was so keen to raise the bar this time around. In the opening match of the season versus Hampshire, conditions were perfect. It was a flat-as-hell wicket at the Ageas Bowl. It was red hot, the surface was white, there was a small boundary on one side. Between our top seven there were four 50s and a hundred in our 473, the first innings of the season. I managed just 10, out to Simon Jones, and I was fuming at missing out.

The good thing about being an all-rounder, though, is that you always get another chance, and an injury to Steve Harmison at the start of Hampshire's reply gave me my chance. The ball was swinging in and out, I was bowling well towards the second new ball, and was given it to share with Callum Thorp. I had three wickets at that point. Then, it all happened in a flash. Another three in two overs, Hampshire were dismissed and I took six for 68 – more wickets in one innings than I had managed in the whole of 2010. That fresh cherry is up on my wall at home.

We had a 179-run lead on first innings, and opted to bat again partly because we were a bowler down. It gave me the chance to make better use of that beautiful batting track. I was my usual aggressive self, taking the attack to the bowlers whenever I could. Another hundred. Mint. That meant it was time to have some fun. My usual attitude kicked in. Liam Dawson, the left-arm spinner, was on to bowl.

Was I thinking of hitting six sixes in an over? No. Well, okay, kind of. I was thinking of hitting every ball I faced for six. And I managed it for the first five, via a combination of running down the pitch and slog-sweeping. At that point it was on. It was exciting.

Bring it on.

But Skeg, or Nic Pothas to those outside county cricket, opted to slow things down as Hampshire captain and talk to his young bowler. He delayed that sixth ball for ages, discussing what Liam should do, and when it eventually came to it, he fired in a quick yorker. I could only hit it for one, and that was that. We declared with me unbeaten on 140.

In mid-May I got the chance to bat on another belter at Chester-le-Street, which might be something of a surprise if you know the ground well. Somerset scored 600-plus and we followed on 373 runs behind. I would like to tell you I played diligently to save the game. But that wouldn't be me, would it? I made 120 off 136 balls, and we saved the game comfortably despite having to occupy 151 overs in the second innings.

Batting at the Riverside can pose problems for batsmen, but my first two seasons were that good, I was on such a roll, that I didn't worry about the pitch. See ball, hit ball, that was my motto. Only later, when I started worrying about it, did my performances decline, triggering some bad spells. Negative feelings crept in whereas I previously played off the cuff. My first-class batting average dropped significantly over the next couple of years as a result, from the high 40s to the lower 30s, and I don't blame the pitch for that. I blame me.

Then came a game of mixed emotions against Lancashire. I hit the ball as cleanly as I possibly could in making a career-best 185, and sharing a 331-run stand with Dale Benkenstein. Batting with the tail, I just kept trying to hit Steve Croft's off-spin to the short boundary. I managed to get one over the Riverside pavilion in that innings, which people said had not been done before, but I eventually got out playing the same slog-sweep, bowled.

When I got back into the changing room, Ruel Brathwaite, my West Indian team-mate, said to me: 'What ya doin' man, ya darn wan a double?'

He was deadly serious, and stirred me up. Could he not just say well done?

Let's face it, I've had a lot worse said to me. And worse was to happen to me too when it was our turn to field. Paul Horton smacked a ball from Graham Onions, a short and wide delivery, for four, and I had just completed the long run to collect it. We were playing on the near side of the square and it was a fair old journey to retrieve it from under the scoreboard, which meant I was not fully back into position when I looked up to see Bunny halfway through his run-up for the next ball.

Same ball, same shot, it turned out, but this time it was a low catch. I got my hands just behind the ball as it thundered towards the turf and it hit me straight on the end of my right index finger. There was no pain, but straightaway I could see it was bent out of place. Jogging off, I knew that Nigel Kent, our physio, would have to bob it back into place. But, back in the dressing room, he just couldn't get it back into position and, after several attempts, it meant a trip to A & E in Washington.

The first couple of X-rays showed the dislocation; the last one, from a different angle, exactly how bad it was. My finger was completely shattered. Where once was a joint, there was none. So we went to another hospital in Sunderland, had anaesthetic injected into it, and the medics managed to get it back in. Or so they thought. Five minutes later, it had popped back out, because there was no socket there to keep it in place. The only option therefore was for me to have an operation.

I don't think I could have had a better first two months of the season. It was 3 June, and I had surgery that was going to sideline me for the foreseeable future. Only it proved to be even longer than feared. When I went back to have the bandage taken off my hand, and the pin sticking out of the joint removed, it felt like the first step on the road back to playing. Unfortunately, it was nothing of the sort.

After another X-ray, I was told I would need the same operation again. It was devastating news. In total I was out for eight weeks, and then I came back of my own accord, not waiting for the doctors' say-so. I just needed to get the right protection on my finger. I did so, and returned for the academy, batting at number three. The fixture against Australia A was a perfect way to get back into things. Good opposition but no pressure like a Championship match. Then, after another couple of games, came the silver lining to my mid-season cloud.

Without much cricket behind me in recent weeks, I was picked for the one-day internationals against Ireland and India. I was going to wear those three lions. That's what I'd wanted for so long. I rang Mam and just dropped it into the conversation: 'Oh, by the way, I've been picked for England.'

'Whaaaaat?'

Dad just gave it a very casual, 'Well done, mate'.

I was unable to play as an all-rounder, which was a frustration, but they still picked me as a specialist batsman. At this point, I could not bend my finger whatsoever despite three physiotherapy sessions a week. Dawn Gillie, a hand specialist in Newcastle, would sit there manipulating and massaging it and I was willing to go through whatever it took to maximize the flexion. I spent hours with my hand in buckets of ice to stop the swelling in a bid to free the finger up. There was simply no joint to work with. Once with the squad, Andy Flower wanted me to bowl off two fingers, so he had me experimenting without using my index finger any spare time we had. But I just couldn't grip the ball.

I played at number six, which meant I didn't bat in the first couple of games. I got done a couple of times by Ravichandran Ashwin in the next two, but the important thing was that we won the series against an Indian team that were top of the one-day rankings, doing so by virtue of a tie at Lord's when Ravi Bopara steered us to the Duckworth-Lewis score as the rain came down. Stuart Broad ripped his bicep, which caused a few laughs because none of us knew he had one.

I missed out on the last game at Cardiff after being hit in the indoor nets, trying to reverse sweep a delivery from Merlyn, our spin-bowling machine. It ripped the skin off my already damaged joint and proved so painful that the medical team, after consultation with Andy Flower, decided it was best for me not to play, and for the injury to be re-assessed immediately. X-rays showed what I had didn't even resemble a finger, so it meant a big trip to America to get this surgery done properly once and for all.

Doing so became a priority for them, and for me. It was a stroke of luck that I had been selected in the first place, because if I hadn't been playing for England nothing would have happened. No one would have been the wiser. Without damaging it in front of England staff, I could have gone on for months.

The two guys I saw in America at the start of November specialized in fixing the fingers of basketball players from the NBA. After one of the previous operations in Sunderland I felt groggy, and Clare literally carried me to the car, so this time, I wanted to stay awake. So I opted for local anaesthetic.

They were chatting about the Super Bowl, working away, slicing and breaking. I fell asleep because I was so comfortable. Yet they were so brutal. They seemed to take little care over it. I know because Mark Young, the ECB physio accompanying me, took a video of it. Of course, they looked so casual because they were just so awesome at what they do – and the final result was much better than the previous two. I was really happy with what they had done for me.

They snapped the finger, pulled it back, chiselled some bone out of the back of my wrist to make a ledge, then took another piece out of the back of my hand to make a new joint. At one point, to show the details of exactly where it had been broken, and what they were doing, they had bent my finger so its tip was pointing completely the wrong way. Then came the pins and screws to give my finger movement once more.

These days, it's still not 100 per cent functional. For example, I can no longer swing the ball away from the right-handers like I used to, and every now and then, because it sticks out at a funny angle, catching is a problem and I end up getting hit on the end of it by the ball.

When I was fit again the following season, breaking back into the international set-up proved hard. England were just becoming *the* team in terms of world status. They were number one as far as the rankings went and I'd got my little bit of action when they were picking new players. Now they were doing really well with a settled side. Contrary to what Andy Flower would tell me in that Hobart hotel room, I was desperate, really desperate to play for England again.

9

I cried my eyes out when Layton was born in the autumn of 2012. It was the start of a pretty emotional period in my life. There is nothing to compare to the high of becoming a father. But an Ashes hundred comes close, and it was an incredible feeling to start my Test career on such a personal high.

These two events make it all sound like such a happy 18 months or so, but it was far from the case. Remember that in between I had been evicted from the England Lions tour of Australia, and the first three-quarters of the 2013 season proved to be a chain of false starts and major disappointments. Up until August there was nothing like the kind of form to merit an international recall.

Things started okay. There was the 111 I took off the Durham University attack in the opening first-class fixture of the season. I was desperate to improve on my return for 2012 when my County Championship average had dipped below 30, and this was a decent start. Yes, it was only against the students, but it was nice to feel the ball out of the middle of the bat all the same.

After that, a 49, the highest score from a Durham perspective in a bowler-dominated win over Somerset, and another start of 33 in the first innings of a heavy defeat against Warwickshire at Edgbaston. This was typical of the way things were going for me – I was getting in, getting set and getting out.

Then, there were the occasions when I wasn't even getting in. There were seven scores of 20 or fewer in my next eight visits to the crease, the only exception the unbeaten 35 to secure victory over Surrey at The Oval in early May. By the end of that month I was in despair, feeling sufficiently bad to grab my phone one day and tweet: 'Any danger?' It was directed at myself. Was there any danger of me getting runs? There certainly didn't seem to be.

Suddenly, I was questioning myself for the first time in my career. I wasn't even asking whether I was a good player or not. I was asking if a score would come along again. After the wet weather draw against Middlesex at Chester-le-Street, I changed clothes and got out of there immediately after we finished.

Paul Collingwood was clearly concerned as my county captain.

'Everything alright, lad?' he texted me.

In reply I told him I was down about not performing. That I hated not contributing; struggling; failing. His response was to tell me not to worry because my bowling was still fine, and that I would come good.

Did I believe that? I'm not sure. But that text exchange was a first step for me in confronting a developing issue. I was angry and frustrated. Not that anyone knew. I was keeping it to myself, and so with every passing week it was building up inside me. As far as I was concerned, it was a weakness to admit that I was feeling low. I was a bloke. I had to man-up and get on with things. Only, I had broken my code of silence by letting Colly in on my feelings.

There were a couple of cracking team wins, the best a fourth-innings chase of 184 inside 21 overs off a Nottinghamshire attack including Stuart Broad and Graeme Swann, after we had been up all night due to faulty fire alarms at our team hotel. There were even some half-centuries in midsummer: 57 versus Somerset, 61 off Warwickshire, 51 against Middlesex. But for every one of them came a low score to offset.

With disappointment brewing, I chose to go one step further than a text exchange with my county captain. Sulking would do me no good. I should speak to someone. I had good people around me, and that's what they were there for. Enough of this bravado; this idea that I was a bloke reinforced by steel. The only way I was going to get help was by confiding in someone who knew what I might be going through, and in the first instance that someone was my agent Neil Fairbrother.

As soon as I began explaining how my failures were doing my head in, it felt like a load off my shoulders. We spoke about me, and my relationship with cricket – how I was in a rut and felt I wasn't going to score any runs whenever I went to the middle. At first it was awkward, but as a former player he knew where I was coming from.

Then, after being invited to train with England ahead of the 2013

Ashes Test at Lord's – which showed me that I wasn't going to be banished following my winter misdemeanours in Melbourne and Hobart – I had a long session with the ECB's psychologist Mark Bawden. We sat in the stands for an hour or so after training, just chatting about the whole subject.

Mark applied instant healing. By talking to him, things actually felt better straightaway, and I liked the fact that he was there to listen specifically to me, not just to someone else in the dressing room. I didn't want to tell a team-mate, because I didn't want it to alter their view of me as a player. I had a certain on-field image I guess, and a certain style as a cricketer. My character is quite in your face. I like to play that way, so I didn't want anyone questioning me, thinking in any way that I had a weakness.

Sharing my innermost thoughts was not a weakness at all, as it turned out. Leaving them to fester was only going to make the situation worse, Mark explained, as he told me some techniques to use to deal with such a build-up of frustration and negativity. He told me that I was suffering from *Bottle, Bottle, Bang* syndrome. In other words, I kept storing up everything in a certain bottle – inside of me, effectively – and I was bubbling it up until that bottle want bang and I exploded with frustration. Instead of letting this happen, I had to find another way of dealing with it: to let it out in a positive way, and accept that good things might happen too, if I let go of the bad stuff. If I didn't do this, the bad stuff would still be waiting for me next game.

● ● ●

It was the second week of July, and the Twenty20 competition was in full swing. From London, I headed back north – and bang! In the space of seven days, I won three man-of-the-match awards for Durham: an unbeaten 72, off 48 balls, against Nottinghamshire, 46 off 24 versus Derbyshire and 41 not out off 26 when we faced Leicestershire. I hit 13 sixes.

I had tackled the issue that was stopping me, my freedom was back and I was somewhere near my old self as a player. Without that chat with Mark, who knows what would have happened? Would I have carried on experiencing a run of low scores? It didn't matter. I'd had it, and it provided a mixture of relief and hope for the rest of the season. I remembered what kind of batsman I was. A dangerous one.

I'd bowled against plenty of players who, if you were not at your best, if you gave them anything, would murder you. It's hard to bowl at players like that. It can be demoralizing. At my best, I knew I could make the opposition suffer. I rediscovered that aggression at a time when I came to realize it's not weak to open up about struggles. Speaking about things got me out of my rough patch.

Throughout the season, while my batting wavered, my bowling thrived. I ended up with 42 top-flight wickets. Two years of struggle with the bat coincided with me becoming the all-rounder I always wanted to be. I loved the fact that I had double the chance to change the course of matches. I wanted to be considered a match-winner.

As my bowling workload increased, so did my threat. Geoff Cook, our director of cricket, told me I was going to have a bit more of a role with the ball in 2013, and as soon as I realized I could get frontline batsmen out, I started to take more interest in our net sessions. I no longer just bowled at training. I bowled with meaning. I worked on swinging it in the way I used to make the windballs swing on the outfield at Cockermouth Cricket Club.

As the County Championship season reached its final month, I was feeling in my best form again. We faced a crunch top-of-the-table match against Yorkshire at Scarborough on August Bank Holiday weekend, the stakes for which were raised when Mark Wood announced in the build-up that if we won this game we would win the league. It was effectively a shoot-off between us and Yorkshire. They began with a 25.5 point advantage but we had a game in hand. Talk about putting the pressure on, Woody.

Over four days it was red hot, the ground was packed, the atmosphere raucous. It was the closest to international cricket I have ever felt county cricket to be. Yorkshire were a strong side, full of England players, plus a former Australian Test batsman Phil Jaques, as well as Kane Williamson, the New Zealander, one of the world cricket's rising stars.

We lost two wickets for spit to Ryan Sidebottom with the new ball, and another before lunch on that opening day, the third inviting me to the crease at 67-3. One of the by-products of me bowling more was kind of instigated by me. I had started as a teenager in the Durham first XI at number six but was soon switched to number four. Now, with the extra workload, I asked to be slipped down a place to five. The number of times I came off the field after polishing off the tail, having bowled a six- or seven-over spell was increasing, meaning I would get no respite if an early wicket fell.

A poor season it might have been for me, but the rediscovering of my batting form in the Twenty20 appeared to have flicked a switch, and now when I struck the ball it seemed to be going into the gaps. It was racing away on Scarborough's notoriously fast outfield. The pitch had good bounce and was true. Even defensive blocks down the ground were timed so nicely that I was picking up twos and threes.

It meant I scored quickly from the off. That is exactly the manner in which our opener Mark Stoneman likes to play too, and taking the attack to the bowlers meant we built a decent stand. In relatively no time, it was worth more than a hundred. Rocky set the tone for all of us, and I certainly need no excuses to play my shots in the right circumstances. Even after he was out, having made 122 out of 197, we rattled along. Another hundred stand with Colly, and I went to my first Championship hundred of the summer. Not long after, Adil Rashid got me, but on we went, with Michael Richardson, playing as a specialist batsman at number eight, becoming our third centurion. Colly got to within 19 of being our fourth. We made 573 in total – Durham's highest total against Yorkshire, our title rivals.

Despite it being a good pitch and quality opposition, it allowed us to enforce the follow-on after their first innings folded for 274. But when they reached the close of day three on 276-1 in their second innings, it looked as if they might be out of the woods. With Graham Onions missing through injury and Mark Wood ruled out with a side strain during the match, I was thrown the ball for the fourth morning. Phil Jaques was 151 not out. I had bowled five bouncer-filled overs at him the previous evening which Colly wasn't too happy about.

'Mate, it's gonna get him out,' I'd argued.

He top-edged a few over the keeper, then hit me for a few fours as well. I loved the situation. I was running in trying to bowl as fast as I could, as aggressively as I could on a pitch of great pace and carry, and he was trying to hit everything. I hit him, then the next ball just missed his helmet. He crunched me for a few decent boundaries too, but the number of times it went flying over Phil Mustard's head caused Paul Collingwood to remove himself from slip and place himself at a kind of fly wicketkeeper position. It was quite funny to see such a crazy field setting. That's what it's all about for me – the contest between two individuals within the bigger picture of the game itself.

After the day's play, Colly instructed a change of approach. 'Right, we've done that, and he's still in,' he reflected. 'Now it's time to nick him off.'

Right at the start of the next morning I did just that, having removed Kane Williamson a couple of minutes earlier. Those two dismissals opened the door again, but the conditions meant a lot of hard work still remained. The hot weather left the pitch dry, and contributed to quite a bit of rough being created for Scott Borthwick to aim at with his leg-spin. He bowled beautifully into it as the final day progressed, and his patience was rewarded with three wickets.

We wrapped up the innings before tea, and it left us to chase 121 in 37 overs. From that position, we were never going to lose. Scott wound it in with 65 before I took the glory with an unbeaten 11. It was an absolutely class game to be part of, a really good advert for Championship cricket. If it had been on TV, people would have been like, 'Wow, what a game.' As it was, the 19,000 who did turn up were served an absolute treat.

To beat Yorkshire at Scarborough was good for all of us, not least Colly who was devastated after declaring four wickets down in the reverse fixture earlier in the season only for Joe Root to score 182 not out to turn the game on its head. We clearly held the advantage now at the top of Division One, and there was no let-up for the final month of the season. We won the Championship with a game to spare.

The 19th of September was a special day. We sealed the title at around 2.30pm, within an hour of the delayed start to the third day of the match versus Nottinghamshire. From a personal perspective, things could not have gone much better. I had been recalled by England for the one-day series against Australia, and took five wickets – albeit in defeat – at the Rose Bowl. That was a day-nighter on the Monday. The Championship fixture started on the Tuesday at the other end of the country, and a further complication was that I had a bit of a niggle in my hamstring. It would mean an early morning scan, followed by the 310-mile drive home for what was a 10.15am start – Nottinghamshire had requested play to be brought forward each day so they could make a quick getaway for their Lord's one-day final on the Saturday.

But I was desperate to play – to be there to help the team over the line. So, as per the ECB regulations on allowing England players to join or leave County Championship matches as long as they are available for a minimum of 50 per cent of its duration, Usman Arshad began the match as my stand-in.

The MRI scan was more of a precautionary thing; it was never going to stop me playing, only delay my arrival until the afternoon session. We were batting when I got to Chester-le-Street, after Nottinghamshire won the toss and folded for just 78. I made a two-ball duck at number six. The following day, I developed a problem while bowling and hobbled off twice. Pressure had built up in my big toe, requiring me to have a needle put through my toenail to let the blood out. It was worth it for the three wickets. I so wanted to contribute to success with Durham.

I didn't get to bat a second time, and despite being next in, I didn't want to. We only required 62 for victory with all wickets standing heading into the third day, and I was with the rest of the team, stood on the balcony when Mark Stoneman punched the winning runs through the covers to seal a third title in six seasons, and my first. It was pure class.

The match was over before lunch, and we spent the whole afternoon around the dressing room drinking to our success. Geoff Cook was back with us by this stage, and that in itself was fantastic news. Geoff was already an established part of the furniture at the club when I arrived as an Under-15. He is Mr Durham.

Admittedly, he is a lot closer to other players at the club, like Phil Mustard, who lost his dad to a sudden heart attack in his youth. Geoff became a real fatherly figure to Phil, bringing him through the academy system; always there for him; looking out for his best interests. Phil and Scott Borthwick were among the first at his hospital bedside after his cardiac arrest on the towpath next to the Riverside on 20 June. For two weeks in mid-season, we really didn't know what was going to happen, so to see him pull through and return to the club (sporting a beard, not a scruffy one, but a real shaped and lined affair) for the final month was a real boost. Everyone was really worried for a time that we were going to lose a legend of our club.

Geoff's ill health was one of a series of setbacks for our team that year. We began with a two-and-a-half point deduction in the Championship for breaching the salary cap, yet the financial state of the club meant we couldn't afford an overseas player. Nor could we afford to go abroad in pre-season. Instead, matches were planned at Loughborough, only for arctic weather to wreck that. So we forgot about cricket and headed to Loch Lomond for a bit of golf, shooting and fishing. On one of the days, we climbed Beinn Dubh. Despite the hostility of it all – icy winds and deep snow made it treacherous – every single player and member of the coaching staff got to the top.

Dale Benkenstein, the leading run scorer in Durham history at the time, injured a shoulder in May and didn't return. Crucially, though, we never stopped fighting through all the challenges, and to reflect on all of it was sweet. Later that evening, we headed to Newcastle in our whites, with names and numbers on the backs of our shirts, and carried on our celebrations at the House of Smith nightclub: stinking, sleeves rolled up, champions masquerading as layabouts.

● ● ●

A few days later came the news to top it all. To be picked for the 2013–14 Ashes tour was an incredible feeling. It's the boss of all cricket series. Nobody knew how excited I was. Nobody knew how prepared I was for this. Except for Clare.

I would be heading back to Australia nine months after being sent home in disgrace. 'You think you're scared of Andy Flower right now. Wait until I catch up with you,' Clare had told me in February, when I broke the news to her that I was being dismissed. I had ruined her holiday in Lanzarote with her mum and four-month-old Layton. Now she was helping get me ready for the step up to the full Test team.

I so wanted to make an impression. To the extent that when we were given sketchy details of a pre-tour, team-building camp in the Midlands – we knew it was going to be 'out-doorsy' – we made sure all eventualities were covered. This new boy was going to be properly equipped. We went out and spent over £1,000 on outdoor gear: a lined jacket, pants, thermals, gloves, hiking boots, the works.

Some of it has yet to come out of the wrappers. I suppose living in the north-east I could wear it half the year. It certainly wasn't required on the surveillance exercise we took part in. I spent two days as a driver, tracking a mock criminal gang who were trading in guns. One morning, at six o'clock, the whole episode became so ridiculous it was funny. Stuart Broad and I were sat in the front seats outside the location we were given when a guy – who was clearly not one of the 'actors' in the task – parked right next to us, wound his window down, and decided it was the perfect time of day to get a big spliff on.

I didn't know Broady well at the time, so in many ways it was a good ice-breaker. The England team management had organized the police-style operation to get us all working together outside of our comfort zones. I'm not sure anyone, those management people included, got anything out of it. A weekend in Las Vegas would have been better, I reckon.

That would have given us some fun in what otherwise turned out to be a pretty sorry winter for the England cricket team battling for the Ashes.

We were already 1–0 down when, for the second Test in Adelaide, I got my opportunity. When Jonathan Trott announced he would be going home, it was quite a shock, and an upsetting time for some of the lads who were close to him. It was a blow to the team, obviously, to lose someone with a record as fantastic as his. We didn't have much time to think about it, though, because there was lots of cricket to play, and it meant someone had to come in. I'd been batting well in the nets, and bowling okay too, and imagined I had a good chance. The other candidate for a top-six place was Gary Ballance and he and I were constantly asking each other: have you heard anything?

So, imagine how I felt when I got pulled out by Alastair Cook at training and told: 'You'll be making your debut, batting at six.'

I was on cloud nine. How do you keep calm in that kind of situation? It was so exciting to be a Test cricketer. I was no longer just Ben Stokes. I was Ben Stokes: England's number 658. But I had to keep a level head. I walked back to the group, started fiddling with my kit, and there were a few 'Well dones'.

I had two battles on my Test debut. Oh, well, I suppose you should start as you mean to go on. The first was with Brad Haddin. I was having one of those frustrating spells. I was really annoyed with myself. We were desperate to break a big stand between him and Michael Clarke. Haddin had just reached his 50, and I managed to bowl a good ball, which he nicked. Matty Prior caught it. It was my first Test match wicket. Wow. Forget how crap I felt about my bowling. Now, I was absolutely on fire. I pumped out my chest. I felt mint.

It was not until Hadds was halfway off the field that Marais Erasmus began checking for a no-ball, and I was like, 'Oh, no, oh, no, oh no.' I can't describe how flaming angry I felt when it was confirmed that I had overstepped. How had I done that? I felt like an idiot.

So the last thing I needed was for Haddin, with his annoying, cheeky grin, to say: 'That's your first and last Test wicket.'

Eh? I was already devastated. I didn't need that. What an arsehole. To say it hit a nerve was an understatement. Of course, I now ran in even harder, looking up at the speed gun every ball to make sure I was hustling him.

I was at boiling point, and Erasmus knew it, stopping me from carrying on my walk towards my opponent at the end of the over as I gave him a good old spray. I was so pumped up, I couldn't hold back. It didn't stop there, either. I kept chirping away, and others, without my knowledge, joined in too.

Jimmy Anderson was stood at slip, off Graeme Swann, and he and Matt Prior had their own fun.

'Hadds, I wouldn't get yourself much further into this one with him, mate,' Jimmy said.

'Why, mate?'

'Well, he doesn't quite know the difference between on and off the pitch – if you know what I mean?"

'Nutter,' said Prior.

'Yeah, he's the type of bloke who, if he saw you in a nightclub, wouldn't care about who he was, who you were, or where you both were. He'd just run across the dance floor and headbutt you.'

I was oblivious to all this. But, I kid you not, I didn't hear another peep from Haddin that match. Since when I've got on really well with him. He likes to have words with the new lads in opposition teams, as most keepers do, and that's all part of the game. He just played on my anger, and I bit. Both he and Clarke scored hundreds, and Australia were controlling the game with 570 runs on the board.

The second incident came on the fourth evening. It was the second innings, and we were trying to bat as long as we could, not trying to go anywhere, just survive against the hostile Mitchell Johnson. We were five wickets down and Matt Prior and I had been together for over an hour. Australia had just taken the new ball, we were in the 84th over of the innings, and Johnson opted to bowl a couple of short ones around the wicket at me.

I watched them through, ducked out of the way. He was mouthy, as usual, and as you can be when you bowl as fast as he does. He had pulled some faces at me, so I pulled one back. George Bailey was sticking his tongue out at short leg. Next ball, I flicked a full one off my legs and set off thinking it was two. As I ran down the pitch I kept an eye on fine leg at the same time. Next thing – *boom*. We smashed into each other.

'What the hell ya doing, ya little shit?'

I just stood and stared at him, silent, and Kumar Dharmasena separated us.

I do seem to attract it. Perhaps because of the way I play. Arguably, because of my physicality, my build, the aggressive way I need to play to be successful. Other teams seem to target me, to try to push me off the front foot and onto the back one. Maybe they think getting me riled will result in me losing focus on what I'm doing. I'm not going to lie, sometimes that does work, and I honestly cannot say either way if it did here, but Ryan Harris did dismiss me from the next ball I faced.

As a competitor on the field, my emotions do get out of control at times, but once the game is ended I believe in shaking hands, and saying, 'Well played'. No matter what has happened. If someone is having a verbal spat with me, it's over once the game's over. The only exception, I guess, is Marlon Samuels, someone who makes a habit of carrying on like a pork chop wherever he is.

Sure, I attract confrontation but I get on famously these days with some of the people I have had run-ins with. Going back to an Under-17 game at Norton Cricket Club between Northamptonshire and Durham in July 2007, I got into a real war of words with David Willey. He said something to me; I said something to him. It went on for a few more overs and then, suddenly, we were at each other, walking towards one another on the cricket field. That's not good. It was something and nothing that started it, but we were going at each other quite hard with our comments, and didn't stop.

I got a hundred; he got me out. So, I'm not sure who won that one but the next time we saw each other, he said to me: 'We going to have another fight, or what?' From then it was as cool as ice between us. It's the way we both play, but we leave ill feeling on the field.

I don't always instigate trouble. But it follows me about, no doubt.

When I first played against Jimmy Anderson, during my first season with Durham, he referred to me as a 'young Ian Blackwell' with the emphasis on my weight rather than my talent. I was a bit podgier than I ought to have been, fair enough, and it was after I hit him down the ground for a four and ran past him that I got Jimmy's full assessment. He didn't look as if he liked me much, but afterwards I thought it was funny.

Jimmy and I are not dissimilar in one regard. I will do anything I can within the laws of the game to overcome my opponent in a one-on-one battle, for the good of my team. That's 100 per cent me. I want to win so much. I hate losing.

That incident when I was 15, against the senior Workington player, was triggered when I hit him for four through extra-cover. 'I've just hit the guy for four.' That's all I could think about. At 15, if you could bat for a while against someone like that it made you feel good about yourself. Of course it did. Imagine it from the other side, though. How would you like to be struck to the boundary by a kid? He exploded.

I explode too. When it's not going well, or I'm not helping towards changing things for the better, I hate it. If I don't feel like I am pulling my weight in a certain bowling spell, or in a certain innings, I tend to get really angry with myself.

Once adrenalin and competitive spirit combine, the red mist tends to descend, and it's nothing to do with whether you like the bloke you are up against or not. When you're cursing your own luck, it doesn't matter a hoot who it is, or whether or not they have a go back. Misbah-ul-Haq is a good example of someone who gets me going. I have found it agonizing to bowl at him at times, and he's a pleasant guy, but when pitched in a one-on-one he gets me wound up something rotten.

Quite honestly, though, getting into states like that actually gives me extra drive. If I feel engaged in a duel, it gets the best out of me. Countless people have told me that it's best not to muzzle that competitive beast completely as they fear they will lose the player I have become. That's really good to hear, because I think I would find it hard not to get into these fights.

Confrontation adds to my game. I loved the theatre of those altercations during my debut. There were 50,000 people there, there were boos, woos and jeers from the Adelaide Oval crowd, responding to our spats in the middle. To me, Test match cricket had confirmed what I had suspected all along. It was class.

Being barracked by a noisy home crowd was far from the toughest part. It was the result that was hardest to take. The tour was getting harder. We were 2–0 down. But I would not have believed that we would go on to be whitewashed.

The two blokes I had the run-ins with in Adelaide were instrumental in the result. We were ruined by Brad Haddin and Mitchell Johnson. The pair of them undoubtedly had the biggest hand in each of their wins. We reduced Australia to 100 and not many for five on several occasions, only for Brad Haddin to come in and smack it everywhere.

When you get Mitchell Johnson in this kind of mood, you know there's going to be a challenge on. He was frighteningly quick, to the extent that he got me out lbw with the first ball he ever bowled to me. In the first innings at Adelaide, he hit me on the pad before I could react. I knew it was going to be rapid – but 'bang', I was motionless as it struck me.

Even though he decimated our batting with seven wickets in that innings, there was a conviction in the England dressing room that he had a variation of the yips in him. There was a lot of talk about that.

Sure, he's got six-for, he's got seven-for, he's bowling well, but we know he's going to yip.

Unfortunately, 37 wickets later, he still hadn't yipped. He was bowling fast, and when it's swinging at 93 miles per hour, it's tough to play, believe me. When someone like Johnson gets on a roll it's so hard to stop.

To average more than seven wickets a match in a five-match Test series, hats off to that. If someone asked me to describe fast bowling – and I don't mean fast-medium – I would just have to show them the clips of him bowling at us that winter: hitting people on the gloves, getting them jumping, knocking poles out, that's what it's all about. It's a lot better viewing 90 yards away, in the changing room, than from 22 yards up a pitch.

The third Test in Perth followed a familiar pattern. Australia were 143 for five when Haddin walked in to bat; 267 for six when he was out. Despite a decent start from our openers Alastair Cook and Michael Carberry, we conceded a 134-run lead, and Australia declared leaving us 504 for victory.

Kevin Pietersen's dismissal gave me a second go, from a position of 121 for four, on a funny-looking WACA pitch. There were cracks all over it and they were huge – an absolute joke on the final two days. But it still played true, and if the ball did hit one of them it would jag miles sideways, not upwards, and that meant you weren't in any danger.

The thing that got me going was the challenge of taking Johnson on. He was at his adopted home ground, traditionally Australia's bounciest surface, but no matter how quick he was bowling, I decided I would go for it. What had I to lose?

You know the pull's one of your shots, so take it on, I muttered to myself. If he went short, hit it. And because I was thinking 'attack, attack, attack' it helped me pick up line and length a lot quicker. By taking on those short balls, I also got fewer of them. Then, I found I was hitting drives on the up nicely too.

From the grass banks, I could hear the Barmy Army song 'The Stokey Cokey' and it was a class atmosphere to bat in. I reached the close on 72, and was just intent on giving it back to Australia whenever I could. It was that 'fight fire with fire' approach again.

I remained positive. Despite Ian Bell and Matt Prior being dismissed, we lost only two wickets in a 46-over stretch, and I felt that we could still win the game if Tim Bresnan and I could stay together because he is a good batter. I was in the 90s at that stage, but not for long. Johnson peppered me with short stuff, I retaliated with a host of cross-batted shots and in taking a dozen off one over I had done it. What a high it felt. The best thing about the moment – as I pumped the air with my fist – was that it had come in an Ashes series. My first Test match hundred was against Australia, and that will always be something cool to look back on.

It was only my second Test match, and in terms of the toughness of the tour, to get a hundred was pretty special. I would have enjoyed it more had there been more team success, to make it a less one-sided series, but as far as enjoying personal achievements go your maiden hundred is slightly different. I have no real time for hundreds in matches in which my team didn't win. That's the end goal for me – the result. But your first one naturally holds a different place in your thoughts.

This time when I got to three figures, perhaps the big shots were ill advised. I didn't need to explode. But that's the option I went for, skipping down the track to hit Nathan Lyon for aerial boundaries before lunch, and then bottom edging a massive sweep shot outside off-stump, after it. I don't think I played a sweep before that.

It was a pivotal match. With defeat, we went 3–0 down and the Ashes were back in Australian hands. With my performance, I had hopefully proven people wrong.

You don't want to play for England. You just want to piss it up the wall with your mates, and have a good time.

When the tour moved on to Melbourne for Christmas, Clare and I were walking in the lobby of the team hotel. Sat in the distance was Andy Flower, having a cup of coffee with the other coaches.

'I really want to tell him I told you so, that I *did* have it in me,' I said to her.

Clare told me that was exactly what Andy had known all along, and that it was the kick up the arse I needed – that Andy had wanted me to stop coasting, to stop being a big fish in a small pond. He knew what he was doing, alright. And I knew she, and he, were right.

When I knew I was going to be making my Test debut in Adelaide, I got in touch with Scott Borthwick, who was with the England Performance Programme in Australia, to see if he could pop across. Unfortunately, he couldn't due to his own commitments. Scott is one of my best mates, godfather to Layton, someone I have played cricket with for years. So, I was made up when I found out he would be making his Test debut on the tour too.

He was called up over the festive period after Graeme Swann announced his retirement mid-series. Scott and I made our one-day debuts together in Ireland in 2011, and he was one match behind me in Twenty20 internationals, against West Indies in late September of that year. This was like, 'Sweet, I am playing with my mate, against Australia at the SCG.'

Unfortunately, the match in Sydney was like watching a replay of all the other games. We had made changes. But all the same stuff was happening. We dismissed David Warner and Chris Rogers early, Michael Clarke, Shane Watson and George Bailey were gone before 100 runs were on the board too. Once again, though, Haddin and Steve Smith blew us out of the park.

I came out with credit for adding a six-wicket haul to my hundred in my debut series, but I didn't think that first-innings display was anywhere near the best I'd bowled in an England shirt. Obviously, I was proud of what I had done, that I'd proved I could perform at this level – but I'd gone for one run short of 100. It was a good job I took those six wickets because the figures would have been quite ropey without them.

Once again, we conceded a three-figure lead. Once again, we headed in a second time faced with a huge, unattainable target.

In less than one and a half hours, I was in. Wickets were tumbling at the other end, and when Stuart Broad came out to bat, it looked like he had just woken up. That's because he *had* just woken up.

'Shall we have a bit of fun?' I asked him.

'Yeah, happy with that.'

When Nathan Lyon came on, I told Broady that with the turn and bounce he might be better off trying to hit straight, rather than going for a cross-bat sweep.

'Right, got ya.'

Third ball, he slog-swept him for a huge six.

If we were going down, we would go down swinging and we tried to hit as many fours and sixes as we could. We had needed 350 when we came together. There were seven wickets down. There was no chance, so we wanted to have a bit of fun. Lyon was the one we targetted but after putting on 44 in just half an hour, I ran down the pitch and tried to hit Ryan Harris out of Sydney. I failed.

There was a lot of criticism for the way the England team had played in that fifth Test. But we weren't trying to slump to defeat inside 32 overs. We weren't intending to lose. Of course, we wanted to win. It was just that we were mullered by a superior team. Australia never took their foot off our throats. They were so much better than us in all they did – catching, fielding, bowling, batting, everything. It was an indication of how much we would need to improve ahead of their tour of England 18 months later.

10

For accuracy's sake it ought be noted that I did not punch the locker in the dressing room at the Kensington Oval – even though the end result would arguably have been the same.

It was the slamming of my open-handed palm that resulted in the broken wrist, causing me to miss the World Twenty20 in Bangladesh, and relinquish my England place across all three forms of the game. It was totally irresponsible, if I'm honest, and an incident that I would deeply regret. It hurt me much more than the physical pain. It made what I viewed as a deteriorating situation for me in international cricket a whole lot worse.

It was only three months earlier that I had truly arrived as an England player – scoring the only hundred by a visiting batsmen in the Ashes had given me immense inner belief. So how had it come to this? My head was all over the place. I was desperate to repeat all the good stuff I had shown in Australia, but, try as I might, I just couldn't.

It was an unusual tour to the Caribbean in 2014. Because of its positioning in the calendar, we had travelled with some different players from those we used in the limited-overs matches in Australia. We were scheduled to play three ODIs and three Twenty20 internationals, but due to the proximity of the World T20, the emphasis was on the 20-over specialists. Instead of sending two separate squads, the England hierarchy opted to send just one. So, Alastair Cook and Ian Bell, two mainstays of the top order in 50-over cricket, stayed at home, and players like Michael Lumb and Moeen Ali made their one-day debuts. Stuart Broad, the Twenty20 captain, was due to lead in all six.

I was genuinely excited about heading off to face West Indies, the reigning world champions in T20. Ahead of departure, there was a delivery of fresh kit – tell me a player who doesn't like that – plus a new batch of New Balance bats arrived from India.

The ball was pinging off those bats in the nets when we landed in Antigua, and I resumed the position of number three, where I had finished up in the Australian one-dayers, for the warm-up match against a University of West Indies XI. I had failed twice with a 70 in between, when batting at first drop against the Aussies. I have always enjoyed that position in white-ball cricket – the field is up and the ball is hard, maximizing scoring opportunities for those who, like me, place the emphasis on attack.

It was a decent start to the tour. I made 58, Joe Root scored an unbeaten hundred, and we won our practice outing by 29 runs. I was told I would be starting the series proper at three. I was on a high. I felt I had seized the chance offered to me.

But then I was told on the eve of the first match that there had been a change. I was no longer three. I would be coming in at five. I cannot lie. That was a disappointment. I had been switched about in the matches in Australia too. Having started at seven, I slipped to eight. Then, from nowhere, I was tried at three. I hoped that the man-of-the-match performance in the win at Perth might persuade Ashley Giles, the England one-day coach, to persist. But from these changes, it was clear that uncertainty remained about my best position.

It's horrible when you are out of form both in the nets and in the middle, but what I was to experience over the next fortnight was much worse. In every practice session I felt class, as though I was just around the corner from a big score. But I was going into games and unearthing ways of getting out. What's the point of batting well in the nets, when that's going on?

In the first match of three at the Sir Vivian Richards Stadium, I was bowled by a delivery from Sunil Narine that just clipped the bail. In the second, I got a tickle off an inside edge that was taken by wicketkeeper Denesh Ramdin, running around on the leg-side, off the left-arm spinner Nikita Miller. Typical of my luck, I had already started walking and given myself out before the umpire Joel Wilson shook his head and said, 'Not out.' Then, after being promoted back up to three for the final match, it was like I couldn't wait to make an impression – taking the positive option against Dwayne Bravo's first ball, I top-edged a pull. My combined total: nine runs off 17 balls.

Things didn't get any better when we moved to Barbados for the Twenty20s. Needing 11.5 an over when I went in at 55 for five in the opening match, Marlon Samuels bowled his quicker ball, it ragged and, trying to hit it for six, I missed by a country mile. I didn't get picked for the second match as we rotated the squad across the three matches, and by the final one the frustration was festering.

So, when I got out first ball to the left-arm Twenty20 specialist Krishmar Santokie – a slower ball that jagged to take out middle stump, a delivery that would have got any left-hander out – it was the culmination of everything. It was agonizing to walk off with nothing next to my name again. It felt like I had been served up a collection of deliveries I could do nothing about.

It was not as though I was able to get over this low with success with the ball. We were spin-heavy in the Caribbean conditions, and so my chances were limited. When I did bowl, it wasn't the best.

All I could think about when I left the field was what a failure the whole tour had been. I had contributed nothing. Zero.

Dug-outs are common in Twenty20 matches around the world now and four days earlier, after the dismissal to Samuels, I had taken my place on the England one. This time, I wasn't prepared to sit simmering. I was so angry I walked straight past my team-mates, up the stairs and into the dressing room.

The next bit wasn't planned. I promise you. It just happened.

I drew my elbow back. And with everything I had, fingers bent in but palm facing, I hit the locker with the heel of my right hand. Subconsciously, I perhaps knew not to punch because of what such an action might do to my knackered index finger. I also broke a finger punching a door as a young Durham academy player.

There was the same amount of force as you would use in a punch, though, and it obviously caused some damage to the locker itself.

What have I just done?

The glass at the back of the locker smashed into what seemed a thousand pieces. I felt such an idiot, and now I had to sweep up the mess.

What I didn't know at the time was how much damage it had caused me. With the adrenalin pumping, I couldn't feel a thing. But 10 minutes later when it had gone, and our innings was drawing to an end, I knew something was wrong. I tried to convince myself I had just jarred my wrist, and taped it up to go out for fielding practice before the switch of innings.

When the West Indies began their chase, I got put into slip. That was not the best place for someone in my condition, was it? I whispered to Jos Buttler: 'I'm stood here at second with a broken wrist.' I'm not sure whether he took me seriously or not. He creased up laughing.

At that stage, I didn't know for sure, but I had a fair idea. When I got shifted to long off by the stand-in captain Eoin Morgan, and had to throw a ball in from the deep, things came to a crunch. It hurt so much I had to run off. When you jar a thumb it can be sore for quite a while – but not this sore. After half an hour, the pain tends to reduce. But my whole hand was throbbing.

I had to tell the management team there and then that I thought I'd fractured my wrist. Whenever you leave the field, usually the first person to get interested is the physio. I had just informed Craig de Weymarn when Ashley Giles walked in. A coach tends to be concerned when one of the best fielders comes off. It's fair to say he didn't have much to say to me in response to my mishap.

People must have thought I was mad but I felt I was letting the team down because I was not scoring runs, that it was possible I would not play for England again. It seemed as if my chance was going up in smoke before my eyes. I had had the chance to improve England's position in a match five times and failed five times. I knew these performances were not what was expected of me. They were not what I expected of myself. I was simply not influencing matches in the way I wanted to.

Next day I was sent for an X-ray and my worst fear was confirmed.

For all the frustrations, and it was a really tough time to handle, there was a World Cup around the corner, and that offered a fresh start. England had considered me good enough to be in that squad, and I would have a chance to turn things round in Bangladesh.

Later, at a team meeting I got to address the group.

'Sorry for letting you all down. I won't be out there with you,' I explained.

I considered whether or not it was appropriate to offer up a little bit of humour by adding: 'But every cloud has a silver lining, and if ever there was a tour I was going to miss . . . .'

On balance, I didn't think it was the right time.

Gilo called me a 't**t' and he was probably right. I could hardly argue with him, could I? I told them I would be watching at home, supporting them from afar.

I felt pretty stupid returning home on my own.

The surgery – a pin was inserted into my scaphoid to re-form the joint – was carried out by a consultant called Doug Campbell at the Spire Hospital in Leeds. I was frustrated at underperforming but now, for the next five weeks, I wouldn't be able to perform at all. I would rather have been trying to put things right on the field than sat on the couch. Unfortunately, I had brought it on myself.

Around this time, there was some nonsense spouted about me being forced onto an anger management course. Nothing of the sort happened. However, I did seek further chats with psychologist Mark Bawden.

This issue was different; but somehow the same. It was all about processing disappointment. We spoke about what I would do if I ever felt this way during a poor period of form in future. When that feeling built inside of me, what was I to do? When it was bubbling up, how could I release it? It certainly wasn't an option to hit solid objects with my bare hands.

We chatted a little about the feelings and how they developed. We discussed how it was important to find a way of dealing with isolated failure, and not bind it all together to create a much bigger problem.

Instead of lashing out, letting my temper get the better of me, we devised a routine for when I got out in frustrating circumstances. From that point onwards, whenever it happened, I was to immediately pack my kitbag.

Not very rebellious, I know. Previously, I'd have been looking around the room for a place to smack my bat. Now, I was supposed to methodically fold things up, making sure all the straps were done neatly and place things in an orderly fashion. These days, if I hit anything it tends to be using one of my batting pads, and I'm pretty confident I can't break anything with one of those. I may swear like a trooper too, but the focus of packing the bag certainly takes my anger level down a notch or two. Time helps the process of calming down. And packing your bag takes time.

Some of the lads were able to see the funny side of things when we returned to the Kensington Oval a year later for a Test series. I walked into the changing room one day to find a boxing mitt taped over the locker nearest to my spot – the handiwork of Ian Bell. It was the screensaver on my phone for a while.

● ● ●

There were serious repercussions for my behaviour at the start of the 2014 English summer; or the 'Summer from Hell' as Clare christened it, and how we refer to it in our household even now. I'd made such massive strides in Australia the previous winter and now it was like they never happened. I went from feeling on top of the world to someone nowhere near solving international cricket.

Being on the sidelines in April and May cost me my place in the England team, and allowed others to prosper. Moeen Ali made a great transition into the Test XI against the Sri Lankans in the first Test series of the international season, and his form meant that despite enjoying a personally successful Ashes, I wasn't going to be straight back in at number six once fit. Instead, I was to find my way back in as a bowler who batted. It was my fault Moeen had been given the opportunity and now I was paying for it with an unfamiliar role, bowling second change, batting at eight. Ahead of the five-match series against the Indians, I took career-best figures of seven for 67, among 10 victims in the match, a crushing win over Sussex at Chester-le-Street.

The first Test against India at Trent Bridge was played on the worst wicket imaginable. There was no pace in it whatsoever, to the extent that the first ball of the match from Jimmy Anderson didn't carry through to Matt Prior behind the stumps. It was embarrassing. Groundsman Steve Birks did offer a public apology after the first day, but having lost the toss, we spent 161 overs in the field. We had a five-man attack and the four seam bowlers ended up bowling 30 overs apiece.

I got a couple of wickets and went at less than two and a half runs an over, but it was really hard work. When it was my turn to bat on it, I got a duck, starting a rather unwanted trend. As a team we outscored India on first innings, but there was simply no chance of forcing an England win on a surface that sluggish.

Then disaster struck at Lord's. We didn't play well as a team, and went 1–0 down in the series as a result. I took five for 91 in the match but bagged a pair. Before I went out to bat in the second innings, I was watching on TV and Ishant Sharma was bowling at 84–85 mph. When I went out to bat, it felt like 95 mph. That said something about where I was at, I think. Whenever I pulled on an England shirt and padded up, batting felt so hard.

After that defeat, I got left out which just led to further frustration. I had been picked as a bowler, and fulfilled that role pretty well, taking seven wickets in two matches – yet I was being dropped for what appeared to be a lack of runs. Liam Plunkett was also omitted from the next Test and he'd been successful all summer. Because we weren't winning, the team was changed around. Did I really deserve to get dropped?

This is the first time in my career I was properly annoyed about selection. I can take being left out for poor performances, but this didn't feel fair. My head was all over the place, and I was confused as to the role I was meant to play as an England cricketer. Was I the batting all-rounder they had backed in the biggest Test series of them all the previous winter? Or was I guy who slotted into the gaps other people left? I felt like the dispensable option, when I wanted to make myself one of the first names on the team sheet.

It certainly wasn't the role I filled for Durham. Despite a winless streak in Division One that spanned the entire months of April and May, and half of June, we finished the season strongly again, just as we had in 2013.

This time it was the Royal London Cup that got us going. We snuck through the group stage, then beat Yorkshire in the quarter-finals when we really shouldn't have. It was not long after that England Test defeat at Lord's, and I was driving to a chiropodist to get moulds of my feet done for some new bowling boots. I listened to the commentary on the radio, and, despite defending only 237 at Headingley, the wickets kept tumbling.

All England players were made available for the semi-finals, and despite my struggles wearing the three lions, every time I featured for Durham I held my head up high. My hundred against Nottinghamshire in the last group game contributed to a third straight win and the securing of fourth place by a whisker. Now we faced the same opposition in the last four.

It was a Saturday and the game was televised live on Sky Sports. I truly felt that the 103 I scored the last time we faced them in a white-ball game turned round my season. More big runs would show England, and England supporters, that I could still play with the stick in my hand. So the

164 I made in this game, as well as being my highest List A score, represented one of the best knocks of my life. To help Durham to a Lord's final felt really good.

Where did I stand with England, though? The answer, in the short term at least, was provided when I was recalled for the one-day series against India and found myself back down at number eight. The one good knock for England all summer was a rapid 33 not out at Headingley between the Notts semi and the Lord's final at the end of September. One good knock . . . in the season that followed my maiden international hundred at Perth. That was my lot.

Pitiful season it may have been, but at least it had a sweet ending.

Ahead of the 50-over showpiece against Warwickshire, Neil Fairbrother told me: 'You don't know what it's like to play in a Lord's final until you're part of one. It's a brilliant day. You will only appreciate it afterwards.'

I chewed over Harv's words on the coach journey down. Even the training beforehand felt like something else, truly it did.

Weather-wise it was a miserable day, gloomy as hell, the floodlights a permanent presence. It was overcast, drizzling, but it was still awesome. We bowled Warwickshire out cheaply on what was a strange Lord's wicket – on the slow side, but offering a bit off the seam.

The atmosphere created by the 16,000 crowd gave the contest a bit of extra edge, particularly after Warwickshire took a couple of early wickets in our pursuit of a 166-run victory target. These kind of low-scoring games can be brilliant to watch, and when Jeetan Patel started to spin one delivery miles, then skid on the next, this one took another twist.

After Jeetan pinned a couple of our batsmen lbw, Mark Stoneman pushed me down the order, doing so twice actually. First he promoted Keaton Jennings, then Scott Borthwick, to numbers four and five, and held Paul Collingwood and myself back. Rocky's feeling was that as we didn't need six an over, and they batted up the top in Championship stuff, it was a situation suited to their skills.

When I eventually went in, at 86 for five, with 81 required, it was my intention not to do anything stupid whatsoever. Jeets was bowling around the wicket from the pavilion end and the ball was either skidding on or ragging. To sit in and block would spell my downfall, I felt. They put a man back straightaway at deep point, as they obviously knew I would want to reverse sweep. They were right, of course, I love that shot in limited-overs cricket. It cut off a boundary option for me, but I could still knock it there for one to get off strike.

Varun Chopra, the Warwickshire captain, had to be quite canny. He knew Patel was his main threat, and even when he took him off it wasn't so long before he was back on again. It wasn't a question of containing us, they had to get us out if they wanted to win. Both sides knew the simplicity of it all. We knew if we saw Jeets out, the cup was ours. They knew another wicket or two and it was theirs.

He had four of the seven wickets to fall when he returned to the attack. The game was in my hands, because I was the one batsman left. The way he was bowling, the only way I felt confident about picking up runs was that reverse sweep. Only this delivery was a lot straighter than the others, meaning I had to reach behind myself almost. I got the tiniest amount of bat on the ball, it missed leg-stump by a smidgeon and ran through all the way to the boundary. I was like 'whatever', but the first thing I got hit with by the lads later was, 'What the f**k were you doing there?'

Colly told me: 'If you are ever going to take a risk, why not run down and hit it straight for six?' I just shrugged my shoulders. I had given a similar reaction when we had been batting together, and gave Patel the charge to produce a forward defensive stroke.

'Why do that?' Colly asked.

Simple, Jeets was on the spot every ball, and I knew if I got to the pitch I wasn't going to miss it. I smothered it. It was one fewer ball left of his allocation. Yes, if I had got out the result might have been different, but it was important not to sit in. I always believe you are at your best as a batsman when you are decisive, whether that is in attack or defence.

As we ticked those last couple of dozen runs off, I thought about what Harv had said again. I could see why all those cricketers over the previous four decades had so wanted to perform at a Lord's final, and being in the middle for the winning moment is one of the more special feelings I have had in the game. Even though it wasn't a run-fest, it was eye-catching. It ebbed and flowed from start to finish. And at the end I was still standing, 38 not out.

At the other end, Gareth Breese struck the winning runs to make it a memorable farewell. He was leaving the Durham playing staff after 10 years. After somehow squeezing a leave-alone to the third-man boundary for four, there was a hug between us and then he ran off to see his wife and kids. It left me in the middle, stood there like a bit of a melon among the Warwickshire lads.

An hour and a half later, Breesey was drinking rum out of the trophy.

He ended up dropping it, and passed out on the dressing-room floor. He had to be wheelchaired out of the ground to the hotel.

It was such a great way to bow out for a hugely popular member of our squad. Breesey batted a bit, bowled a bit and had great hands. He was also the nicest bloke you could wish to meet, always the first to text 'well done lads' to others on personal successes. He had the worst body frame I have ever seen on a West Indian – but it was made for life in the north-east and he's still around coaching now.

● ● ●

I knew my role with Durham. There was clarity. But the struggles with England continued. If they were going to bat me at number eight, I needed to bat like a number eight. Trouble was, I didn't know how. I had no experience of it.

What was I meant to be practising? The most balls I was ever going to face realistically was 40. And that would most likely be in a scenario in which the England team had done badly and the opposition well, potentially in helpful bowling conditions.

Do I practise smacking it? *Yes.* Because if I face 40 balls, I can change the course of the game with 70. I have always thought positively about the game of cricket, and so I wanted to come up with an aggressive attitude to what I was being asked to do. Unfortunately, I got into some filthy habits doing so. I was turning myself into a slogger.

I went to the nets thinking like a batsman but knowing I wasn't considered one by the selectors. What was the point of me practising a block or a glorious cover drive? There wasn't one. It was the big shots that would be needed.

As the number eight batsmen at pre-match net training, you have to slot in when you can, and that sometimes means slipping in before the openers are ready. I wasn't getting any meaningful practice at all. It was no good me facing the new balls against the pace bowlers, because I wouldn't be up against that in a match situation.

I was feeling lost. I was being strangled as a player.

Any lingering confidence I had in my ability was wiped out on the tour of Sri Lanka. I batted twice in three matches, managing scores of 16 and 6. We lost the series 5–2. My bowling, rarely used, went at 10 an over when it was. As a group we were talking a good game. This is how we were going to do such and such, this is how we were going to do something else, we would say in pre-match planning. We just never delivered anything like we pledged we would, once we got on the pitch. On the eve of a game we needed to win to stay in the series, we reviewed some psychology work we had done in London earlier in the year. We spoke about how once you wore the England cap, you wore it forever. How was that going to help us over 100 overs against Sri Lanka?

When I got home, after seeing Clare and the kids I excused myself for the evening. The only thing I wanted to do was go out and get blitzed.

I sought refuge in alcohol and with proper mates who knew the real me. I was absolutely nowhere in life at that point. My head was scrambled. So I went round to the house where I lived when I was in the academy. Stuey Poynter, Graham Clark and Keaton Jennings now lived there.

I hang out with those three guys most of the time. They are not just drinking buddies, they're good mates. All three make sure Clare's alright when I'm away on tours, popping round for an hour every week to see her and the kids.

That night, I wanted their attention. I needed a decent craic, away from cricket. I just wanted to get smashed, basically. There are lots of different ways to enjoy yourself in life and my main way is cricket. Unfortunately, I hadn't enjoyed myself in the previous five weeks. So my only chance came through alcohol.

We began by playing a drinking game called Flipbox. The rules are straightforward. You place a cigarette box on the table and have to flip it. The way it lands – on its side, flat or on its end – dictates how much you have got to drink. Afterwards, we headed into Newcastle. I was stumbling through my front door at 1.30am after red-carding myself. If you want to get an idea of my state of mind, I cried in the shower. All my emotions were pouring out. I was completely gone. It just wasn't me.

11

Despite everything pointing towards it being bad news for me when the 2015 World Cup squad was chosen, I always retained that glimmer of hope that I would be wrong. That the England selectors would pick me, regardless of whether my recent performances merited a place or not.

Throughout the build-up towards the announcement on 20 December, I was not expecting to be in, knowing deep down that I didn't deserve to be among the 15 names remaining from the original 30-man party. But the waiting was the worst part – because of the little 'maybe' that was lingering in the back of my mind. It wasn't 100 per cent dead cert my name was not going to be amongst the 15; that I would be missing out on a chance that only comes around every four years.

'I might still have a crack, here,' I persuaded myself as the hours towards that phone call ticked by. I had only been back in the country a day or so, after that horrendous tour of Sri Lanka. After all the crap going on in my head there, all I wanted to hear was, 'Yeah, we're going to go with you.'

My numbers were not good, and the run of low scores and irregular bowling opportunities meant I didn't deserve to go to Australia and New Zealand in the new year. Yet somehow I retained an inkling that they might gamble on me. After all, they were still picking me through that poor run – probably because I fielded, batted and bowled. Potentially, I was offering something in one department even if I was failing in another, and that can be useful in limited-overs cricket. Potentially, they might recognize I was the kind of player that could just click in an instant, and produce something match-winning in either innings of a game.

There was to be no honey-coated conclusion. Everything I suspected would happen on the balance of probability happened, and there is no preparation for the moment negative news comes that makes you feel any better. When reality hits, it hurts like hell.

Jimmy Whitaker's phone call, ahead of the public announcement, began with him asking how my family was, what the kids were up to, what was going on. It was all quite friendly. Then came the hammer blow.

'The bad news is that we have not picked you,' he continued.

Nah, please don't make small talk before telling me I'm not going on the World Cup trip. It kind of made it worse, if you know what I mean? There is no doubt he was trying to make it easier, to be more personal, to step away from being a hard-faced chairman of selectors to soften the disappointment. But, nah, that ain't my way. Just tell me.

I was at home with Clare when the phone rang, and left the room to take it. No matter how resigned you are to being overlooked when there is a selection issue, it's still devastating when the news is confirmed. I stood motionless. Then I felt an urge to hit back. To challenge. To question. To show how much I cared.

I was not deliberately looking to be argumentative. I was frustrated. Of course, I knew what I needed to do – make bigger contributions. I had failed to do so for a period of time, and that period of time had now gone. Quite simply, it had proved too difficult for me to deliver batting at number eight.

But what about the future? There was no point looking at the past. So, I asked Jimmy, what could I do to help myself? I wanted to know what I needed to improve on to get given a chance, from a white-ball perspective, higher up the order batting-wise.

I was told I required greater consistency, more runs.

'I totally understand that,' I said. 'But if you look at my last couple of seasons with Durham, batting at five, sometimes four, positions where I want to be, positions that suit my game, my numbers are very good.'

'We are talking about England,' Jimmy told me.

'But I've been batting seven or eight for England – and that's my problem,' I said.

The conversation to-ed and fro-ed like this for a few minutes. I just wanted an answer on what I needed to do. Without it, I might not have got another chance to stake my claim; to air my grievance, in a reasonable manner. If I had let that call end as it normally would have with an 'Alright, cheers, thanks, bye', then maybe they wouldn't have gone away and looked at those statistics from Durham. To acknowledge that from a county cricket perspective, I had averaged something like 70 that previous season and that, perhaps, was being ignored. Maybe later, they would take that into consideration and agree that I was a number five batsman. Maybe they took no notice whatsoever. Who knows? The point was, I'd had my say. Jimmy his. And it was a chat worth having. I didn't hold any grudges.

My biggest problem, though, was that there was no scheduled cricket for me to prove my point. My next opportunities with Durham in limited-overs action were more than six months away. So later that day, during the conversation to tell Neil Fairbrother the disappointing news, I asked him whether he could find me a solution.

'I just want to get away and play some cricket. I don't want to be sat here at home, pulling what little is left of my hair out, thinking what could have been,' I said.

I just wanted to get somewhere booked – to get out, play some cricket. That's what I do as a job, and I wanted to be doing that job.

Clare was as broken as I was about the whole situation. She knows how much I love playing, and at the same time how much I hate being out of the game. She almost feeds off my mood. World Cups happen every four years. There aren't that many chances to play in one, and this one had slipped through my fingers.

Clare acts as my sounding board. When we discussed what the exclusion meant for me, I told her I was keen to discover whether there were any Big Bash opportunities out there. She was all for it. There was no 'Oh, really?' She was just 'Go for it.'

From a selfish perspective she might have been looking forward to a rare family Christmas and New Year at home. Not a bit of it. She always makes sacrifices like that. Cricket comes first, even though she plays on that by calling me selfish, tongue in cheek – as if I am choosing to go and have a knockabout with my mates in the street rather than spend quality time with the four of us all together. Deep down, she means it, I reckon. But she knows it has to be that way, because it's what I do.

● ● ●

The Big Bash was already under way down under but Harv got onto the case, and we went down to Clare's mam's for Christmas. It was while we were down in Somerset that I got the call I'd been waiting for. I was to fly to Melbourne two days into the new year as a replacement for Jesse Ryder, who had been ruled out of the tournament by a back injury. Dwayne Bravo and Andre Russell, the two West Indies all-rounders, filled the overseas spots for the first four games, but I would play the latter ones in the group, alongside Bangladesh's Shakib Al Hasan.

This was it. I would show everyone. I still thought like that. As if I could prove them wrong. Not in a told-you-so way. Just to remind the selectors the reason they had picked me in the first place. I now had the chance to produce the kind of innings I spoke about in county cricket, and to be fair, England were good with it. They had no problem with me going abroad. As a centrally-contracted player you are at their mercy when it comes to events outside of ECB control, and they could have refused. Instead they provided me with a No Objection Certificate.

Left: Fourth Test, Trent Bridge, Ashes series 2015. I snaffled Adam Voges in the slips and the look on Broady's face says it all.

Below: On my way to a career best 6 for 36 in the second innings. I'm fit to bust after Mitch Johnson's wicket.

Right: Clinching the 2015 Ashes urn at The Oval, with a little help from JR.

Eoin Morgan's positive captaincy has been one of the main reasons behind England's stunning improvement in the white-ball game.

Below: The fastest-ever double-hundred by an Englishman. My 258 at Newlands in the second Test against South Africa in January 2016 took my batting to another level.

Top: In what must rank as one of my best-ever catches, I was buzzing after snaring AB de Villiers in the deep in the first ODI at Bloemfontein.

Above: T20 World Cup final, Kolkata, April 2016, and the picture really does tell the story. Nothing Joe Root can do to ease my pain after that final over of the match.

On the attack at Old Trafford against the mercurial 2016 Pakistan tourists.

I can't explain it. Misbah-ul-Haq gets me wound up big time.
But then again, not reason enough to smash up his helmet.

It felt like a sniper's bullet. My calf goes in the second Test
of the Pakistan series, making 2016 an injury-plagued year.

Tatts with a meaning. I'm proud of my tattoos and my part Maori blood. It's Kirihuti art on the left arm and a tribute to Layton and Libby on my right.

Top: With Clare and Layton and a particularly sleepy cheetah.

Above, left: No better way to celebrate an Ashes triumph than with the family – Clare, Layton and Libby.

Above, right: No idea where he's putting all that. Like father like son. Layton and me celebrate Durham's semi-final victory over Nottinghamshire in the 2014 Royal London One-Day Cup.

Right: Who said it was fancy dress?

So, without any obstacles in front of me, I flew to Australia on 2 January 2015, arriving in Melbourne on derby day – the Renegades got well and truly pumped by the Stars, a score of 57 all out the lowest in Big Bash history. The margin of defeat was a massive 112 runs.

I didn't make it to meet my new team-mates that night, instead meeting up with one of my pals from Durham. Ryan Pringle was playing Victorian grade cricket and was thrilled when I called him to tell him I was on the way. He wasn't having a great time at that point, we both needed a night out, and I was intent on arriving in style. As soon as I landed I was on a mission – to the hotel, quick shower, I didn't get back in until seven the next morning. Perfect cure for jetlag, I reckon.

It was a good job the Sunday was a day off. Not that I would have done any worse than on the Monday when I arrived at the Etihad Stadium for my single practice session with my new team. I did not middle one ball or bowl a delivery where I wanted to. I felt like I had never picked up a bat before. My bowling was rusty, to say the least. It was embarrassing. I had come over to be the overseas player and I was worried: What the hell are these guys thinking?

On the flight to Hobart the following day, 6 January, I could only imagine thoughts such as, 'What have we signed here?'

But it's amazing how things work out sometimes, without any explanation as to how. From feeling like I couldn't hit a cricket ball out of the middle of the bat ever again, everything fell into place.

Having clanged the ball in the nets in Melbourne, I was probably not expecting the Renegades coach Simon Helmot's question ahead of my debut: 'Where do you wanna bat, mate?'

I was the overseas player, and they had signed me to make an impact. My answer didn't ooze confidence. Neither did it shy away from the responsibility.

I gave him what people will tell you is *the* typical Ben Stokes answer: 'Wherever you want me.'

'Do you wanna bat up top?'

'Well, I've never really done it. I've batted three a few times . . .'

'Right, there you go – three.'

It was all so uncomplicated. The Renegades had signed me. They believed in what I could do. They weren't signing me to bat low down. Far from it. They wanted me up top.

The thing about Twenty20 cricket is that you have to take advantage of the powerplay, to look to score runs heavily during those initial six overs of the innings; and walking out to face the eighth ball of the innings, after Hobart Hurricanes won the toss, that mentality undoubtedly helped. It made me commit to playing aggressive cricket shots.

An early clip off the pads for four told me I was in good touch. But the one shot that really got me going was in the third over when, having faced seven deliveries, I hit Tim Bresnan straight back over his head for six. When I am hitting the ball down the ground, and hitting it well, I know I am in decent order. I couldn't have struck the ball more cleanly. Nor made a better impression. Another one of my five sixes, off Ben Hilfenhaus, struck the top of the roof at the Blundstone Arena. My 77 runs came off just 37 balls.

Apparently, the Channel Ten commentators were debating how on earth I wasn't in England's World Cup squad. At around the same time, the England World Cup squad were landing in Sydney for the triangular tournament against Australia and India that would serve as warm-up matches for the main event. Some media reports suggested my innings would be a timely reminder that they'd omitted me. But I didn't necessarily look at it like that. Yes, I wanted to prove a point. But for me, not against anyone else, and the thing I had done for me was show that I was in form, and in the right place, should I be required by England due to injury.

We won that match but things weren't brilliant from a team perspective. The results were up and down, and we were unable to pull back a poor start of one win and three defeats. We finished third bottom, with six points from eight matches. However, I look back on that stint in Melbourne fondly. Upon arrival, I knew Aaron Finch from playing against him in international cricket, but not many others. I knew names, not faces. But it was such an easy group to get into, and I got friendly with two of the younger lads, Nick Winter and Tom Beaton, spending most of my days off with them.

The pressure of being an overseas signing? There wasn't any, really. I had been successful playing a certain way in the past and I didn't want to do anything differently because I had switched domestic competitions. Ultimately, the person who is most crucial in you being successful is yourself – the same person who gets in the way of that happening. I wanted to be true to that self by playing in the most natural way I knew. The way I played as a kid. That was what had made me successful in the past, and so I decided that was the way I should go about things at the Big Bash.

When I got all those ducks in a row for England, I was hitting the ball as well as ever in the nets. So I couldn't quite understand why I was unable to transfer it onto the pitch. I would go out there intent on playing in the manner I had always done, but it just wasn't happening in the middle.

But it was only after getting left out of that Test team during the 2014 summer that I truly began to question myself. You might think that when I was called up for the one-day internationals against India, a different format might have freed my mind up. After all, I had made big scores in county matches. The truth, however, was that there was still a bit of a hangover from underperforming in the Tests.

It was hard to get the confidence back that I was showing in a Durham shirt. It was as if the badge on my chest was having an effect. As though those three lions I love so much were telling me: right, you haven't really performed with us on the last few times you've tried. It was still in the back of my mind that I had been next to useless. It was a hard cycle to get out of.

Now, though, it was way past the point of trying to be anything else, trying to fit into roles that I could not fulfil as was required. In one innings, I had realized that I had to keep being me. That it was the only way I was going to come out the other side. If that wasn't good enough, so be it. But I had to give myself the best chance of being successful.

That knock of 77 against a good Hurricanes attack got me going again. In subsequent matches I tried to play the same way, and contributed another good innings in the last game, a top score of 33 off 19 balls, chasing down a challenging score against Adelaide Strikers at home. An unsuccessful chase, as it transpired. Selfishly, though, despite the result, it reinforced the feeling that it had taken one visit to the crease to get all my confidence back.

The responsibility of being an overseas player had positive effects too. Suddenly, I was asked opinions on all different aspects of the Renegades' cricket. When I was younger I had so much to say, but never would open my mouth because I didn't feel like I deserved to share that opinion. Now, I was actively encouraged to do so, and there is no doubt I came out of my box a bit more during that fortnight. At the end of my three-week stay, Simon Helmot, the coach, asked me for my views on where the team needed to go in future years.

They had not had a great season, and he wanted to know from an objective perspective where I thought they were at, in terms of both their batting and bowling. My conclusions batting-wise were universal rather than Renegades-specific. I said to him that for any team to be successful in Twenty20 tournaments, the positions one, two and three were vital. Those three batsmen have to take advantage of that powerplay, and then the players from five downwards have to finish the innings off in a similar manner. From my experience, the crucial bit they were unable to master was the art of batting at the start and end of innings – and those are the periods in which games are won.

They had a great bowling unit, both in terms of variation, and how they used them, as far as I could see. Peter Siddle and James Pattinson, to use the new ball, Nick Winter, a left-armer who swung it, Fawad Ahmed, the leg-spinner, and Nathan Rimmington, an excellent death bowler. They had that half of the T20 gameplan sussed, as far as I could see. I said as much, and it felt good to get asked stuff like that – to be valued as a crick-eter both on and off the field.

● ● ●

I was feeling my old self again, and soon to be re-acquainted with a few old mates thanks to England giving me further opportunities to play some cricket. When it became obvious that I was not going to be staying on for the latter stages of the Big Bash, I was asked whether I would like to join the England Lions in South Africa. Crucially, I was going to bat at number five.

It was cool to see a few of the lads I'd grown up playing cricket with at England age-group levels. It only served to improve my mood. Even so, there were still some of my old habits re-surfacing to cause me a few problems.

Within 24 hours of me arriving in Bloemfontein – I did so on the pen-ultimate evening of the second unofficial Test – we were invited to an end-of-series function. Both teams were in attendance, there were a few beers laid on, and some food. That was just the warm-up, of course.

Later, a large group of us went on in search of a night out. One thing led to another, and several lads sloped off back to the hotel, leaving myself and somebody who probably wouldn't want to be named in these pages out a little bit later than we should have been.

As I say, I had just flown across the globe to meet up with some of my old England Under-19 mates, and I was pleased to see them. We were enjoying ourselves. So much so that we completely ignored the instructions of the ECB's security officer on the tour, when he asked us to leave the club we were in.

Later, we were told that we actively evaded him, doing everything we could to throw him off our trail – ducking for cover every time he came into sight. We had argued with security, putting forward our case to stay, and he had just left us to it. We assumed he had accepted it, and gone back to the hotel.

'Well, we've been here before,' Guy Jackson, the England Lions manager, said when I was summoned before him next morning.

Guy was also in the management team on the trip to Australia two winters earlier when I was dismissed from the tour for one transgression too many. I argued that I had been a victim of circumstances. On this particular occasion, I had landed amongst a group of blokes who share similar personalities to myself. Put them all together and you are guaranteed an interesting night. And yes, it got chaotic.

That's the problem with me, I guess. Once I set my mind on something, I generally try to do it. So, if I decide 'I am going big tonight' it generally tends to end up in a big night. That's why I only tend to drink if I'm going out. To be fair, most of those big nights come from winning games of cricket or being handed a day off next day while on tour. They don't tend to involve defying management or security detail orders. This time, we were given a rap on the knuckles, a 'don't do it again', and it was pretty much forgotten about.

That South Africa trip got off on the wrong foot on and off the field. Bowling-wise, it was the worst I have ever felt during those opening days in the nets. In Sri Lanka before Christmas, the batting was rubbish, the bowling was as bad, it was just a terrible tour. But the bowling bit had annoyed me most.

I told Ottis Gibson, our bowling coach: 'Mate, I've got no idea where it's going. Can you help me?'

To say I was concerned was an understatement. My bowling was literally all over the place. Throughout all the talk of me losing my England place, and regaining my confidence in Australia, it was the batting that remained the focus of attention. But there was clearly a lot of work to be done in the other half of my game.

So we had a few sessions working on my alignment. Some age-old habits of jumping out and jumping back in again during my approach to the crease had crept into my bowling. Only after a few sessions did I feel like I was back somewhere near to where I wanted to be again. My batting was just so. Now, if I could just get my bowling right . . .

I know my form can fluctuate with both bat and ball, but I never stop working to try to be the best I can at each discipline, and when things are not going well, I will work even harder. People will never see the effort we put in behind the scenes, and how coaches like Gibbo dedicate their time to improving you or ironing out flaws. I have never moaned about the hours required. We are in such a privileged position. What does annoy me, though, is when we are on the receiving end of smart comments on social media about spending our days playing golf, when, apparently, we 'should be working harder'.

Bizarrely, just as I thought I would never straighten up my approach, everything clicked. Technology showed I had been down five or six miles per hour when bowling in training, stemming from an inability to get through the crease properly. Then, one morning I came off half a run, putting only half effort in, just to try to get loose. The first ball came out of the hand so easily, swung and hit Gibbo's baseball mitt hard.

What's going on here? It was almost like my muscle memory had come back to where it previously was without even realizing it. Who cared?

I didn't bother dwelling on what had happened. I was just so pleased that whatever I had been doing over the previous week had produced a positive effect. Admittedly, I didn't feel 100 per cent right when I came out of the opening win over South Africa A in Bloemfontein with figures of 6.3-1-22-4. But I did feel a lot better.

It all started with an off-the-cuff delivery, of course, but one result of those practices in January 2015, is that whenever I now come to a bowling session, I never approach it off my full run. I concentrate on staying nice and straight, and strong, at the crease. If I feel like the ball is coming out at a nice pace without charging in, I know everything is in good order, and that everything should be fine when I switch to a match scenario. It's worked for me so far, and I intend to stick to the policy.

As for the batting, things were going from strength to strength. I hit 31 in the four-wicket win in Bloem, then 30 off 17 deliveries in a Jason Roy-boosted total of 376-9 in Kimberley. You don't tend to lose with that kind of score on the board, and at 2–0 up we were oozing confidence as a team.

There is no doubt that collective confidence influenced my actions in the Pretoria township of Mamelodi. The third game in Potchefstroom had been abandoned, we could not lose the series, and in such an equation you have everything to gain. The pitch we were playing on was surprisingly quick for an outground, and they had an attack with some pace in it, including Marchant de Lange, the fastest of South Africa's quick men.

We were plenty for not many – 215-4 to be exact – when Jonny Bairstow got out, and Sam Billings walked in. I had 55 off 50 balls, and had played pretty normally, other than punishing the spinners by hitting them for six.

I gave Sam a couple of overs to settle in, and then informed him: 'Right. I'm going to go now.' We were 225-4, and there were 10 of our 50 overs remaining. My consideration was that getting another 100 off 60 balls, rather than think about my personal landmark, was what was required. If anything I was focused on getting to 150 rather than three figures.

There was a lot of focus on how England were approaching one-day innings at that time during the triangular tournament involving Australia and India. But my mind was a million miles away from that. Here, I was faced with a small boundary on a good wicket. And with another batsman who loves to dominate, as my partner.

'I could get out any ball – but if I don't, I'll see you at the end of every over,' I told him.

The boundaries were on the small side. I'm not sure I would have managed 15 sixes on a normal-sized ground. But it was mega fun. Together, Sam and I put on 132 in 10.4 overs. South Africa A tried everything. But I was swinging, I had my eye in and there was nothing to lose. Even when I plinked a couple they still carried the rope. I managed to get four over the boundary for six in De Lange's final over of the innings, and we bettered our previous best total in the series by two runs. I hadn't given much thought to that hundred – it all happened in a whirl, but I enjoyed myself, and walked off 151 not out off just 86 balls.

This England Lions XI was playing in a certain way, and it was mint. Later we would be asked why we were able to do this against South Africa's second string attack, while the senior England team struggled to score with any freedom at all against the white ball. I could only answer from a Lions perspective, and say that it was 100 per cent the nature of the players we had in the side.

A team with Jason Roy at the top is always going to be adventurous. His presence seemed to rub off on Alex Lees, who is a bit restrained in terms of strokeplay but suddenly fed off the way other guys were playing and became more expansive. Then came James Vince, Jonny Bairstow, myself, Sam Billings in the middle order.

The combination of the players we possessed, and their attitude to cricket, were decisive factors. It wasn't like we were aiming for this target or that when we went out to bat, we were just looking to express ourselves without any fear of the consequences.

We had a dynamic team, and it shouldn't be a surprise that we have taken that kind of character and attitude effectively to the next level. All the young guys that come into county cricket now are looking to entertain. Why is that? You would have to think it's the influence of Twenty20.

They have been brought up in the era that the game has been established. The way cricket is going, everyone wants to be scoring at a certain rate. I feel a part of that.

In a high-scoring series in South Africa, I was showing how much damage I could do given half a chance. Since joining the Renegades, everything had been on the up and up for me. I had gone from one end of the spectrum to the other. I was no longer thinking about the England team, how badly I had done, or how far off a recall might be. I was simply enjoying doing well again. Sure, it wasn't the team I was wanting to be doing well for. But I was back to where I wanted to be on so many levels. My enjoyment level was high and I was playing in a position in which I was happy and effective. It felt like I was on the rise again.

After that telephone conversation with Jimmy in my TV room a month earlier, I was furious. I hadn't even been given an opportunity. I had been batting at number fricking eight. Picked as a bowler, when I had always considered myself as a batting all-rounder. I was not playing the role I was used to playing.

I carried the anger through the tour of Sri Lanka. But as I was playing for England, and I love playing for England, I would have done anything asked of me to be on the field. It was the only way I could get into the team, so I had to grin and bear it. They were not going to bat me anywhere else. The frustration of it all was festering. I kept reminding myself I was a batter, that I needed to make some runs, but I simply could not make that transition to going in six wickets down.

I couldn't find a tempo. I was out of sorts. I was spewing how badly I had done. It was embarrassing. I tried to be calm about things. I didn't want to rock the boat. The last thing the England team needs is a moaner. So I tried, unsuccessfully, to fulfil the requirements. I just came up way short. But at least the chairman of selectors knew where I was coming from. I was quite blunt but certainly wasn't an idiot about it. Crucially, I had got my point across. Even more crucially, I had backed it up.

12

The 2015 World Cup was an absolute disaster for England. Sometimes maybe you become a better player when you are not in the team. But it was clear there was support for me to be selected again from former players and the media.

I had not been involved in the matches England played in the first three months of the year, but, back in the reckoning as I flew out with the England squad to the Caribbean in early April, I knew I had a huge chance of getting into that first Test team. Moeen Ali was sidelined with a side strain, and it meant there was a place open for an all-rounder. I was hungry for the opportunity. This was my chance for a fresh start.

Did I put more pressure on myself to go well in the nets? No, not really, because I know deep down that what you do in the nets hasn't much bearing on selection. Nevertheless, I worked extremely hard to get myself into form with ball and bat, so that when it came to that first team selection I gave Alastair Cook and Peter Moores concrete reasons for picking me. In my mind, I wanted to force their hands rather than them favouring me over someone else in a 50/50 selection call. I wanted them to be clear: 'Yeah, we're picking Stokesy.'

It worked. The warm-up games were good; it felt like a real achievement to be told I was back in the team. Jonathan Trott was back too, and it looked like being a happy return for both of us in Antigua. We dominated the Test, and were on course to win, all the way up to lunch on the final day. But from that point, Jason Holder, the West Indies captain, played really well. He is an extremely talented all-round cricketer and his form in that innings in particular was that of a Test match number five or six batsman, not a number eight. His disciplined, unbeaten hundred saved the match for his side – and the series as things turned out.

During the first innings of the next Test in Grenada, we all gave Marlon Samuels some verbal stick. I already had some history with him from the England Lions tour four years earlier, and was not shy in joining in while he was batting. In fact, just about everyone in an England shirt was having a word. 'You've got 35 now, your average is in check, you can get out' – all that kind of stuff.

Marlon has a reputation for getting very focused on personal landmarks. He is someone who traditionalists would call a red-inker. Once he got to his 50, off 142 balls, he tried to hit every ball for four. Then, when he got to 80 he took his time again, went into his shell, to make sure he got to three figures. It was no surprise that immediately after he did, he went on another counter-attack and fell trying to hit Jimmy Anderson out the park.

Quite honestly, it wasn't as though it was uniquely an issue between the two of us. It wasn't as though I was saying anything he hadn't heard before. Nor was I saying anything different from the rest of the England lads. It became personal on the third evening when I received a filthy long hop from the leg-spinner Devendra Bishoo that screamed 'whack me'.

How on earth did I toe it straight to the man at deep square leg? It was so infuriating.

I have no idea why Marlon saluted me, as I trudged off the field.

'You might look good on camera, Marlon, but no one f**king likes you,' I told him.

I was fuming. Later, the other lads like Joe Root – who was stood at the other end of the pitch as I made my walk of shame – made me see the funny side of it. The following day we laughed about it. Even then, I felt I couldn't allow him to have one over on me. Sometimes things cast a long shadow. So when we won the Test match 24 hours later, Ottis Gibson, our bowling coach, and I saluted each other in full view of all the photographers. I had to have the last word.

Unfortunately, West Indies had the last word in the series, and the result in Barbados was a really bad one for us. It was an unusual pitch for the Kensington Oval; it lacked its usual pace and bounce and there was quite a lot of rough for their spinners to work with from the start. Aside from Alastair Cook's hundred, we just didn't bat well, and even though we were in a good position for the first half of the game, our second innings contributed to that position being eroded.

Credit where it was due, a chase of 194 was not straightforward in such a low-scoring match and Darren Bravo played a nice innings to seal their win. From our side, though, it was a disappointing way to let the series slip. We had dominated the majority of it, made all the running, and so to allow them back in at the very last was really poor.

Afterwards, it wasn't very positive chat that filled our dressing room. We had been given a lesson in ruthlessness; our opponents shouldn't be allowed back into contests that we dominate for such long periods. We need to beat teams like West Indies in Test cricket every time we play them, if we want to be universally accepted as the number one team in the world. Failing to do so is not negotiable. We knew we had to be so much better in the kind of situation we found ourselves at Bridgetown. Not for the first time, a bad spell let us down.

It was our last series under Peter Moores. I really got on well with him as a bloke. Frankly, though, I don't think I quite got him as a coach. He was a little bit too technical for me, used too many big words and probably spoke a bit too much to get the best out of me. On several occasions, I listened to him speak and didn't quite get where he was going. If you talk to me long enough, I hear but I don't listen.

I thought he overanalyzed stuff. Sure, cricket can be a difficult, complex game but if you play it as well as international players do, it can be simplified. That's the way I have always viewed it. But I often found Peter wanted to go more in-depth and that lost me. I left a few chats thinking, 'I've not gained much from that.'

But I had no issues with him, aside from one that cropped up during that West Indies series. When Moeen Ali came back to fitness in mid-April, I got dropped back down to seven in the batting order, despite scoring 79 and 35 in the draw in Antigua. Immediately, it struck me that it was a decision I needed to challenge. But I didn't want to rock the boat, so I carried on playing, and waited for the end of the tour.

My question to Peter, and Paul Farbrace who was in attendance with him, was simple: I had scored runs trying to push the game on, so didn't I deserve to be staying at number six? I thought so. I wanted the recognition I believed my efforts merited. Peter's argument was that Mo had done well at six previously.

'Yeah, so have I,' I countered. I was averaging 40 at six. Well, 38.66 to be exact.

Peter challenged me on the number of games I was talking about. The answer was five, stretching from the start of my career in the 2013–14 Ashes to that first Test at the Sir Vivian Richards Stadium. I wasn't in his face, I just felt my point warranted being made. I would rather talk straight, and he is a similar kind of bloke.

When we got home, there was a bigger change. Peter was sacked as England coach. It had been debated in the media for over a week, and for him it had probably been a bad time to get the job in the first place. He took on the role when England weren't doing very well, and the coach gets the blame if results don't go as anticipated.

● ● ●

From a personal perspective, I assessed my performances out in the Caribbean. I felt I had been playing alright – there were runs in the first Test and starts in the other two – but I noticed a bad habit from my youth was prominent. My back foot was moving towards the leg-side, meaning

I found it hard to score when balls were hung out on what we call a fifth or sixth stump line. I was so far away from the pitch of the ball that I was lacking control when driving through the off-side.

The best players in the world hit through cover, extra-cover and point, but the only way I could score square or backward of it was to run the ball down to third man. Eventually, though, West Indies worked this out, countering it by placing fielders at gully and third man. They dried up a scoring area and opened up the potential for a dismissal. Twice I got out on the tour, caught in that region.

Back at Durham, I decided it was necessary to find a way to stop my weight moving away from the ball and get it going towards it, so I worked with Alan Walker, one of our coaches, in the nets, for half a dozen sessions of half an hour each, trying to get my foot to go from middle stump to middle and off, rather than towards leg. Where previously, it was slipping a stump's width to the right, I wanted it to be no further than middle from this point onwards.

Whack kept his eye on my movements, making sure they both reduced in size and appeared as natural as possible. After just a few sessions, he reckoned everything looked better. He had never seen me hit the ball as consistently straight down the ground, he said, and any vulnerability against lbw was reduced. I had got into a habit of playing balls on middle stump to the leg-side. Now I was hitting them back down the pitch.

I'm not a person to study my technique unless I feel something is not in order – and when I do it's the back foot movement I look for. If I'm hitting the ball sweetly through the 'V', it's a sign my feet are where I want them to be. Eventually, I want the newly imposed trigger to be second nature. I used to be so open, and if you look at footage of me when I was first breaking into the team at Durham and now, there is such a huge difference.

The challenge was to come in the first Test match of the summer, and for all the work you do to change your technique, the biggest worry is taking it into a competitive environment. So you can imagine what the two scores against New Zealand at Lord's did for my confidence.

People talk about breakthrough moments in careers and this was undoubtedly mine. Although I didn't score a hundred in the first innings, the manner in which I played summed up the style I want to be known for. Skilful, combative and most importantly entertaining: these are the qualities I seek to show in my game. To be portrayed as an exciting cricketer.

I live for the kind of buzz that this match gave me, and there was a real feeling of 'this is me' when I walked off that field, after scoring 92 to put us into a good position. It was certainly a much healthier position than we had been in when I joined Joe Root at 30 for four. The reception I received was addictive. As a performer, how could you not want more of that? Most importantly, it showed that I could be successful at international cricket by trusting in my methods.

One thing had been massively significant when I walked through the Long Room that morning. Not what the scoreboard read. No, that didn't bother me. There was a spring to my step because of the faith Paul Far-brace had shown in me on the eve of the series. To be told I would be back at number six did wonders for my confidence.

Later, the New Zealanders told me that when they saw Moeen Ali frantically running around the boundary, after we lost a couple of early wickets, they presumed I had padded up in an emergency. They weren't the only ones expressing surprise that I was batting there.

After all the stress of the winter, being snubbed and then shifted back down the order in the Caribbean, I finally felt where I wanted to be in this England team. On my previous Test appearance at Lord's I'd bagged a pair.

In swinging conditions, Tim Southee and Trent Boult are a real handful, but in a way that played into our hands this time. Sure, you have to be fully on your game when quality bowlers are moving the ball around at that kind of pace and testing you with every single delivery. Boult has two different gears, I find. He can bowl at 80 mph and swing it prodigiously and he can also slip himself up to 86 mph and still get it hooping enough, and that makes him a difficult customer to deal with. I'm not sure if it's just a rhythm thing or if he is a master at finding the right pace for the conditions, but he wasn't at express here. His main threat was movement through the air.

You can tell you are up against a Brendon McCullum team by looking around the field. You won't see conventional and defensive field settings. There will be three slips, two gullys and no mid-on, and that might be the case in one-day cricket, as he showed in the 2015 World Cup, as well as Test matches.

Some captains place their hands over their faces when things don't go well for them. Not Brendon. There's no biting of nails, cursing or grunting, just a smile and a positive attitude. One of his signatures is to chase the ball as hard as possible until the second it hits the boundary. His attitude is infectious. He's totally carefree and it's a great way to be. New Zealand also fully respect the game. When the Australian Phil Hughes passed away, they didn't bowl a bouncer as a mark of respect. There is no sledging. It's just cricket with a smile on the face.

Because of the gaps in the field, anything loose was flying to the boundary, and I got into the 20s at better than a run a ball. It was clear at this point that the New Zealanders were trying to bump me as often as possible. My response was to try to tap the ball on its head for a single. It was a rare piece of caution from me, and I got a flea in the ear from Joe. The pull shot has always been a big one for me, one I've always had confidence in executing.

'Forget that. Just whack it. That's what you do,' he told me.

It made a huge difference. I was still finding the guys on the fence but it was reaching them a lot quicker, and it's a completely different feeling when you are nailing the ball out the middle of the bat. Joe and I share the same philosophy. If you get a ball that's hittable, you hit it. If you get a good ball, leave it alone.

They were offering some full half-volleys because they were desperately trying to nick us off, and there were gaps to hit those half-volleys into because they had so many catchers around the bat. New Zealand's positive tactics played into our hands. And we carried on from there. It created quite a different atmosphere from what we were accustomed.

The customary Lord's hum, which comes from everyone talking, gave way to lots of roars and cheers. I have not played in a Test match there, even the Ashes Test that was to follow that summer, in which the crowd was so energetic and loud.

Perhaps it was the way New Zealand were playing, or because of the way we responded; perhaps it was just the excitement of a first Test match of the summer, or because they were anticipating the great Test match it turned out to be.

What was clear was that it felt like we had turned over a new leaf. In the build-up, we had talked about wanting this England team to play more positively. But it was one thing saying it, another doing it. Typical me then that the way I got out, after playing so positively, was so lame. I had a complete 'mare against Mark Craig, the off-spinner, and left a straight one.

New Zealand were miles ahead of the game at halfway in the match, after scoring 523 at a similar rate, but from my point of view I just wanted to carry on where I'd left off when my chance came again at 220 for four. We were 86 runs in front, and Alastair Cook was anchoring the innings, two short of his hundred. I took 10 balls to get off the mark and rode my luck a little but, just as in the first innings, New Zealand's attacking intent played into my hands.

I got to 50 at a run a ball, taking advantage of those gaps again. Then they went back to the short plan against me to try to get a soft dismissal. In my head, I had already decided to hit long. I got three away into the stands, the beans were going and every boundary was greeted by 'Whoa!' It sent shivers down my back.

What a feeling it was to get a hundred at Lord's, and to receive an ovation like that. I had no idea at the time that it was the fastest Test hundred by an England batsman at Lord's. I just loved being able to entertain a full house. The 101 that I scored came in a 132-run stand for the fifth wicket. That buzz, again.

The connection to the people in the stands was something else. On the final afternoon, with the place jammed again, the response to my dismissal of Kane Williamson was incredible. Running in to Brendon McCullum, it felt like a hat-trick ball it was so loud out there in the middle. It was a moment I will never forget. They roared me to the crease, and when the ball got through him it was pandemonium – the lads went crazy, the stands bounced. It was just mega.

New Zealand don't give you anything cheaply, and even at five down in the first hour after lunch, we knew it was still a long road ahead. We tried to dislodge their remaining batsmen by any means possible, but we weren't expecting to get any of them caught at third man like Trent Boult was, off Stuart Broad, to give us the win with less than 10 overs remaining. It was getting quite tense out there and none of us wanted to believe that we would be denied by numbers ten and eleven.

But the fact that it went all the way down to the wire was in keeping with the game, which was of the highest class. Fair play to New Zealand because they refused to let up at the next Test at Headingley. And fair play to the England supporters because they stuck with us despite defeat there.

Little things went against us in Leeds. For a start, Stuart Broad was ill for the entire Test match. He didn't warm up and then slept on the physio's bed before taking the field, towel on his head, bucket by his side. Even off colour, he came out and took five wickets.

Again, it was an even contest and the scores were level pegging after one innings. Quite honestly, though, we should have scored so many more. We were flying when Adam Lyth completed his first Test match hundred, and 135 runs behind with nine wickets intact. In gloomy conditions, the contest changed once the floodlights went on. What had been a fairly placid pitch previously, under artificial light presented a completely different challenge. Give the New Zealand attack any assistance and it can be deadly. They had a brand new ball and it swung around corners. Headingley is not the greatest viewing ground and in these conditions we could not cope. After that, New Zealand simply batted us out of the contest with their attacking style.

As for me, although I failed twice there, I was playing in the style that got me into the England team in the first place and with a technique that was sound. Those two innings at Lord's got me going again. The real me had been lost for a while. I had not been sure what I was meant to be doing within the England team. Now I knew. And it fitted into a new team philosophy.

Only three months had gone by, but the World Cup was now a distant memory. This was a fresh start. Several of us had not been in Australia and New Zealand, and if we wanted to make strides forward as a team there was no point looking back.

The batting line-up selected for the Royal London Series was full of dynamic cricketers who wanted to express themselves. Even those down the bottom – players like David Willey, Adil Rashid and Liam Plunkett – were quality ball-strikers.

Suddenly, it was like, 'Check us out.' There was a big focus on getting spectators to enjoy watching England play white-ball cricket again. There was to be no safety-first option considered, and I would be surprised to hear any fan say that the team that represented them was not fun. The excitement came from batters scoring 60-ball hundreds, ramping, paddle-sweeping, monstering the ball 100 metres, and out the ground. From a bowling point of view, we were looking to take wickets. Our one-day cricket had gone through a revolution, no doubt.

Eoin Morgan, our captain, told us he no longer wanted to impose limits on us. From now on we were to express ourselves.

To be part of the England team at Edgbaston for the first match of five was truly amazing. So much talk preceded it, about how we wanted to play, and it was sweet to deliver everything we had discussed. It's easy to overlook the fact that we lost a wicket to the first ball of the game.

Having watched Jason Roy drive straight to point, Joe Root could have begun his innings conservatively. He chose not to, and to come in at number three to strike a 71-ball 100 gave everyone around him the belief to keep going, to be true to our word, to stick to the plan. There was no going back into shells. In that moment, Joe showed he was becoming a senior player.

We scored 408 for nine in that match. Our batting was relentless. Everyone chipped in. We were losing wickets, but when I went in I was focused on the positive. There was no thought of letting the run rate drop, even though four of us were dismissed in the space of eight overs in mid-innings. We were flying but six wickets down. Jos Buttler carried on as only he can, and surpassed Joe's century achievement by five deliveries – a new England record. Jos was awesome. So was Adil Rashid.

Suddenly, 300 was only an okay score in 50 overs. Ten years previously you won the game with that kind of total. Nowadays, even 350–360 isn't safe, and we showed that by pushing hard to make 379 in 46 overs in the second match at the Oval.

Rain was the only thing that halted our charge. The series was showing that the overs between 25–39, formerly the tick-along period of singles and no risks, were consigned to the past. Twenty20 cricket has enhanced everyone's scoring options and made people realize the greater possibilities that exist.

At the Rose Bowl, Eoin Morgan showed no fear in taking the boundary fielders on when going for sixes. Even when bowlers had two men set back, he was still going for his shots, and when your captain does that it sends out a positive message to the rest of the team. I opted to play like that from the start, particularly against the left-arm spinner Mitchell Santner, and it was fun. Though not so fun later to hear some criticism that we didn't bat out our 50 overs. There was a lot of focus on the 34 balls of the innings we had left unused. I contributed to that, as one of a flurry of five late wickets. But I had also contributed 68, off 47 balls, and I was trying to get us to the score of 350 that would enhance our chances of a win, not play it safe for the 320. I chose the positive option.

Old school had got us nowhere, though, and thankfully the mutterings didn't last long. At Trent Bridge, our new fearless approach witnessed the shattering of the record for England's highest ever run chase – what once was 305 but now stood at 350. We had knocked off a huge total, to stay in the series, with five overs to spare. Eoin Morgan and Joe Root paced their hundreds to get the game done and dusted well ahead of time. Thirty balls ahead of time was quite ridiculous.

It was an infectious attitude, and that was shown in the decider on my home patch in Durham. When Jos damaged his finger on the eve of the contest, in came Jonny Bairstow, a batsman in the form of his life. What a perfect guy to come into a tough situation. It felt normal for him to come in, and rescue a victory with a man-of-the-match knock. It was an amazing environment to be a part of, as records tumbled every match. We hit 14 sixes in the opening match; never before had England managed 300 plus in three consecutive matches; we did that and then made it four; we scored at a rate in excess of seven an over. It's the type of series anyone would want to be involved in.

● ● ●

We were playing well across all formats. Yet the Australians were very cocky about their chances even before their arrival for the main series of the summer. Their guys playing at the Indian Premier League were very confident, Steve Smith being one.

'I can't wait to get over there and play another Ashes against England in their conditions after beating them so convincingly in Australia,' Smith said. 'It's going to be nice to go into their backyard. If we continue to play the way we have been playing over the last 12–18 months, I don't think they'll come close to us.'

Not that we remembered his comments word for word, or played the

Cricinfo video clip back over the dressing-room speakers at Trent Bridge after we won and laughed about it.

Maintaining the enjoyment aspect was a big part of it and our new coach Trevor Bayliss ensured that happened. I first met Trevor at the airport on the way to our pre-Ashes trip in Marbella, and found him to be a man of few words. I wasn't sure whether that was going to change – perhaps he was just getting to know us before opening up? Maybe he was sussing everyone out, letting others speak initially while he just observed. No, as it turns out, that's just him. He's a very relaxed guy, and what you see is what you get. A typical Aussie in that regard.

I can remember one of his first statements to the group when we got to Puerto Banus for a few days of fielding, fitness and socializing. Some of the fitness stuff was done on bikes, and I was one of those at the front on a cycle ride, alongside Steven Finn. We were due to all meet up at the beach for a bit of football. In the distance, we could see a guy walking, and as we got closer it struck me.

He's got no clothes on.

He wore a backpack but nothing else – his nether regions on full show. Another bloke was pushing a wheelchair. Both he and the woman in it were completely naked.

The 15 of us plus support staff were arriving at our destination in dribs and drabs. When he saw what was going on, it was typical of Mark Wood to strip off and bike down to join the rest of us. He's always up for the craic.

Trev was like, 'What the hell have I come into here?'

Truth is he had come into a happy camp. And one with a focus on winning – but winning the right way. We already had confidence from the way we had played in the Tests against New Zealand. Momentum exists in cricket, but only within individual games, I reckon, not from game to game. It wasn't momentum we took into the Ashes. It was a feelgood factor.

Undoubtedly, the way we played from the start took Australia by surprise. They didn't have the same team as they had in the 2013–14 whitewash, and they let early chances to dominate us slip through their grasp. There were changes in their personnel, such as the loss of Ryan Harris from their attack, but, quite honestly, do you think we were giving what they were doing a second thought? Why worry about what they could do? As far as we were concerned, it was all about us.

Things could have been different: for example, if Brad Haddin had caught Joe Root on nought after we batted first in Cardiff. He didn't, and Joe took advantage to hit one of his finest hundreds, building the platform for our win in partnership with Gary Ballance.

Gary's 61 on that opening day was crucial and showed the strength of the England team during the five matches. Even when guys were struggling for their best form, they stood up at challenging times. Gary's innings went unseen in the kind of scorecard we produced, but it allowed myself and Moeen Ali to come in and play our own natural games in adding 50s apiece. It set the tone. Ian Bell would go on to score two half-centuries at Edgbaston. In between, it was the other guys like Joe backing up. We had at least one guy putting in a potentially match-winning performance every Test match. Australia lacked that.

We had opened a 122-run lead ahead of our second innings, which would begin with a tricky 40-minute period before lunch on the third day. Normally, from my experience, you will get a command from the coach at this point, something like, 'Right lads, everyone in.' He will stand in the middle of the room and begin that 10-minute changeover period with a pep talk.

But the music remained on, and Trevor just calmly walked around, while the opening batsmen Alastair Cook and Adam Lyth were putting their pads on, saying, 'Remember, it's not how long we bat for, it's how many runs we score.' That was all he said to us. There were no targets, no guidelines, no do this, don't do that. I was sat with Mo and we just looked at each other as if to say, 'This bloke will do for us.'

When you have your coach saying that, it gives you a licence to play your own way. For many of our batsmen that means expansively, and that is the reason why when we have scored big runs during his time as England coach, we have done it fast. In both batting innings in Cardiff, we scored at a rate in excess of four runs per over. In both bowling innings we caught brilliantly. The work in Spain had paid off, and we headed to Lord's 1–0 up after a 169-run win.

Lord's wasn't a great Test match for us. Australia were better in all departments. It was a slow wicket, it was hard to get anything out of it, and Steve Smith and Chris Rogers played really well. When you are out in the field as long as the Australians kept us out there, I always feel sorry for my team's opening batsmen. It must be so tough to switch back on again.

Adam Lyth went second ball, one of four wickets inside the first dozen overs and there was a feeling of déjà vu when I went out to meet Alastair

Cook at 30 for four, the exact score when I entered the fray against the New Zealanders two months earlier.

This time, I got a partnership going with Cooky, and a few early boundaries on the Saturday morning suggested I was in touch and capable of doing something really special. For a while, it felt like the New Zealand Test all over again. There was a nice reception, the ball was coming out the middle of the bat, and I felt in good order. But the dreaded 87 did me, a drag-on from a Mitchell Marsh delivery that kept low, and left me questioning whether Lord's is a ground for me after all. Some people have got grounds where they feel at home, and always perform well. Yes, I got those two scores earlier in the summer. But I also got a pair against India.

The second innings, after Michael Clarke opted not to enforce the follow-on, was a complete disaster, summed up by my dismissal. It was another brain fart by yours truly. Joe Root pushed a single into the leg-side off Marsh and all I could think as I was running was 'the ball's going to hit me'. I was bracing to be struck on the back by Mitchell Johnson's throw from mid-on, which caused me to hunch my body as I passed the crease, rather than concentrate on running my bat in. It was embarrassing when I looked up at the screen to see how far I was over the line, without having grounded anything beyond it, at the point Johnson's shy broke the stumps.

It's hard for me to deny that I'm one of those people that has these stupid moments. It didn't help the team doing that kind of thing when we were already under serious pressure. We were blown away, by a margin of 405 runs, and people began speaking as though what had happened in South Wales was simply a false dawn.

Around this time, there was a big media debate about the kind of pitches this England team wanted to play on – some nonsense that we were ordering groundsmen around the country to prepare low, slow surfaces. Do you truly think those were the characteristics that best helped us? Come on. What we really wanted was nip, swing and carry, and that's what we got for the rest of the series.

We were wanting a typical English wicket. Our bowling unit relies on swing – we knew Mitchell Starc and Mitchell Johnson would get wickets with out-and-out pace, but generally if the ball is going through the air or off the seam then our bowling attack is a handful for any batting line-up. The first two pitches weren't to our liking, we just adapted better in Cardiff.

In contrast, the one at Edgbaston for the third Test was quite quick throughout the entire duration of the match. It meant the nicks Jimmy Anderson, Stuart Broad and Steven Finn got flew at catchable height.

In between Australia's innings of 136 and 265, Johnson was like his old self. It was fair to say that he clicked on the second morning. From what I had remembered of facing him in Australia two years earlier, he was nothing like that in Cardiff when the series began. He didn't feel as menacing. He just didn't have that oomph. In the winter of 2013–14, he made you mumble to yourself as a batsman: 'Christ, this guy's quick.' Very few bowlers in the world possess that ferocity.

Over the first two Tests of the summer, it hadn't felt anything like the Johnson of old that we were up against. Perhaps it was a rhythm thing, because suddenly in Birmingham it was like I had been transported back to Adelaide, and my Test debut, all over again. The two throat balls he bowled to Jonny Bairstow and myself on that second morning were unplayable, quite frankly. It was all we could do to get touches on them.

But we won the match because our own pace bowlers used the conditions so well. The only negative was that Jimmy, who took six wickets to start Australia's demise, was injured and ruled out of the next Test at Trent Bridge – one that would potentially end with us regaining the urn.

Although unable to play, Jimmy was asked by Trevor and Cooky to stick around the group, and just having him around on warm-up days, for a chat if we wanted, was good at a ground where he had enjoyed so much success.

In Jimmy's absence from the Test, Stuart Broad produced one of the great Ashes spells to leave us on the brink. Those first morning figures of eight for 15 were insane. It was a one-man show and the Australians just couldn't handle him. Eight edges, eight catches behind the wicket. Australia 60 all out.

The most pleasing thing about it all for me was that I had been complaining to Chris Taylor, our fielding coach, in the build-up: 'Mate, we do so much work with you on these speculative catches – 10 minutes every fielding session – yet it never pays off in a game. Those kind of catches just don't come along.'

Funnily enough, I had nearly latched on to a full-length drive at Edgbaston in the previous Test, but the ball had just gone over the top of my fingertips. What chance of another coming along?

Broad's reaction to my one-handed claw at gully to dismiss Adam

Voges will forever be an image synonymous with the Ashes. The crowd ooh-ed and aah-ed as they showed the replay on the big screen, and then his ridiculous shocked face, goggle-eyed with hands over mouth, came into view as the cameras panned around.

The first thing I thought when I took it was, 'At last, I've finally got one.' My response when I got up from the turf was to raise the ball up towards the home dressing-room balcony. Then, as my team-mates mobbed me, I raised the other arm to point again. It was an acknowledgement to Chris that all that extra work *had* paid off after all. I have never taken one better. I'm not in the catching positions that often, the ball had gone past me, but the intensive practice had made the difference.

It was the start of a stunning seven sessions of cricket for us – the time it took to move into an unassailable 3–1 lead. By the end of the day, Joe Root's second hundred of the series had put us 214 runs ahead. By lunch on day two, Australia had begun batting again needing 331 to avoid an innings defeat.

Yet for a 90-minute period either side of the interval we became passive. Waiting for something to happen, it felt like we had switched off completely. Australia's opening pair of David Warner and Chris Rogers had put on more than 100, and for the first time in an England shirt I was close to losing my rag with my team-mates.

We were bossing them but it didn't feel like we had the kick in us we had shown the previous day. Mark Wood had taken a wicket off a no-ball, some Australian fans were getting stuck into me in the crowd, and I wasn't having it. I felt we were in need of a gee-up, so when Woody did make the breakthrough I roared into the huddle: 'For f**k's sake, lads, you would think we were the team however many behind, not them.'

People have suggested I couldn't bowl any better than I was to do for the remainder of that innings. Yeah, I bowled well and of course I enjoyed myself, but quite honestly I didn't feel I ever had 100 per cent rhythm.

Jimmy's ability to get aerial movement at Trent Bridge had served England so well over the years. Now, in his absence it was my turn, and because it was swinging so lavishly I was letting the ball do all the work. I was running in quite wildly, dipping in and out on my approach, and the ball was coming out at only 82–83 mph.

Sometimes you hear commentators praising bowlers for finding the right pace to bowl to allow the ball to swing. However, I have to admit that this was not the case with me. I was putting in all my effort but the ball was just plopping out, and that's what happens to a bowler when he doesn't have rhythm. It comes out a lot slower than you are aiming for. Normally I would be up at 86–87 mph, so I was 3–4 mph down on average. But because I was putting it into decent areas, things were happening for me. On a flat deck, without that kind of movement, it would have been a different story.

Sometimes when the ball is swinging, it hits the pitch and seems to picks up pace. This was one of those occasions. I was especially effective to the left-handers. From experience, as a left-hander myself, I know that when a bowler is coming around the wicket and swinging the ball away, it's hard to line the ball up. Even more so with the way I jump out, delivering from wide of the stumps, angling it in, before it veers away.

I have had a couple of masters to learn from in this regard in Jimmy and Broady. My skill execution has got a lot better since watching them.

The confidence to do it also increased throughout the summer. It coincided with feeling like a fourth seamer on merit in the eyes of Alastair Cook. The fact he was giving me more opportunities was an acknowledgement I could hold my own as a bowler, and it was important for me to know my captain had faith in both aspects of my game. As a genuine all-rounder it was great to know I had a chance to be an influence across all four innings of a match.

Despite the early afternoon lull, it was developing into an amazing atmosphere. As the wickets tumbled, people around the field were reminding each other, 'We haven't won the game yet.' Of course, we knew we had. There was no chance they were going to come back from this. It was only a matter of when, and that was exciting.

I claimed five of the seven wickets to fall on that Friday, yet it still might have been considered a surprise that Cooky ignored the claims of Stuart Broad to open the bowling – especially given his first-innings carnage – to throw the ball to me and Mark Wood at the start of that historic Saturday. I was hoping that would be the case and you can imagine it felt pretty cool when he told me in the dressing room I would be starting at the Radcliffe Road End. I loved being at the centre of things. I still take more joy out of scoring a hundred but I haven't taken as many five-fers in my career, so I was raring to do it in an Ashes series, and to make that six before Woody delivered the final blow just before midday.

To win the Ashes back meant we achieved the main goal of our 2015 summer. When conditions were in our favour we were clinical. When they were not – at Lord's and in the series finale at the Oval – we were not so good and were defeated by huge margins. But a series victory by any scoreline was what we were after. We knew that Australia would come at us hard in that fifth Test. They may have lost the series but they play it tough and there was the added incentive of giving Michael Clarke, their outgoing captain, a send-off.

Sometimes Australia play it too tough. Now, I have been dismissed in some pretty unusual manners over the years, but to be a victim of Law 37 in the one-day series that followed the Ashes was infuriating.

It was the second match at Lord's, and we were 141 for three in the 26th over, chasing 310 to level things up at 1–1. Myself and Eoin Morgan were in the process of establishing a partnership when I played a punch down the ground and initially thought it had beaten Mitchell Starc, the bowler. Next thing, though, I saw him ready to load up to throw and natural instinct just took over.

As I turned, I put my hand up to protect myself. When a fast bowler bowls at you, it's from 22 yards. Now he was in his follow-through, and I was out of my ground, that distance had reduced by about half. With my head turning, my body twisting to dive back into my crease, the ball somehow struck my outstretched palm. I was not looking and I don't know how my hand managed to be down there in the line of the throw. It was not intentional; it was a reaction to protect myself.

I'm not even sure Starc appealed to start off with, only joining in after being prompted by a 'howzat' from the wicketkeeper Matthew Wade. Next thing Steve Smith, the Aussie one-day captain, is carrying on. So I took myself out of the crowd of Australians, to avoid an argument, and joined Eoin, leaving it up to the umpires Tim Robinson and Kumar Dharmasena, who appeared to be in agreement that I was simply taking evasive action and therefore not out.

As tends to happen in these kinds of incident, though, the decision got passed upstairs. Joel Wilson, the third umpire, viewed it in slow motion, and that, of course, made it look a whole lot worse than what it was. But just think about it. And think about it in full speed. I was turning as he took aim, and he threw as hard as he possibly could. To judge that I willfully handled the ball was ridiculous. I was really annoyed. The best placed people to judge whether my actions were intentional were the on-field officials, in my opinion. Did they really think so? When Eoin discussed it with them, they had thought not.

Once the decision was made, that was that, but if England had been fielding I think common sense would have prevailed and we would have recognized that there was no chance our opponent had purposely done it. We would have withdrawn our appeal.

England v Australia matches are always going to be competitive. During an Ashes summer things get heated and because of the rivalry, that heat is turned up a notch or two. But any aggro remained on the field. We had beers together after every individual series, and I didn't hold a grudge. When you move onto the next game everything that has gone on is forgotten about, as far as I'm concerned. We weren't going to replay it, were we? So there was no point in dwelling on it, and the whole episode probably masked the fact we had not played well in the first two matches of the Royal London Series.

Our better games came in the next two, and although we lost the decider in Manchester, we had finished a hugely enjoyable summer with a combined score of 5–5 against New Zealand and Australia, the two World Cup finalists. We defeated both in Twenty20 internationals. Few would have believed that possible five months earlier. This team had come a long way.

13

Remembering how England received a bit of a bump against Pakistan immediately after the great Ashes series of 2005, I wanted to make sure that I was fully prepared for the challenge we faced at the start of the 2015–16 winter.

It was going to be completely different from the kind of cricket we had been playing throughout the summer, both conditions-wise plus the way Pakistan would play in comparison to Australia. We had just come out of a full-on, all-action series, where things happen quickly.

Facing Pakistan in the United Arab Emirates was going to prove quite a contrast, and I needed to tailor my practice with that in mind. So, after a couple of weeks off at the end of the 2015 season, I headed into the indoor school at the Riverside. I wanted to try to replicate some of what I was going to encounter in those desert-type conditions, by finding an old ball that wouldn't swing. In the UAE it doesn't do anything off the seam, and swings conventionally for only short spells when the ball is new, before I tend to come on. So I would have to unearth a different way of being successful before it starts reverse swinging later in the innings; of playing my part with the ball as the team's all-rounder.

I set myself the task of bowling dots and lots of them – area, area, area – to try to get into a groove before we flew out there. I wanted to be so well drilled, to get a head start. I knew the kind of cricket we were going to have to play out there. Discipline would be key for our bowlers.

With regards to batting, I didn't really feel anything I could do indoors would replicate the actual experience of grass wickets that turn square at times, so I just concentrated on hitting lots of balls. Preparation for spin would come later, and would be needed because I had never played in a series in which spin dominated before.

I'm not bothered by having to do different work. The way I look at it, I don't want to be the same player for the next 10 years. Of course, I want to retain the positive attitude, the instinct to attack, to pressurize the opposition at every opportunity, but I also want to develop the good stuff within my game, and add more to it to get better. That's the way the best players progress.

● ● ●

Patience was going to be key at Abu Dhabi, a ground that has a reputation for sending the ball soft very early in the innings. Similarly crucial was the toss. It's a real 'bat first and apply scoreboard pressure' kind of venue. You don't have a lot to work with as a fast bowler, so when you get the opportunity, if you want to help your team put any authority on the game, you have to do it quickly. Unfortunately, it was the England attack that were asked to meet that challenge when Misbah-ul-Haq began his sequence of coin flip wins on the first morning of the series.

With such a narrow window of opportunity, there is no time for looseners, it's flat-out from the start. It was like a furnace. Exhausting. Once your four overs were up, you were cooked, quite literally, and your bowling lost its zip. At the end of a day's play in those conditions, you tend to get back to your hotel room, have some food and melt into your bed. Trust me, you get no better sleep than when you play in that kind of heat.

For me the prep also extends beyond the physical. If I know I am going to a hot country, I go on sunbeds a couple of times before we travel, just to get my skin used to the high UV levels. It's quite a contrast to a winter back in England, and while some might go on for vanity, as a pale-skinned lad I have to give myself the best chance of not frying. There is a lot more focus on hydration too. I was drinking half-water, half-Pepsi, for the extra sugar required to keep going – the liquid you lose through your body is unbelievable. So much sweat poured off us throughout the day that it felt like we were losing five kilos. Unless you are Alastair Cook, of course, a man who can score a double-hundred without changing batting gloves.

That first innings was hard work, and relatively joyless for the seam bowlers, the rewards coming later when the Pakistan batsmen started trying to hit the ball. Sometimes you can have no luck, but come back later and, even though you're bowling slower, pick up some cheap wickets. That was a fair summary of what happened to me in their first innings of 523 for eight declared. We were flogged in the field, and a couple of late wickets massaged my figures to four for 57.

It was such a good surface for batting that it was a boring Test match for the first four days. It doesn't sound great, saying that, but it was genuinely the first boring Test match I have ever played in. I knew playing cricket out there was meant to be like this – going at under three runs per over, sitting in, biding your time. But it was hard to be part of. Don't get me wrong, Shoaib Malik and Cooky were equally impressive in scoring 245 and 263 respectively. But it meant the game was going nowhere.

Then, boom. From out of nothing, the match turned. Pakistan were almost playing as if they were resigned to a stalemate, and allowed themselves a bit of fun after we secured a 75-run lead. It proved a dangerous policy. They tried to slog a few, their attitude gifting us a few wickets, and getting us interested in the possibility of a positive result. Three down while still behind, they just got a bit lackadaisical and Adil Rashid, with his googlies and leggies, proved a real weapon for us against the Pakistan tail. Hardly any of our batsmen can pick him and their lower order had a similar problem.

We all knew how good Rash had been the previous summer, and I felt sorry for him in the first innings because of how good the Pakistan batsmen are – Malik and Mohammad Hafeez being examples – at playing spin bowling. They were running down the track, missing the pitch of the ball by a couple of feet, it would spin and they would whack it anyway. If that was us, we would have been stumped. And they were sweeping balls against the spin, perfectly into the gaps for four. Sure, a leggie bowls the odd bad ball. You take that. Shane Warne sent down a few in his time. But Rash did not deserve figures of 34-0-163-0 in his first bowl in Test cricket. So, I was overjoyed for him when he got his second-innings five-fer.

Rash is one of those characters you hear people talking about on the county scene. A player really respected for his talent by opponents. I remember when I first played for Durham as a teenager, the talk was: 'Adil Rashid, he's awesome. Bowls leggies, smacks it.' He went away after being picked for England early in his career and returned at a level that was testament to how hard he works.

It was manic. It was exciting. Bowling Pakistan out inside 58 overs gave us a sniff of the most unlikely victory. We needed to chase 99 in about an hour of daylight for a 1–0 lead. We knew it was going to be tough. We knew there would be some time-wasting from the Pakistanis. Moeen Ali and Jos Buttler strode out to open. There were mutterings of, 'Bloody hell, get on with it . . .' from our dressing room towards our opponents.

'Hang on a minute,' Trevor Bayliss said. 'We would be doing exactly the same if it was us bowling, wouldn't we?'

Fair enough. Of course, we would. The light was not going to last long, and Pakistan were going to bowl their overs as slowly as possible without facing a reprimand, but we retained a positive attitude.

Come on, let's chase this down.

We gave it a crack and nearly pulled it off before the umpires Bruce Oxenford and Paul Reiffel took us off the field. We were 74 for four, 25 runs shy, having faced four overs fewer than we hoped. It had been a chase in vain, but it taught us that a Test match is never truly gone. They had a bad session; we nearly won. It was part of a painful lesson for us. We had two bad sessions; we lost the series 2–0.

● ● ●

I was ill in the days leading into the second Test match in Dubai. All the family had come out, and we headed out for dinner, to a restaurant just in front of the Burj Khalifa. We were all sat at the table, when I began feeling really ropey.

'You alright?' Clare asked.

'Just feeling knackered. Must be the heat.'

At that point Clare's mam excused herself to go to the toilet. As soon as she was back, I went. We had both got the same bug, it seemed. We got back to the hotel thinking that might be that. For me, no such luck, though. I spent the next hour wedged between the toilet and the bidet, with it coming out of both ends. Not the ideal preparation for a Test match.

I missed training the following day, confined to bed. The only good thing about the whole episode was the chance to watch the first two series of *Peaky Blinders* – how cool is Tommy Shelby?

With an injection up my backside, and 24 hours to sweat it out, I felt okay to play – not 100 per cent but good enough. I could have done without us bowling first, but I was keen to build on a few wickets and a first-innings 57 the previous week.

As a bowling unit, we did well to dismiss Pakistan for 387, and we were certainly well placed in the contest at the end of the second day at 182 for three, with Joe Root and Jonny Bairstow in tandem. But the whole complexion of the match changed when we lost seven wickets for 36 runs in 17.5 overs. I'm not sure why it happened, really. It's a question you have every right to ask but not one to which I can provide a satisfactory answer.

When we got bowled out for 103 against Australia at Lord's, Trevor Bayliss asked us a similar question: 'How do we stop a repeat?'

But we couldn't figure out why we got bowled out by the Australians. All you can say when things happen, like they did in London and Dubai, is that opposition bowlers are allowed to get on a roll in helpful conditions. Credit to them for doing their jobs. Who knows why these things happen in cricket? How one team is bowled out for 60 and the other gets 400 on the same wicket. Good bowling? Obviously, yeah. Bad batting? Perhaps, to an extent.

One thing that you can guarantee with this England team is that it will never stop fighting. Yes, in the circumstances, Pakistan held a more than useful lead, and we were back in the field a lot quicker than we anticipated. Don't forget: spells of four overs were common for the pace bowlers in this series. Remember though: rules are there to be broken.

Sometimes you can bowl for longer, and not know where the energy comes from, like I did on that third afternoon. Misbah-ul-Haq, who scored a first-innings hundred, was batting. He'd played and missed against me throughout the whole series and it felt like I had to get him eventually. There were nicks, plays and misses once more; it was doing my head in.

I bowled my four overs and asked Cooky to give me one more. After my fifth, I felt like I hadn't even bowled. I felt so fresh it was weird.

'Done?' he asked me after it.

I didn't feel like I was. I had gone from being absolutely knackered to feeling comfortable as anything. The ball was reversing a bit, I'd hit the edge of the bat a couple of times and it was going through nicely. I was in the heat of the battle, pumped up at the prospect of finally getting him out.

'No. You're not taking me off unless I bowl a ball under 84 miles an hour.'

'Deal.'

Every ball from then on, I was looking up at the big screen to check the pace. When one finally did register sub-84, he told me that was it.

'Nah, you know the speed guns always register shorter ones slower than the full ones,' I argued.

I bowled nine overs on the bounce. Misbah played well, though. Along with Younis Khan, he steered them to a total that put the game out of our reach, and forced some of us into a change of tactics.

I always go out to bat with intent. In this match, however, a different approach was required. Pakistan's attack had been strengthened by the inclusion of Yasir Shah, who was deemed unfit for Abu Dhabi. Yasir is a fairly quick leg-spinner. I wouldn't say he's easy to pick, but I felt like I had all his variations sorted in my head. His biggest strength, I reckon, is that he is on the money every ball. He is also quite low and skiddy, and that makes him harder off a pitch offering natural variation. One ball would bounce, the next would skid on, making him more dangerous than he otherwise might have been. We were set to face plenty of overs from him and Zulfiqar Babar, the slow left-armer.

I have always felt fine playing aggressively against spin. I know the areas in which I can score, but I have also been nailed by commentators for playing that way when the team doesn't need it. So this was a time to put my usual approach to one side. You won't hear me talking about survival very often, but this was a necessity. Test wins feel amazing. Test defeats suck. If we weren't able to experience the first one, I wanted to play my part in preventing the other.

All the hard work I had done in the build-up made me feel a lot easier at the crease. I faced 66 balls for 13 – obviously, the intention was to face a lot more, but I honestly didn't feel I was going to get out to the spinners. I was playing very late with soft hands, off the back foot. Alastair Cook is a great player of spin and that's what he does. It brought out another side to me that I didn't necessarily know was there as a batsman. I am an instinct player and things happen without me even thinking about them. On this particular day when I was just trying to survive, I concentrated so hard on watching the ball and making sure I didn't get out.

I know that teams regard me as not being great at the start of my innings against the slow bowlers, but I don't want opposition captains to be thinking, 'Right, let's get the spinner on.' I don't mind them thinking, 'We need to get him early,' because I'm a dangerous player. But not that I have a weakness. So that's something I have been working on really hard.

My goal here was to bat as long as possible, and I managed 80 minutes, before getting suckered by the pace bowler Imran Khan, outside off-stump.

Others took even bigger chunks of time out of the game. Adil Rashid managed four hours, all but a minute, and Mark Wood two hours. It was so close to us salvaging a draw. It showed the collective effort to improve against spin that we made the three Pakistani spinners bowl 98.3 overs between them. I have played a number of years with Woody at Durham and I would never have given him a prayer of doing that. I have seen him score counter-attacking runs before as a nightwatchman, but this was different gravy, against a ball spinning sharply from high-quality bowlers, on a worn surface.

Nobody expected it to be cut as fine. We had been eight wickets down before tea, and yet there were only 6.3 overs remaining when Rash hit straight to cover. He was cursing himself. Some were critical that it was a soft dismissal in the circumstances. But it wasn't the reaction of us, his team-mates, in the dressing room.

What an effort. Unbelievable.

It was ridiculous how well he had batted. Like Woody, he was devastated. It was not either of their faults, though. It was a collective responsibility that put us in that position – one session of madness, and the game was away from us, as far as winning went.

● ● ●

Another day, another toss won by Misbah. Pakistan's batting tempo didn't alter throughout the series – they didn't seem to come out of their box unless we offered them a half-volley. They were happy to block and leave all day long. And that was not about to change in Sharjah now they were 1–0 in front.

They hardly played a shot against our pace bowlers, and Jimmy

Anderson and Stuart Broad were outstanding, finishing with figures of 28.1-15-30-6 on a pitch with nothing in it for them. Their more aggressive approach against spin, however, cost me big time.

Fielding on the 45-degree angle behind square on the leg-side, I saw Sarfraz Ahmed go to sweep a delivery from Samit Patel, and began running round, guessing where the ball might go. As it happened, I guessed right. Unfortunately, though, in trying to pull off the diving catch the ball popped out and I landed awkwardly on my right shoulder.

The pain was incredible. To the extent that I felt like I was going to be sick on the field. Craig de Weymarn, our physio, and Rob Young, the England team doctor, were concerned when I told them that, and they put my right arm into a makeshift sling, before escorting me off, suspecting I had dislocated it.

Back in the dressing room, they lay me down and I fell asleep for 20 minutes. When I awoke they gave me an inspection, and began telling me what they suspected was wrong.

'Speak English. Stop trying to impress me with your doctor's speak,' I told them.

They confirmed it was a suspected dislocation. I couldn't move it at first above 90 degrees, and the range was limited by the sling. The problem whenever I get a run-of-the-mill injury is that I tend not to tell the truth when asked questions; I become a compulsive liar. I am Craig's worst nightmare. He has come to learn that if he asks me if I'm fit to play, I will never say no. So what is the point of asking, I tell him.

For example, in the 2015 World Twenty20, I had a bad groin. It was being iced regularly.

'Shall we go for a fitness test, mate?' he asked me ahead of the semi-final against New Zealand.

'Eh? Even if it's sore, you know I'll tell you it's fine, don't you?'

We have come to understand each other now. While yanking on an injured limb, if he asks me, 'Does this hurt?' I tend to respond through gritted teeth: 'N-o-o-o-o-o.'

It's fair to say I have spent a bit too much time with him recently. Not that I'm the only one who will do all they can to get on the field. There are some right tough nuts in our team. Jimmy Anderson is an obvious example, and Alastair Cook would have to be at the stage where he couldn't walk to be ruled out.

Craig has developed a saying: 'Help me help you.' All he wants is to protect my long-term interests. In the short term, though, I needed to find a way of batting again in a series that was still on the line, and that meant addressing the fear of hurting it again. I didn't know what I would be able to do when the time came to give it a go. From a cricket perspective, I might be able to help Stuart Broad increase our 62-run lead to 92. If so, brilliant. I couldn't do much else than prop forward and in the end we settled at 72.

Ahead of the second innings, I actually went out to the nets to check what I could do. I was thrown a few half-volleys. I started hitting them tentatively, working through to hitting them harder and harder. Pull shots weren't really a goer, and I couldn't sweep. The general idea was to go in with Cooky and block. He could still bat properly, and I could try to get him on strike. We were 138 for eight, still requiring 146 runs, but we had to try to pull off the unlikely.

Yet when I got out there, instinct took over. Wahab Riaz bowled me a short delivery the fourth ball I faced and I could not help myself pulling it. *Aaarghh*. At the other end, I ran down the pitch and clipped Shoaib Malik, the bowler who dismissed me first innings, through mid-wicket for three. Next ball I faced, I tried to slog-sweep for six, and top-edged into no man's land. My grip on the bat was ridiculously tight from my bottom hand but my top hand was loose, so I spooned everything towards leg.

Unfortunately, the plan to provide Cooky with a partner lasted only three overs, as he was stumped. With only Jimmy for company, I swept Yasir for four, but it was game over. Officially so, two balls later, when I was stumped down the leg-side. We had lost a series we had been competitive in for long periods, 2–0.

● ● ●

I was already missing the one-dayers that were to follow, as the England management decided I was in need of a rest. At the end of the 2015 Ashes, Joe Root and myself were told that we would not be playing all series for the remainder of the year, because they were concerned about our workloads. He was told he would not be playing the Aussies in the one-dayers, and I was to be left out for the white-ball stuff in the UAE.

Although a voice inside my head was telling me to protest about sitting out – all I want to do is play – I was generally okay with it. Things would have been different for me if I had been given Joe's lot and told I was missing cricket against Australia. I never want to miss playing in those matches.

If the same situation had arisen two years previously, and I had been 22, I would probably not have accepted the argument about the need to prolong careers. Naturally, it's flattering that they view me as someone they need to look after for the future. But there remains a part of me that is still not a massive fan of resting. What if someone else comes in, takes your place and performs to a standard that makes them undroppable? Hundreds and five-fers in my position are gold. If my replacement manages that, they're picking him not me next game, aren't they?

I also hate missing out on cricket. The thrill of being a part of an exciting England team, the love of the battle, the addiction of performing in front of big crowds and in dramatic matches. But I have been made aware of the need for breaks by our medical people – I field, bat and bowl, with intensity, so I put my body through a lot, and the odd rest here and there is not the worst thing.

This enforced one gave me the chance for rare family time. The next five weeks were the best I have had at home. I miss out on a lot of activities with the kids, being away so much, and so going to things like Layton's nativity play was awesome. To see your lad up on stage puts a tear in your eye. How proud can you feel?

It also gave us a chance to visit Disneyland Paris as a family. I reckon I had nearly as much fun as the kids did. While the rest of the England team were developing their white-ball cricket in the build-up to the World Twenty20, I was taking a Buzz Lightyear laser gun ride to new levels, not only to beat the three-year-old Layton but achieve the high score, which looked on when our carriage stopped suddenly, placing us alongside one of the red circles. I just kept shooting – ding, ding, ding, ding.

Around this time, I was not overly concerned about missing cricket into the new year. There were weeks in hand, the scans had shown a relatively small muscle tear near the collar bone and I wasn't noticing any pain moving around in everyday life. However, I was soon to discover that doing anything strenuous was a problem. One day I went to pick up Layton and felt the sharpest pain. At that moment, several weeks after the Sharjah Test, I thought I was in trouble. It felt like one of those injuries you leave to heal but never does. Such was the soreness I experienced that I feared missing the tour of South Africa.

14

Confidence that I was going to be alright for the series against Test cricket's number-one ranked team increased after I returned to the indoor nets in early December.

I did quite a lot at the Riverside, training with Durham, and that told me I could bat and bowl, and that left only diving in the field to be checked. That would be crucial, and was to wait until the first outdoor training sessions over in South Africa.

From the very first training session, Craig de Weymarn wanted to be satisfied that my collar bone would be up to the task. I was fairly positive that it would be, but there's nothing quite like confirming there are no issues. It wasn't an injury I had encountered before, so I had no experience to fall back on. In one way that was a good thing, as there was no habitual weakness in the area.

So for the first four days of training I was like a performing seal, being thrown the ball to either side, leaping one way, then the other, testing the injury's ability to withstand impact. I left the field smiling after the final individual session, pleased to get back to catching practice with the rest of the squad. I was ready for what is one of world cricket's biggest challenges – South Africa had risen to number one in the Test rankings because of their consistency over a long period of time, and they don't lose series very often.

But things had generally gone well for me over recent months and I was keen to test myself against bowlers like Dale Steyn and Morne Morkel. Then, there was the challenge of bowling to batsman of the class of AB de Villiers and Hashim Amla. When they're at the top of their games, they are just about the best players in the world.

It was also the big winter tour for us as a team. Tours like this only come around every couple of years – Australia is one, South Africa the other – when you head out late in the year and spend two to three months in the country. The nature of the tour is demanding for that reason. Because you are away for Christmas and New Year, your families are with you, and that potentially provides an off-field distraction. It feels quite weird to be together but away from home at that time.

From a business point of view, we want to be the world's number one team, so getting ourselves up the rankings as quickly as possible was at the forefront of our minds. Having dropped down to a mid-table position, that goal would not be achieved on South African soil, but we knew a win on the board would take us a big step further towards achieving it. We knew if we went out there and did well, people would view it as a statement of intent. It would send a message that this England team was a serious one to be reckoned with.

Our ambition is no secret. Alastair Cook spoke openly about it in press conferences after we won the 2015 Ashes, and I want to play a full part in achieving that – to help us win games, to get up the rankings. Whenever a new player comes into the team, they are made aware of our goals and naturally that stays in your head. It is not as though we need go back over it after every couple of months. It's part of being an England Test cricketer – to contribute towards making the team as successful as possible.

But talk is talk. It is another thing achieving your targets, and I much prefer to make my impressions on the pitch. Yes, I have been more vocal with my opinions as I have established myself in the team, but you don't get anywhere just talking. I am not someone that is motivated by words. I prefers actions. A 150 in the warm-up game against a South Africa Invitational XI in Potchefstroom gave me confidence in my batting, and the shoulder was fine with regards to bowling too.

The night before the first Test began in Durban, I could not help building it up in my mind. The status of the series added to the excitement, and it made it even harder to sleep. It's the excitement that goes with a big occasion for me. Once the next morning gets going, and you start your pre-match routines, everything settles down, and your concentration is turned on fully.

● ● ●

We started the series with a new-look top order. There was an opening combination of Cook and Alex Hales, followed by the recalled Nick

Compton at three. In a weird way because Cooky was out early on, after we lost another toss, it created the perfect scenario for Compo. Being a wicket down early meant we couldn't afford to lose another, and that's *his* situation. It allowed him to play the perfect Compton innings. Some people might have thought there was pressure on him going into the Test, after coming back into the team, but the early success for South Africa suited him, in my opinion.

He did well, by playing his natural game. At the other end, Hales started looking good but played one of his big drives on the up and was caught. It was unfortunate he got out, but I believe you accept a player for who he is. Just as Compo was contributing by building an innings, Hales was trying to move the game forwards for us. You tend to get comments like, 'What's he doing?' when someone gets out in an attacking manner like that. Pundits and commentators are not so critical, though, when the ball flies for four or six. I don't believe you can have one without the other. Occasionally, a top-class bowler will nick you off trying something expansive, and that is what Dale Steyn did.

A half-volley is a half-volley whether you are 100-0 or 13-3. The danger is you nick it, but regardless of it being your first ball or your 50th you want to try to hit it for four, because the best attacks don't serve them up that often. I never get too fussed when or how people get out. It's all the same. You have reached a certain level playing a certain way. Be true to it – because out is out whatever the mode of dismissal in the scorebook.

The high price Compton placed on his wicket meant we were well set to put 300 on the board in that first innings and I ended up unbeaten at the close on that opening day. I had to survive an over that night and it was nice to get a full toss off Dane Piedt, the South African off-spinner, to get me going.

I sensed we were in a decent position the following morning and that, even though it was only day two, it was time to move things on a bit. I got a couple away off Dale Steyn, and he was funny in response.

'Hi Ben,' he said. 'I've never played against you before. You going out tonight?'

He kept chatting to me, not in a sledging way but in a way to get me engaged, to put me off my game. I don't mind it one bit when people say things to me on the field. They're trying to do what I'm trying to do, win games for their country. If talking is a part of their game, and it makes them be the best they can be, then I have no issue with it.

Dale might claim he succeeded in distracting me. I would argue my downfall was self-inflicted, as unfortunately I got out trying to go up two gears when one would have done, and ended up attempting to pull one that wasn't wide or short enough off Morne Morkel.

But with Jonny Bairstow at number seven and Moeen Ali following at eight, whenever there is a batsman set at the other end, there is licence to try to change the tempo in our favour. Some would say that it's lacking responsibility playing in that way, using the insurance of the long batting order. I would counter that in that situation, I am trying to take responsibility for moving the game on. If the counter-attack comes off, with the depth of batting we possess, we have the potential to blast the opposition out the park. As it was we got to 303, and that gave us a decent score to work with.

The pitch was very two-paced; some balls would skid on and occasionally some would explode without warning. It spun though and Moeen Ali bowled really nicely for us from the start. He set the tone for the whole tour with his performance in that first innings. Normally, you would expect your spinner to have an impact later in the game, but Mo gets a lot of revs on the ball – a really good action on it – particularly when he's deep into a lengthy spell. With Jimmy Anderson out injured, I was at slip, and I could see how well Mo was bowling. I know from batting against him in the nets what he's like when he's at his best and it was on view here – the ball starts ducking halfway on its journey to the batsman. The nice dip comes thanks to the revs, the ball was landing in the same area and because of the nature of the surface some were going on straight, others were spinning. It is probably the best he has bowled for England, I reckon. It was lovely to see him get the ball up and down like that, unconcerned about drag-downs or full tosses. He was in such a rhythm.

On a pitch like this, with no real pace to work with, you can't get away as a batsman. Equally, the bowlers aren't able to take wickets in clusters. Runs do not come freely; batsmen are not easily removed. It was more of a chip-away than blow-away wicket. Even though we got a couple of early wickets, it was a real patience game for us, and our search for a third featured an incident I would later regret.

South Africa were on 36 when Steve Finn got one to ride up and strike AB de Villiers on the glove. The ball looped into the air, forcing me to dive forward from gully. I was confident I had caught it, but there was a tiny bit inside me that said: 'Tell them you're not sure.' In passing it over to the umpires, I was just trying to be a good bloke, but after what transpired I really wish I hadn't. The decision came back as not out, yet every subsequent replay I saw showed the ball go straight into my hands. If I had confidently told them, 'Yes, I caught it' he would have been out; showing uncertainty resulted in a 'not out'. No one wants to be out to a catch on the half-volley, but this was a case that left me annoyed. One of the problems with low catches is that the angle of the cameras nearly always gives a false visual impression: the ball looks like it's hitting grass when it's not, and the pixellations when they zoom in make the picture unclear. The fingers and the grass tend to merge into a bit of a blur.

Despite that incident, our bowling attack kept coming at them, and the fact we were able to deliver in those conditions threw down the gauntlet for the rest of the series. South Africa were taken aback a little bit by how well we bowled, I think, particularly without Jimmy Anderson. Steve Finn, Stuart Broad and Mo took all the wickets but Chris Woakes held an end up, and that's not to be underestimated.

A 241-run win was an unbelievable start for us. With the bat, Compton, James Taylor and Jonny Bairstow, all guys recently recalled to the team, made good contributions in each innings, and so we were confident as individuals as well as a team going into that second Test, the first of 2016. When you win the first game of a series as big as that, it gives you a real lift. South Africa knew victory was essential in Cape Town to get back into it. In a five-match series it probably wouldn't be the case, but the threat of going 2–0 down over four matches, or even trailing by one with two to play, creates pressure.

South Africa are aggressive. They're an abrasive team. I sensed they were up for the challenge when I walked out to bat at Newlands on a hat-trick ball at 167-4. *Just don't get out,* I told myself. After negotiating it, though, everything felt normal. Better than normal when I got my first boundary away. I simply stuck my bat down to a ball from Chris Morris, gave it no more than a flick, and yet it rocketed off to the boundary. When that happens, you know you're in fine nick. I felt very early that my movements at the crease were in good order.

Getting through the tough bit at the start — a mini rescue with Joe Root — set up that period of great fun. At the start, Joe was doing his usual 'Just another five runs, lad.' I always let him get on with that kind of non-sense, as I know it helps him concentrate. *What an idiot* — or *wonderfully talented idiot*, I should say to make clear we are the best of pals — I tend to think when he talks like that. *What good's five going to do?* We have similar outlooks on a lot of things in cricket, but not this subject. I let him get the fives. A few hours later, all I was interested in was sixes.

I was loving it. There was no pressure on me, thanks chiefly to the work of our top order, and that suits the way I like to play. The only pressure I felt on that second day was self-imposed: *score quickly*. There is no better feeling when you have middled one and you are confident it's going for six. You watch the flight of it, cast your eye towards the boundary, check where the fielder is, and egg the ball on to clear the ropes. One of my bugbears is that when training in the nets, there is nothing to hit the ball into — a stand, a pavilion, a grass bank. More often than not there is a huge meshing at the end of the bowlers' run-ups. It's why I prefer practice on the square. Give me a target and I will go for it. At Newlands, I really wanted to hit it into the brewery.

Growing up, I always wanted to score a double-hundred. I guess most people dreamt about hundreds. I always thought bigger. I got close a couple of times, but fell short playing in the same manner as I did in Cape Town: caught on the boundary, or slogging one straight up in the air. So I was pumped that it happened in a Test match. Occasionally in net sessions you will hit consistent long balls without a mishit. Rarely does it happen in a match. This was an exception.

When I first walked out on the practice day, across the square, towards Table Mountain, it took my breath away.

'What a ground this is,' I said.

To do it there, at such a picturesque venue, in front of a healthy English contingent, made it a dream day. It really is one of the most iconic backgrounds for any sporting stadium, and after Trent Bridge it is probably my favourite ground. The reason those two are up there for me is that they both look like paintings. They have such beauty about them.

It was so loud, people were well oiled all around the stands and half of them were more interested in having a party than watching the cricket. But I was doing my best to distract them. What did surprise me during that 258 was breaking the England record for the number of sixes in an innings. I assumed someone would have hit 11 before.

I want to be known for turning games around, changing the momentum of matches out of nowhere. I feel as though I have done it on a few occasions now. Sure, I want to be a consistent performer, but more than that I want to be the one who wins games for his team. I want to influence as many matches as I can and love the idea of using the freedom I have been given by the people I play for, to try to entertain.

While I am given that freedom, I will continue to pursue this way, and with that comes an acceptance that one day I can get 258, the next it might be three off 40 balls. That's me. I'm like a pendulum, swinging from one extreme to the other, but I have come to appreciate that I am able to produce things out of the blue. I never want to fear trying.

One of cricket's regular expressions is 'He understands his game.' Guys would churn out 1,000 runs a season year on year, and you would hear 'He knows his game.' When I was younger people used it, wrongly, in relation to me. To be honest, I never quite got its meaning. I always found it slightly weird. To me players were able to perform, because they are good players. It is only since my international recall in 2015 that I have begun to understand the phrase, and apply it to myself, because it's in that period that I have begun to understand myself as a cricketer. And with that understanding comes an acceptance that with trying comes failure.

I'm not looking for excuses for doing so. I don't want to cruise through the rest of my career, thinking 'That's me.' I will try to adapt; to do more; to get better. Part of me moving my game forward is an ability to deal with failure. Two or three years ago, I couldn't. I would go chasing something, look to do things differently, go away from my true self.

Scoring at five runs an over in that innings gave us control of the game, and put us in a position to push for another win. There was a real sense of fulfilment in contributing to the team cause. Jonny Bairstow played brilliantly but afterwards as he was slumped to his seat in the dressing room he said: 'Any danger of me middling one?'

He was 100 per cent serious. He's never satisfied with what he's done, and sure that can be a good thing. But he had just got 150, for goodness sake.

As it turned out, the pitch beat us, and on a surface like that when Hashim Amla is in form you know each ball has to be good, or it will be punished. Certain players, if they're in, will make you suffer if you are slightly off as a bowler, and Amla is one of them. Some might argue this quality borders on intimidation.

Just as Pakistan had done against us earlier in the winter, we got ourselves into a bit of a pickle playing positive shots when the game was supposed to be petering out. It would have been a miracle for the Saffers had they turned that around to chase a win, having conceded 629 on first innings.

Not that time was on their side. Jonny and Mo steadied things for 90 minutes to snuff out those hopes and it meant we went to Johannesburg, and a result pitch, with that 1–0 lead.

This match was the only time I felt targetted during the series. Perhaps it was partly due to what I had done in Cape Town – the South Africans wanted to fight fire with fire. Undoubtedly, it was partly due to the fact that the Wanderers is home to a quicker wicket. It actually got faster on the second day, after we bowled the South Africans out for 313.

It was all on the line. South Africa had us 91 for four, they were up for it, and Morne Morkel was steaming in. The first ball I faced was a snorter. The second hit the bat handle and veered off to long leg. It was a delivery that broke my bat.

But the pull shot is arguably my best shot, and when, with a new bat in hand, Kagiso Rabada tried to bump me with his second delivery to me, I was standing and waiting for it, ready to swing as hard as I could.

Thwack.

I got it straight out the middle and it flew cleanly over the boundary.

The bouncer plan didn't last very long. Generally, I think people have realized playing the short ball is a strength of mine.

For my first Test back at number six, against West Indies, Jerome Taylor bowled me a bumper early on that I just didn't see, that resulted in me throwing my hands up in front of my face. Thankfully the ball dropped safely at my feet. But the fact I had played it like a mug encouraged them to carry on with the bumpers – they thought they were exposing a weakness. That actually got me going. I kept on pulling, and my international career was back on track again.

Growing up I always took the short stuff on. It was my way of saying, 'Yes, you're fast, but I can hit fast bowling pretty hard.' The faster they bowled, the harder I would swing. Even if I was made to look like an absolute novice, I would go for it. If I know someone is targetting me, even if they post two men back, I will take them on, and it has served me well so far.

With the bounce on offer in Johannesburg, you are well served getting the ball full and looking for outside edges. Although it's good for strokeplay, bowlers are also always in the game because of the carry, and that meant both sides fancied their chances. Play your shots and there are runs on offer, but it also comes with a risk. One mistake and you're gone.

This was the kind of scenario that suited Joe Root and myself. I'm not sure what we average together, but over the past decade it would be good. When one of us gets good runs, it tends to have come after a decent stand between us. We are different players but have a similar mindset. No matter the situation, if we are bowled a bad ball, it's going one way or another. We keep things simple, touch gloves, have a laugh.

You tend to find you bat better with some people better than others. There is a chemistry there between Joe and me and we feed off each other. It was the same with Dale Benkenstein at Durham. He was at the end of his first-class career just as I broke into the England team, but he always seemed to be at the other end when I was playing the innings that got me international recognition. It always felt comfortable being out there in the middle with him. There wouldn't be any analysis unless the ball was doing a bit. I enjoy a craic. Other guys are very focused on talking technical but, trust me, I'm not the guy to ask about whether your shoulder is too far over.

South Africa ditched the short stuff for a while after I hit Rabada over the ropes, but then Hardus Viljoen, the big lad on debut, came bombing in. Viljoen bowls a heavy ball. Sometimes he felt 7–8 mph quicker from one ball to the next, and admittedly he did me a couple of times with that.

At the other end, Joe was playing his shots on the way to a fine hundred, and it felt like we were matching each other boundary for boundary. It was fun, while it lasted. The end, when it arrived, seemed to come in the middle of a spat between Morkel and me.

The band, playing in the stands, was so loud that the umpires told them to stop when the bowler got back to the top of his run. It caused a moment which was deceptive upon appearance. Morkel ran in, then pulled away just before entering his delivery stride. He told me he wasn't sure if I was ready, if I was able to concentrate, because the musicians had not stopped playing. I replied it was fine, and he should have bowled it anyway.

Next ball, I instinctively hit him back over his head for four. It felt great. I had just got to 50 at better than a run a ball, and I was in no mood for hauling it back in. Unfortunately, though, Morkel had his revenge later in the over when I popped one back to him off the leading edge.

Our exchange certainly drew some attention, with people presuming we'd had a huge spat. Back in the dressing room, I had just taken my kit off when a couple of our lads asked: 'What did Morkel say to you there, mate? It looked like he was having a right go at you.'

They couldn't have been further from the truth. But when I looked back at the footage, I could see where they were coming from. The way he celebrated his caught and bowled suggested he had won a bit of duel. It kind of said, 'Up yours'. But he was just celebrating a Test wicket as anyone should – certainly the way I would.

The hundred partnership with Joe brought us back into the contest, and a first-innings lead of 10 made it anyone's game at the halfway stage. Who could have envisaged what was to happen next? Wicketless before lunch, once we got the first one afterwards the floodgates opened.

Stuart Broad produced a spell that, in my opinion, was better than his one in the Ashes at Trent Bridge. There, the pitch was green and he had a Duke ball in his hand. Here, at Jo'burg there was a little bit in the pitch, but not as much, the Kookaburra ball didn't swing as much, the seam wasn't as big – and he ransacked their top order. Games move quickly at the Wanderers but this was incredible. In a flash, Broad single-handedly had South Africa five down, and only 25 runs in front.

Cricket is a rollercoaster of a game. Everything is calm one minute. Then a wicket goes down and it starts swinging and seaming, nipping all over the place, balls explode off the pitch. Broad has the ability to flick that switch, probably because he has that great fast bowler's habit of just doing enough with the ball. The batter always tries to hit the ball with the middle of the bat, so you only need to do just enough to hit the edge, I guess; and that's what he does.

He was helped by the sensational low catch by James Taylor at short-leg to get rid of Hashim Amla. The ball was turned firmly and was taken only an inch or so off the turf. It was simply stunning.

Actually, it's funny how guys take worldie catches on days like this. He should never have caught it, but moments like these tend to lead to wins. They energize a side. It's like when I took that catch in Nottingham. It came on a day when Broad took eight for 15. On a run-of-the-mill day, nothing happens, and nicks fly between the slips. Whereas things out of the ordinary happen on these special occasions – twice in the case of this match. Not satisfied with one stunning piece of fielding at short-leg, Titch produced a second, arguably better, to grab a flick off the full face of the bat one-handed to his right to dismiss Dane Vilas. Steven Finn was bowling at a really good pace, so the reaction time was hundredths of a second.

When you get wickets quickly, and through moments of individual brilliance like that, the atmosphere on the field is infectious. Everyone goes berserk. You are playing for England, but it brings out the enjoyment you experienced as a kid. The other thing it does is increase focus. Everyone is so switched on. All series I had wanted to get my inswinger going and here it finally paid off, to bowl Chris Morris. Soon, Kagiso Rabada was nicking off. Then Broad and Anderson wrapped things up. It was such a ridiculously fast Test match.

That night we toasted a really special series win in the away dressing room at the Wanderers. Every time England win a series, the winner's ale tastes good. It was a tradition long before I came into the team, and will remain long after I am gone I guess, to pour beer into your cap and drink it. A Test series win is a special achievement, and toasting it with your team-mates provides great memories. It's the first thing you want to do after victory. The last thing I want is a beer when we lose.

There was the usual drinking game, too, with Gary Ballance taking his usual prominent role. The rules are simple – touch the bottom of some-one's glass or bottle and they have to down its contents. Of course, it always leads to disputes, which is where Gary, playing the role of Marais Erasmus, provides third umpire adjudication.

'Yes, hello, rock 'n' roll, please.'

'Right, let's see the other angle.'

'Yes, you're on screen, the decision is . . . Out.'

'Pitching in line, hitting in line – that's out.'

It was buzzing later at a nightclub in Sandton. Somehow I broke my Rolex watch on the dancefloor, and struggling to piece it back together, handed it over in two halves to our security guy. You can imagine what's coming next? Yep, the panic well and truly set in next morning. I couldn't remember a thing. Of course, I like the watch – I never take it off unless I'm playing cricket – but it is actually of greater sentimental value. I bought it immediately after I won my first Test match in an England shirt, in Grenada in 2015, having been given the idea by Stuart Broad, who mentioned he bought himself watches to represent mile-stones in his career. The next one on my radar is for winning the annual

Test mace or a global trophy. Thankfully, my current one was returned that evening.

South Africa were very vocal in the build-up to the final Test – AB de Villiers suggesting we had 'weaknesses to expose' and Dean Elgar suggesting it was not a dead rubber in their eyes. They had not won a Test match for a year.

It was not a dead rubber in our eyes, either, but I'm not going to lie – it's very hard when you know you've won a series to keep the motivation at the level it should be. Of course, a Test match always contains that energy, that electricity, that excitement about it. Whenever you walk onto the field in an England shirt you are desperate to do well. But it is almost inevitable that you get drawn into conversations, about how the match doesn't matter as much. We had done what we had set out to achieve when we arrived in South Africa a month earlier, and it's hard to feel the same intent as when a series is alive.

And I certainly felt sore and heavy-legged after bowling in that first innings at Centurion. After the first evening, with South Africa 329 for five, the next day already felt like a long one. Previously, we'd enjoyed some success getting South Africa's makeshift openers out early, but Stephen Cook bucked that trend and played well for his debut hundred. We were always chasing the game from then on, and after conceding a 133-run lead on first innings we got hammered. Frankly, it was embarrassing to fold for 101 on that fifth and final morning.

It was something highlighted by Trevor Bayliss and Alastair Cook in our post-match debrief. They wanted us to be in no doubt how badly we'd let our standards drop. They always finish their talks on a positive, so they reminded us that we had achieved our target of winning the series. We had just defeated the best team in the world but, going forward, we were asked to be better. Trevor never gets angry, keeping the same pitch, the same tone to his voice whether good or bad. But we were left in no doubt as to his feelings.

Just as in the Ashes, we couldn't find that extra push heading into the last game and, just as Australia had, South Africa seized their opportunity. They had their best game, and we had our worst.

15

The World Twenty20 heartbreak was put into context for me just nine days later when the news broke that James Taylor was being forced to retire at the age of 26.

Unlike him, I can go out and play again, and I am so thankful for that. I also know that Titch would accept any kind of on-field scenario to be back out there again. If he was a bowler and the opposition needed 35 from the last over, and he got hit for 36, he would take that over the situation he found himself in early April 2016. I might have got smashed for those 24 runs in the final – but I can still play.

He had done nothing wrong, committed the previous 10 years of his life towards a professional career, and the sport he loved was taken from him.

It proved such a big fight for him just to get into the England team, and when you look at his record – his raw numbers – he should have played a lot more during his career. The volume of runs he scored was phenomenal. It was just unfortunate that they came at a time when everyone else in the England reckoning was churning them out too.

In fact, the cruellest twist when he was diagnosed with his rare heart condition was that he had just started building an international career to match what he had done with Leicestershire and Nottinghamshire. Now, in an instant, it was gone.

No one was fitter, either. Titch was a gym freak. In the end, his arms were like clock hands that got stuck at 9.15. He could certainly lift weights. It was like Arnold Schwarzenegger had been shrunk to a third of the size. I guess being five foot two means you have to do some work on your rig.

I was putting words together for this book when the news broke. It was not an easy subject to process. I literally couldn't believe it. I wanted to show him I cared. I played a lot of cricket with him for England Lions. More recently we were England team-mates across all formats. But just how do you approach something like that?

Everyone's going to be texting him. You should ring him. It's too easy to send a text.

Yet when it came to it, I just couldn't. I didn't know what I would have been able to say. I feared jumbling my words up, not getting across what I wanted, so I sent him a text, saying how gutted I was for him.

'The most important thing is that you're still here with us,' I wrote.

Even then, I didn't quite understand the severity of his situation in the long term, which unfortunately meant I added: 'One day, I hope to God you can get back on the pitch and do what you love again.'

It clearly hadn't sunk in for me that arrhythmogenic right ventricular cardiomyopathy spelled the end, and it must have been hard to accept that a career developing with such promise had taken the most clinical cut. In response, though, Titch reflected he felt lucky to be alive.

The worst thing about it, he added, was no longer being able to drink alcohol.

'I'll miss the nights out,' he said.

'Yeah, mate. You were absolutely mental . . .'

Even in that situation, I felt duty bound to act no differently than at any other time in our relationship. That's team-mates for you. I wasn't going to treat him any differently now.

Titch's news did make me wonder, though. If it happened to me, what would I do? I'm not a person to think about the future. I very much live in the present, only dealing with what's on my plate. Life after cricket can be planned nearer the time. Now, I realized that aside from my family, this sport is all I've got.

● ● ●

It is a privileged position we hold as England cricketers, and on the whole we get an overwhelmingly positive support from the public. I was worried coming back home how people would react after the World Twenty20. Yet, walking around Sainsbury's with Clare and the kids, there would be taps on the shoulder with 'Well dones' and 'We're so proud of you all'. I felt like an absolute moron being the guy who delivered that final over, so to have people go out of their way to say positive things was a massive help.

That was the kind of recognition that means something to me. I'm not so bothered about accolades. I was named a *Wisden* Cricketer of the Year in the first week I was back. It's a prestigious award, and one you can only win once, but I never set out to pick up trophies for personal performances.

What I was really focused on was helping Durham and England win matches again. After all I had experienced, I couldn't wait to get back out on the field, a different field from Kolkata, and put everything behind me. My first match back was a rain-hit County Championship fixture against Middlesex. The weather meant we only played for the equivalent of two of the four days, but from a personal point of view, it was overs under my belt ahead of the Test series against Sri Lanka. I bowled a couple of long spells and took a couple of wickets.

The workload was considerably bigger away at Surrey. It was a typically flat pitch at The Oval and dismissing batsmen was therefore hard work, which meant I ended up bowling enough overs to get extremely sore feet.

Once you are into a spell, and your feet are warm, you tend to be able to keep going, but when I came off the field the problem inhibited me, and when I took my boots off I wasn't sure how I was going to get them back on again. And this was after just one innings.

Surrey posted 457 but we replied with an even more impressive 607, and a chance of victory remained if we dismissed the home side on the final day, with enough time remaining for a dash at whatever target was required. I was desperate to play my part. But a callus on my big left toe was causing a problem. If it pressed against anything, it was agony. Even water hitting it in the shower, or putting my socks on, was painful. But I don't like to be beaten in these kind of situations, so the biggest question on my mind was not how to stop the pain but how I was going to contribute.

Because the callus was on my landing foot, it meant cutting a massive hole out of my boot. I went out there and hoped for the best. The first two overs were excruciating. It was almost unbearable. But getting through them was important. In bowling those balls, I had slammed through the hard crust of skin.

'Keep me going for as long as you can,' I told Paul Collingwood, 'because if I stop, I don't know how many more you're going to get out of me.'

The game appeared to be heading for a draw, but the probability of us forcing a victory increased when I got three quick wickets – among them the prize one of Kumar Sangakkara, caught at second slip by Scott Borthwick. If Colly wanted me for any more overs, he had to keep me on, not think about bringing me back later. I bowled 13 overs in one spell.

It might have looked from afar that Paul Collingwood was bowling me into the ground a week before the Test match. The truth, of course, was I refused to come off. Whichever team I play for I want to win, and there was a little bit of me that felt I should show the same level of commitment for Durham that I would do in the same situation for England. I didn't want any of the other guys thinking, 'If he was playing in a Test match, he would have kept on going.'

Since establishing myself as an international player, I have made a conscious effort to show the guys back at Durham that they are no less important to me than they were when I first called them team-mates, that I will not put the club behind me. Whenever I'm on the field with them, I give it everything and never consider the consequences.

Those three wickets gave us hope but Tom Curran held firm, playing well to hit a 50. One more and they might have collapsed but the hour-long partnership between him and Ben Foakes – they were still 11 runs behind when they came together with half the Surrey side out – stopped us in our tracks.

If I had scored some runs in those two Championship matches, I wouldn't have felt any better or any worse going into Test cricket with England. The main thing for me is bowling well. If I am bowling well, I tend to go into internationals with a lot more confidence. Batting tends to look after itself for me, but you want a rhythm about your bowling and I got that from those two games. As an all-rounder, one skill tends to feed the confidence of the other, and for me batting has always been the stronger suit in terms of statistical returns, and the one I have found easier to regain form in.

It was pretty awesome being back out in the field with all the England lads again, even allowing for a bit of a flunk with the bat against the Sri Lankans at Headingley in the first Investec Test. Then, disaster struck during a bowling spell on the second afternoon when I jarred my knee. Only it was not while bowling that I felt the discomfort. No, it was actually at the other end, in innocuous circumstances, while stood at gully.

The ball was being relayed from Jonny Bairstow, through the slips, as usual. I received it from Joe Root and routinely turned and threw to mid-off – you get such a feel for the length of a throw from your regular fielding spot that it becomes second nature, you don't even think about what you are doing. Almost without looking, with no effort whatsoever, I lobbed it the customary 30 yards. Only this time, as I turned to the side, and drew my arm back, I felt my left knee open out. It twisted and I immediately knew it wasn't right. I sank to the turf. I took a second; two seconds; three; four; five. Whoa, time-out, I thought, as I got back to my feet.

'Stop, Finny,' I shouted.

Craig de Weymarn was soon on the scene, moving my knee this way and that to assess the damage. Instantly, I knew something was up. It wasn't as stable as it should have been. In that situation, you are half in denial and half in hope of a miracle. I got up, pressed my studs into the turf, did a few squats, had a bit of a run-around, and then asked Craig to let me stay out and bowl another over.

I did that, jogging up and down the pitch between deliveries, and it felt okay. Not completely, though. My approach to the crease for the first ball was made rather gingerly, and even though I got through another three overs after that, once the spell was done I immediately left the field. Adrenalin had kept me going out there. It was sore, but like most bowlers my instinct was to try to run it off. I was in the middle of a spell and therefore my body was warmed up. There was no real pain. Only when I cooled down did things really deteriorate.

Once back in the dressing room, it was not good. I was hobbling about, unable to straighten and bend my leg freely, and very cautious of any movement. Craig began a more in-depth assessment of the injury.

One thing in my favour, I suppose, was that this was not a new situation to me. I had suffered from a locking of this knee for some time and on the previous occasions when it flared up like this it was fine the next day. I could wake up the following morning and, seemingly against all odds, everything would be normal. With that in mind, I asked Craig to allow me to return to the field, so that in the eventuality that I did wake up tip-top next morning, I would be able to bowl straightaway, and not have to wait for a couple of hours to offset the time I'd been off.

That night I prayed it was another false alarm and the knee would be back to its normal self soon enough. I took the compression machine to my Leeds hotel room, and switched it on at regular intervals, along with the ice machine.

Only 15 months previously, I experienced similar pain on the Lions tour of South Africa. There, I awoke one morning just a couple of days after flying from the Big Bash in Australia and felt tightness behind the knee. Ben Langley, the England Lions physio, quizzed me as to what might have caused it and I had no idea.

On that occasion we took things steadily. I skipped bowling practice for a couple of days, and later everything felt fine. There had just been some swelling. Bizarrely, it went as mysteriously as it arrived.

Or, perhaps not. It all seemed symptomatic of a long-standing issue. Basically, a loose piece of cartilage in my left knee occasionally flicked out into areas of the joint it should not be in, causing aggravation. In the past, it had always flicked back into place after a period of time. This time, however, in Leeds it had not. This lock of the joint felt worse than those in the past.

I actually tore the cartilage in question early in the 2012 season, and I had been booked in to have surgery to remove the bit causing the inflammation elsewhere in the joint. I was due to play for England Lions in a four-day match against West Indies at Northampton when the problem flared up, and they opted to send me to see Andy Williams, a knee surgeon in central London.

On the way down to the Fortius Clinic, I didn't think there was any option other than an operation. Yet, when I met him, despite the trouble it had given me, everything seemed fine again. Obviously, that was confusing to me. He ran a few tests, got me to do some frog squats – which require exaggerated bending of the knees – and put me through an MRI scan.

Despite the bending, there was no pain, and after spending no more than 10 minutes assessing, he told me that if he was to treat what he saw on scans he would carry out dozens more surgeries. He preferred not to do so unless absolutely necessary, and he had seen enough from the movement and appearance of the knee to treat me rather than the picture his machine would produce.

It was a bit like having a stone in your shoe, he said. One you can't get out. It falls back into the corner somewhere, no longer causes an issue, and you carry on walking. Eventually, however, it will get stuck in an uncomfortable place with greater regularity and you have to get rid of it.

'As far as I am concerned, you can continue playing, but you will have to have this operation eventually,' he told me. 'As you are now, I don't feel I need to operate on you. It's not the right time.'

He explained that he could see the tear and the flap of cartilage on the scan, but the best course of action would be for me to carry on playing until the time came that surgery was an absolute necessity. I was lining up the following week, on 22 May 2012, making 60 and 0 in the County Championship match against Somerset.

Naturally, I was hoping for a repeat result when I woke on the Saturday morning of the Sri Lanka Test in Leeds. Because of the extensive ice and compression treatment, I had not got any movement into the knee for about 10 hours. Other than getting up for the occasional comfort break, I was laid out on my bed the entire time. Craig returned to my room at 8am to see how I was, and although it didn't feel great, I couldn't tell him the whole truth now, could I? I can never bring myself to tell physios that ever.

'Yeah, it's a bit better.'

Headingley that morning was gloomy and overcast. The start of the morning session was delayed and that meant I stood around waiting after pulling my kit on. It would not have been very sensible to join in the football kickabout with the others, so I watched on from the edge of the square with some of the backroom team.

It might have surprised people to see me out there when play got underway at 11.15am, but I wanted to see whether my knee remained stiff after all the compression and ice. Or, would it do its usual and click back into place? I ventured out onto the field and into the slips in the hope it would.

I had done some run-throughs in the morning warm-ups and it hadn't triggered an improvement. Nor had slip-catching practice worked. Going out with the other lads as Sri Lanka resumed their innings gave it another chance. It's a waiting game in this kind of situation. Unfortunately, I realized time was running out.

'Chef, I'll give it 15 minutes,' I told Alastair Cook. 'If it hasn't loosened up, I'm off. Is that alright?'

At 11.30am I hobbled back to the dressing room knowing I faced a spell on the sidelines. It would have been much more heroic had I done it flinging myself full length to pull off a stunning catch, or headlong into the advertising hoardings to save a boundary. Sadly, it was rather less dramatic. I had pounded into that crease, giving it my all, undeterred by the consequences of doing so, for the best part of four years since first incurring the damage, and nothing had stopped me. Now, lobbing a ball around the field was set to keep me out.

It was just a question of how long. Scans confirmed that it was time for the floating cartilage to be removed, and at the very least that meant missing the rest of the Sri Lanka series. It was a shame to lose the opportunity of playing in my home Test match at Durham the following week, as not many internationals get scheduled there and I was going to win my new England cap. Recently, players have been awarded new milestone caps for every 25th appearance at Test level, and I had 24 caps to my name.

Jonny Bairstow received his '25' on his home ground of Headingley, and marked it with a hundred. It's funny how often people rise to the occasion when they are on home turf like that, and I would have relished the chance. Moeen Ali joined the 25 club at the Riverside and, sat watching him bat from the hospitality boxes, I believed there was a destiny about his hundred, a first in two years.

● ● ●

Injuries can plague you at times in a career – we all have to accept that because of the physical demands you put your body through. For all-rounders, those demands are increased. So, yes I felt devastated that I would be sidelined, particularly right in the heart of an English summer when I so wanted to put in the performances that made the difference. But I was not about to mope about. It was not the end of the world; it was something I had to deal with.

Whenever I am out, I set myself time frames for getting back into action. So, after surgery on the Tuesday in London, I set a target of the first Test against Pakistan at Lord's, which was seven and a half weeks away. The surgeon and physio instructed the medical team at the ECB and the Durham staff on what I could and could not do. Whenever there is a challenge like that, I tend to respond to it. I knew there would be a workload ahead and that Craig de Weymarn, the England physio, would be looking at my long-term interests and telling me to be patient. But at the same time, he would have a realistic programme set out. Craig told me immediately after the operation that my rehab time would be between seven and eight weeks.

In other words, I would be back on a cricket field if all went to plan between 11 and 18 July. The first Test was starting on 14 July. Immediately, I felt a slight disappointment – I hate missing Test matches, and I knew it was extremely unlikely the England management would throw me straight back into international cricket without some first-class action as preparation. But I was also determined. I was going to give myself every chance of reducing the time frame.

I am always pushing to play whenever I have a problem; Craig is the one ensuring that I am one hundred per cent right before I can play, pushing me towards the sensible course of action. In this instance, I knew that it depended on how much mileage I could get through my body in the month of physical conditioning. Sure, if England were not 100 per cent happy with the number of overs I had bowled in the build-up, they could make that call if I was not ready for a return to international cricket. I was fully prepared for that. But if I could bring everything forward by a week, I would give myself an outside chance.

Craig gave me loads of drills and I was put on ice and compression machines as soon as I came out of surgery to reduce the swelling as quickly as possible. Another machine kept the muscles active by twitching them even when I was inactive on the couch. I carried out all the rehab religiously, never missing an opportunity. I was soon up and about on it. The step up to more intensive gym work was fine. Things were going well. So well, in fact, that a plan was drawn up for me to play as a batsman for the Durham Academy in the North East Premier League on Saturday 25 May.

There was one problem. That match was in Stockton, 25 miles away, and I had recently been banned from driving for six months. Clare and I moved house in January 2015, while I was away with England Lions in South Africa. Unfortunately, with all that a move entails, I forgot to notify the DVLA of my change of address, and it was only when I sold my BMW X6 that everything caught up with me. I put my new address on the sale documents, and suddenly copies of correspondence that had been going to my old place were landing on my doormat. There were speeding fines, notifications of action for a late reply and court orders. It gave me a pretty nasty jolt.

I already had points on my licence and there were two speeding fines that I knew nothing about. One of those was worth 6 points – I had been caught on camera doing 75 mph in a 50 mph zone. It was on a stretch of the A1 on my way home from England duty, in a roadworks section. I drive long distances – that's a given when you live in the north-east – it was late at night and it was one of those occasions when there was not much traffic about. One of those occasions when you are a quarter of the way through roadworks before realizing how fast you are going. In court, I pledged that I would take more care of how I was driving in future, promising to use the auto setting for the speedometer. I was disqualified from driving until November 2016, and it cost me £830.

Clare was therefore my taxi service. We are only 10 minutes away from Chester-le-Street, and it so happened they were hosting Newcastle – for whom Chris Youldon, who became one of my best mates when we were at the academy together, played – that weekend. So, I was granted permission to register for Newcastle. I was going to be back playing, albeit as a specialist batsman, 19 days before the first Test against Pakistan.

However, things were happening in fast forward. Although I was still a way off bowling, physically I felt great. Nigel Kent, the Durham physio, was happy enough for me to be taking part in full fielding drills, and the England medics agreed. Mark Wood and I were then named as 12th and 13th men for the home County Championship fixture with Yorkshire. And on the Thursday, I was back in competitive action, substituting for Paul Collingwood, who had broken a thumb, and taking a catch at first slip to get rid of Adam Lyth. That evening it was decided, following discussions between Durham and the ECB, to ditch the plan to play club cricket. I was to play in the following day's NatWest Blast fixture between the sides instead.

I didn't make the impact with the bat I wanted, but I was back playing and the Division One fixture against Hampshire at the start of July gave me a chance for time in the middle. I was filthy angry at myself for getting out for 51. As I was replacing Collingwood in the XI, it was also suggested in the build-up I might bowl a few Colly-style overs. But I am an all-or-nothing kind of bowler, and we waited until the following week to step up the bowling in the nets. I was feeling good. However, I had not bowled in a competitive fixture. I had just come back from knee surgery. Would England still pick me?

The answer came when I received a phone call from Trevor Bayliss ahead of the squad announcement on 7 July. He was enthusiastic about my return but told me that they wanted me back for the second Test in Manchester. I was therefore pitched into the match against Lancashire at Southport. In the opposition for the first two days was Jimmy Anderson, who had also been left out of the Lord's party, due to a stress fracture of the shoulder blade. I got the overs under my belt, felt great, bagged three poles in the second innings, hit a few sixes in the final-day chase, and we scrambled home by two wickets. I don't know what it is about outgrounds, but they produce some great county matches, and this was another. Afterwards, we had a knockabout with the local kids on the outfield, and as far as I was concerned everything was sweet.

Remember the feeling of excitement I got when Alastair Cook told me I was making my debut at practice at the Adelaide Oval? Well, I get something similar whenever I come back into the team, and the fact that I received my 25 cap increased the levels. The stakes were high. We were 1–0 down after defeat at Lord's, but we responded brilliantly as a team. Joe Root batted like a god. It was awesome to bat with him in the final stages of his Test-best score. As for me, despite a pretty rough DRS decision, you could barely wipe the smile off my face.

I was like a kid again. The ball was zipping through, and I found the edges of Younis Khan and Sarfraz Ahmed's bats. We bowled clinically as a unit, and it was awesome to be part of the pace group, alongside Jimmy Anderson, Stuart Broad and Chris Woakes. I was back where I belonged.

But not for long. How was my luck? I had the seam position just right, I was creating chances, and bang, 21 overs into our task of dismissing Pakistan for a second time it felt like I had been shot in the right calf. The 330-run victory was completed later that day and not for the first time I was in need of a scan. A grade two tear. It was the end of my series.

Injuries go with the territory, I guess, but to keep breaking down in Test matches was agonizing. All I can promise is that whatever ill fortune comes my way I will always look to fight my way back up. Never give up.

I want to contribute to winning matches for England. Over the past 18 months I have felt liberated as a player, and trusted to provide an influence on matches across all formats, so these periods on the sidelines have done my head in. It was good to be involved in another Test win in Manchester, and to put us back in the series against a fine Pakistan team. But what I would have done to have been given the chance to get us to that number one Test status.

None of us knew it would be on the line when the four matches against Pakistan began in July. But a combination of results elsewhere – Australia's defeat in Sri Lanka and India's failure to beat West Indies by more than a 2-0 margin – meant a 3-1 series victory over Misbah-ul-Haq's side would have sent us and not them top of the Test table. Sure, that would perhaps have been slightly ahead of schedule for this developing team, but we would have taken it.

Our development has been fairly rapid. We all want to keep moving forward, as we have done since the spring of 2015, to continue our upward momentum, across Tests, one-day and Twenty20 internationals. There is a feeling that despite the variations in selections across the different formats, and the fact we have two captains in Alastair Cook and Eoin Morgan, that we are progressing as one England squad. We know we will make mistakes. That goes with the territory when you have young players. We also know that we are capable of ironing out those mistakes, and to achieve our goal of being top across the board we know we will have to be at our very best over a concentrated period of time.

Getting to within one victory of hitting the top shows us that we are not far away now, and also where the room for improvement lies. It is in those pressure matches, when the odds are against us and the stakes are at their highest, that we need to find ways, as we have done at times in other series. We need to master the moments that count.

But the message is that we will get there by promoting our current game plan. Because the different England squads are united by a positive attitude towards the game, and a similar way of playing. We always want to take the exciting option when it's available – to entertain, to inspire, to provide new highs. We have reaped so much from this attitude in recent times, and I want my name to be at the forefront of making things happen. To make English cricket the truly dominant force I believe it can be.

PICTURE CREDITS